Nicene
Christianity

Nicene Christianity

The Future for a New Ecumenism

Edited by
Christopher Seitz

Brazos Press
A Division of Baker Book House Co
Grand Rapids, Michigan 49516

© 2001 by Christopher R. Seitz

Published by Brazos Press   Paternoster Press
a division of Baker Book House Company   and   P.O. Box 300, Carlisle,
P.O. Box 6287, Grand Rapids, MI 49516–6287   Cumbria CA3 0QS U.K.

U.S. ISBN 1-58743-021-5
U.K. ISBN 1-84 227-154-7

Printed in the United States of America

Library of Congress Cataloging-in-Publication Data

Nicene Christianity : the future for a new ecumenism / edited by Christopher Seitz
    p.   cm.
Essays originally delivered as papers at a conference held in January 2001 at the Episcopal Cathedral in Charleston, South Carolina.
Includes bibiographical references.
ISBN 1-58743-021-5 (pbk.)
    1. Nicine Creed—Congresses. I. Seitz, Christopher R.
BT999.N53 2002
23'.142—dc21   2001056603

A catalogue record for this book is available from the British Lirbary.

For current information about all releases from Brazos Press, visit our web site:
http://www.brazospress.com

Contents

Preface   7

Introduction—*Philip Turner*   9

1. Our Help Is in the Name of the LORD, the Maker of Heaven and Earth—*Christopher R. Seitz*   19
2. And in One Lord, Jesus Christ . . . Begotten, Not Made—*Colin Gunton*   35
3. Being of One Substance with the Father—*Alan Torrance*   49
4. By Whom All Things Were Made—*J. Augustine Di Noia, O.P.*   63
5. For Us . . . He Was Made Man—*Robert W. Jenson*   75
6. Crucified Also for Us under Pontius Pilate—*David S. Yeago*   87
7. The Reality of the Resurrection—*Carl E. Braaten*   107
8. Confession and Confessions—*John Webster*   119
9. Confessing Christ Coming—*Douglas Farrow*   133
10. The Holy Spirit in the Holy Trinity—*Thomas Smail*   149
11. He Spoke through the Prophets—*Kathryn Greene-McCreight*   167
12. I Believe in One Holy, Catholic, and Apostolic Church—*William J. Abraham*   177
13. I Acknowledge One Baptism for the Forgiveness of Sins—*Susan K. Wood*   189
14. And I Look for the Resurrection . . .—*Vigen Guroian*   203
15. To Desire Rightly—*Ephraim Radner*   213

Notes   229

Contributors   240

Preface

The essays in this volume were originally delivered as papers at a conference held in January of 2001 at the Episcopal cathedral in Charleston, South Carolina. The conference was made possible by the vision and tenacity of three organizations—two Anglican and one Lutheran. They are S.E.A.D. (Scholarly Engagement with Anglican Doctrine), A.A.C. (American Anglican Council), and C.E.C.T (the Center for Evangelical and Catholic Theology). Each of these organizations has, in its own way, placed itself, as it were, "in the breach" and there stood with faith, hope, and charity (and, one should add, intellectual rigor) against forces whose desire to express Christian belief and practice in a more contemporary idiom has in fact led to their distortion and, on occasion, eclipse.

The conference and the presence of such a remarkable group of scholars were also made possible by the vision and tenacity of certain individuals. Deserving of first mention is the president of S.E.A.D., Professor Christopher Seitz of St. Andrews University. It was his fertile and bold mind that first dared think a conference such as this possible, and it has been his energy and devotion that have made what seemed at first a dream into a reality. Mention must also be made of the Right Reverend James Stanton, past president of the A.A.C. Without his support and that of the A.A.C., the organizers would have never found the financial means to bring this extraordinary group of scholars together. Special thanks are also due to the Right Reverend Edward Salmon, bishop of the Episcopal Diocese of South Carolina; the Very Reverend William McKeachie, dean of St Luke and St. Paul's Cathedral; and Martha Bailey, secretary both to the cathedral and to S.E.A.D.

Philip Turner
Dean of the Berkeley Divinity School at Yale (retired)

Introduction

Philip Turner

The poet Dylan Thomas, in his long prose poem *A Child's Christmas in Wales*, notes that one Christmas he received a book that told him "everything about the spider but why." I confess that I could very easily read everything about the spider and not ask why, but, in my case, I find such a lack of curiosity difficult to imagine when it comes to the creeds of the church. In this day and age, when creeds are regarded more often than not as outmoded restrictions on the free play of thought and imagination, a conference that proposes Nicene Christianity, and in particular the creed associated with this ecumenical council, as the basis of a new ecumenism is, to say the least, out of the ordinary. Even if one does not ask, the very existence of such a conference poses the question: Why?

The short answer is that the sponsoring organizations and the authors of the papers contained in this volume share a set of convictions about the nature of the church and about the place of theology within the life of the church. They believe these convictions provide a necessary basis for the renewal and reunion of the divided church. In contradistinction to the currently popular views that theology is best understood either as an attempt to give metaphorical expression to personal experience or as reflection upon forms of action directed by social and political goals, they hold that theology is properly understood as a practice with a soteriological goal that is properly carried out within the life of the church. They hold that theology receives its charter and subject matter from certain other practices or "marks" of the church that are themselves to be understood as works of the Spirit. In his treatise "On the Councils of the Church," Martin Luther lists them as the preached word of God; the sacraments of baptism and the Lord's Supper; church order and discipline; public prayer, praise, thanksgiving, and instruction; and finally, discipleship in suffering.[1]

I have no doubt that, given time and opportunity, the authors who contributed to this volume would characterize these practices in differing ways and give them differing emphases. Nevertheless, they all hold that theology is a church practice with a soteriological goal that is properly carried out within and in deference to this complex of practices. In keeping with these views, they hold also that theology, as a practice of the church, is responsible to the doctrines of the church as derived from Holy Scripture and given expression in the ecumenical creeds.

Why Nicene Christianity as the basis of a new ecumenism? Properly because it anchors the church in those beliefs and practices without which the church can preserve neither its unity in Christ nor its identity as Christian. Pragmatically because understanding Christian belief and practice either as an attempt to give expression to personal experience or as an engine that provides a religious motivation for political and social goals is an enterprise that, in the end, both distorts the Christian gospel and divides the church. It is not surprising, therefore, that S.E.A.D., A.A.C., and C.E.C.T. should sponsor a conference that focused on the Council of Nicea and its creed. Each of these organizations has a different history and each has developed a distinctive program. Nevertheless, they share a common concern, namely, the distorted and diminished character of Christian belief and practice that so characterizes not only the life of the denominations they represent but also that of the mainline churches in general. Each of these organizations has, in its own way, sought to awaken the churches in America to their plight and to recall them to forms of faith and practice that are both evangelical and catholic. Each has also insisted that such a work of reform and renewal requires more than fervor. It requires, as well, recovery of the full scope of the biblical narrative, a thorough inhabiting of the traditions of the church, and a critical engagement with the age in which we live. Each, in short, has insisted that the reform and renewal of the church simply cannot take place apart from an adequate theological base.

Nicene Christianity, and in particular the creed through which it is generally identified, provides an apt means to focus these shared concerns. From very early days, the creeds associated with the ecumenical councils have been taken as adequate summaries of both the biblical witness and the preaching and teaching of the church. Most, I suspect, know the fable told by Rufinus about the origin of the Apostles' Creed. It provides in narrative form an account of what the church has, from an early age, taken the basic purpose of its creeds to be. In 404, Rufinus said this of the Apostles' Creed:

> As they were therefore on the point of taking leave of each other, they first settled an agreed norm for their future preaching so that they might not find themselves, widely separated as they would be, giving out different doctrines to the people they invited to believe in Christ. So they met together in one spot, and, being filled with the Holy Spirit, completed this brief token, as I have said, of their future preaching, each making the contribution that he thought fit: and they decreed that it be handed out as standard teaching to believers.[2]

The creeds thus served, and I believe continue to serve, as tokens or badges of Christian identity. They provided and continue to provide a norm both for reading the scriptures and for evangelization and instruction. They provide a means of recognition for God's people, scattered as they are among the peoples of the earth. They have served both as a means of identity and as a basis for unity. Perhaps most of all, they contain the basic confession of Christians—a summary of their witness about the truth of God in Christ Jesus. Creeds are outlines of instruction, but they are also forms of witness, and thus they came, in time, to occupy an important place in the public worship of the church.

The confessional and unifying purposes of the creeds serve to explain their original connection with the instruction given people who were preparing for baptism. These purposes also explain why, in time, the creeds came to provide a means of ruling out certain false readings of the bible and certain false presentations of Christian belief and identity; they provided the basis of church doctrine. Thus, for example, to those who held that Christ was not fully God, it was necessary to say that he is God from God, Light from Light, true God from true God, begotten not made. But to those who insisted that he was not fully human, it was necessary to affirm that he was born of the Virgin Mary, became man, and was crucified under Pontius Pilate.

I am, of course, doing no more at this point than providing a reminder of what many already know about the place the creeds have occupied in the life of the church. In a positive sense, they have served as a guide to a correct reading of Scripture and an adequate expression of belief and identity. Negatively, they have served to rule out certain false readings and expressions. The question, of course, is whether they can or ought to continue to serve these functions. The papers here assembled defend the ability of the creeds to fulfill their historic function, but their authors are aware of the major problem the continued status of the creeds within the church presents. Some years back, Bishop, then Professor, Stephen Sykes identified this problem rather well in the discussion of Bishop Gore he included in his study *The Integrity of Anglicanism.*[3] In his attempt to come to terms with modernity, Bishop Gore made ample room for the findings of both literary and historical criticism in respect to the Bible. Nevertheless, he insisted that if anyone was to be a minister within the Church of England, that person must adhere to the creeds. He did not require such adherence of laypersons, but he did of the clergy. Indeed, he insisted that if the clergy could not accept the creedal miracles they should resign their orders.

Michael Ramsey, in *An Era in Anglican Theology, From Gore to Temple,* dealt a deadly blow to Gore's position. "If," he said, "criticism is allowed to modify thus far the presentation of the faith (drawn from Holy Scripture), what if criticism questions the substance of the faith as the creeds affirm it?"[4] In fact, criticism has indeed questioned the substance of the faith as affirmed in the creeds. Nevertheless, criticism can and should be answered. These essays respond to the critics of the creeds both by careful and close argument and by the reprise of the full breadth of their content.

This initial reminder of the nature and functions of the creeds, I grant, borders on banality. I enter it only to call attention to the place at which one must begin—with the nature and functions of the creeds as traditionally understood. However, in respect to the creeds, it would be quite ineffective to end with the beginning. The times require even of those who say the creeds without effacing them by means of a thousand qualifications that they give attention to each article and not simply to certain favored ones. In our time, the baleful results of what might be called *creedal précis* abound. One need look no further than the common habit among clergy of reducing their working creed to but a small part of a single article—for example, "he came down from heaven ... he became incarnate ... and was made man." How frequently does one hear the incarnation depicted apart from the full narrative of Christ's relation to both God and creation? In this truncated form, the second article of the creed (which displays the mystery of the incarnation), by an ironic inversion, becomes little more than a disembodied theological principle that can be used without restraint to bless the human condition *simpliciter.*[5] "He was crucified," the phrase that displays most clearly the full meaning of the incarnation, does no theological work beyond pointing to a moral tragedy. Phrases like "he ascended into heaven" and "he will come again to judge the living and the dead" simply have no meaning at all.

In hands such as these, Christianity becomes a religion of meaning and personal affirmation rather than a religion of salvation. Truncated creeds no longer serve as tokens or badges of Christian identity. Rather, they serve as simulacra of idolatrous attachments. By curious inversion the creeds, partially explicated and partially confessed, can become vehicles of an alien way. I have put an extreme case on the basis of popular usage among some liberal Protestants. The more usual case is less dramatic, but only slightly less serious. De facto creedal abridgements can result in a distortion rather than a complete metamorphosis of Christian identity. I cite but two examples. The Orthodox churches of the East have complained for centuries that the Western emphasis on the second article and its relative indifference to the third have resulted in an inadequate account both of the church and the Christian life. More recently, Douglas Farrow, in *Ascension and Ecclesia,* has pointed to the way in which eclipse of the phrase "he ascended into heaven" within the Western church has led to profound distortions in its self-understanding.[6]

One could, I think, mount an entire conference on the subject of the distorting results of the various contemporary creedal précis. A critical exercise of this sort is not, however, the purpose of these essays. The purpose of this collection is clearly displayed by the fact that no article of the creed is left in the shadows. To leave any part of the creed, as it were, on the academic shelf, does no more than contribute yet another précis to the welter already available. No! If Nicene Christianity, as expressed in its creeds, is to form the basis of a future ecumenism, the unifying identity to which it at one time gave expression cannot be reborn by means of a reduction in its working content—a reduction that is, say, more easily suited to contemporary taste and opinion.

If the creed that gave Nicene Christianity its badge of identity is once more to provide a basis for an adequate reading of Holy Scripture, and if it is once more to provide the grammar for a unifying way of Christian speaking, it must be presented whole and with sufficient force to once again shape and unify the mind and heart of the church. It must, in short, once more provide the basis for right Christian usage. If such an eventuality were to occur, then there might indeed be a future for a new ecumenism. This ecumenism would not be based upon halting and, in the end, vain attempts to pick and choose between the perceived strengths of the various portions of Christ's rent body. Rather, it would be based upon an attempt on the part of each fragment of the body to give up its pretensions and, in a state of humility and repentance, learn again to read the Bible with a common mind so as once again to witness and teach in a way that displays a common badge or token of Christian identity.

If the churches were to look at Nicene Christianity whole and afresh as the norm for reading Holy Scripture and as the grammar for Christian teaching and preaching, the exercise would, as the philosophers like to say, place them "on all fours" one with another. Each would have to approach the exercise "as a little child" learning to walk and talk. None could presume to be parent to the other. Were the churches to place themselves as what the New Testament refers to as *mikroi* or "little ones" under the tutelage of the Nicene fathers so as to learn as children, obedient to the commandment that requires honor to one's father and mother, to read and speak adequately, we would indeed have a new ecumenism—one that has a future.

The creeds can indeed form the basis of a new ecumenism, but having said this it is immediately necessary also to say that, though they can provide a lens for reading Holy Scripture and a grammar for Christian speech, they cannot in and of themselves generate adequate usage on the part of God's people. To change the metaphor, the various articles of the creeds can provide necessary topics for Christian speech, but they do not of themselves provide the full content of what needs to be said, nor do they supply the rhetorical tools to say what needs to be said in a way that is effective. Adequate exposition of these topics requires the practice of theology.

The creeds call for more than liturgical confession. Understood correctly, they invite the practice of theology into the center of the life of the church. The Nicene fathers understood this practice in a way that is different from ours. For us, theology is an academic discipline carried on by a professional guild ensconced in institutions of higher learning. For those at Nicea, theology was an aspect of an entire way of life, the purpose of which was the knowledge and love of God. As Tom Torrance has so well pointed out, for those at Nicea, there was a necessary connection between the rule of faith, explication, and godliness (*eusebeia*).[7] Right knowledge of God comes only insofar as the Scriptures are interpreted through the rule of faith in the context of the life and worship of the church and in an attitude of listening obedience. Reverence and holiness of life were thought by the Nicene Council to be particularly necessary for the practice of theology if in the exposition of Christian belief one was required to go beyond the actual words of Holy Scripture. In their minds, error was linked to ungodliness and ungodliness to error.

Nicene Christianity thus sounds an alarm for the contemporary church. The practice of theology, even a theology structured around the topics present in the creeds, can go wrong if it takes place apart from the life and worship of the church and apart from a form of life in which one learns both humility and charity. At present, the practice of theology takes place in exactly the way the council at Nicea suggested leads to error. If there is to be a new ecumenism rooted in Nicene Christianity, the setting and practice of theology will have to change in some very profound ways. In what will strike us as an amusing manner, the Council of Nicea has sent us a warning across time about the way in which the practice of theology is presently carried out, and it has done so by means of the its second canon. It reads in part as follows:

> For as much as, either from necessity, or through the urgency of individuals, many things have been done contrary to the Ecclesiastical canon, so that men just converted from heathenism to the faith, and who have been instructed but a little while, are straightway brought to the spiritual laver, and as soon as they have been baptized, are advanced to the episcopate or the presbyterate (or we might add to a teaching position), it has seemed right to us that for the time to come no such thing shall be done. For to the catechumen himself there is need of time and of a longer trial after baptism. For the apostolical saying is clear, "Not a novice; lest, being lifted up with pride, he fall into condemnation and the snare of the devil."

In respect to the practice of theology in the church, we might well repeat these words: "Not a novice!" The creeds in and of themselves are not a complete guide to Christian knowledge. On the one hand, they point to a way of reading the Holy Scriptures and, on the other, to a way of practicing theology that is very different from our own. Honoring the Council of Nicea as the source of a new ecumenism requires recovery of its way of reading the Holy Scriptures and its way of "doing theology."

But proper honor requires even more than this. It should be noted that full to the overflowing as this volume is, its content does not itself give the full honor that is due. There is an aspect of Nicene Christianity that is addressed in these essays only partially and in brief. Only but one of the papers addresses church order. Nicea, Constantinople, Ephesus, and Chalcedon did more than agree on creedal statements; they also promulgated canons. To be sure, the content of these canons, on the whole, has less relevance to our situation than does the content of the creeds. One need look no farther than the first canon agreed upon at Nicea to see why, generally speaking, we center attention on the creed and ignore the canons. It reads as follows:

If anyone in sickness has been subjected by physicians to a surgical operation, or if he has been castrated by barbarians, let him remain among the clergy; but, if any one in sound health has castrated himself, it behoves that such an one, if [already] enrolled among the clergy, should cease [from his ministry], and that from henceforth no such person should be promoted. But, as it is evident that this is said of those who willfully do the thing and presume to castrate themselves, so if any have been made eunuchs by barbarians, or by their masters, and should otherwise be found worthy, such men the Canon admits to the clergy.[8]

The evidence before us today does not suggest need for a canon prohibiting self-castration among the clergy. Contemporary circumstances do, however, suggest that the third canon might, with suitable revision, still have some relevance. It reads:

The great Synod has stringently forbidden any bishop, presbyter, deacon, or any one of the clergy whatever, to have a *subintroducta* dwelling with him, except only a mother, or sister, or aunt, or such persons only as are beyond all suspicion.[9]

Citation of these two canons may appear frivolous, but it seems a good way to direct attention toward a subject as necessary for the future of a new ecumenism as a sound grasp of Christian grammar. In passing canons, the Council of Nicea recognized that the order of the church was also a necessary aspect of its unity and identity. Thus, the fourth canon provides what might be called the "joists" of a sound doctrinal house. It reads:

It is by all means proper that a bishop should be appointed by all the bishops in the province; but should this be difficult, either on account of urgent necessity or because of distance, three at least should meet together, and the suffrages of the absent [bishops] also being given and communicated in writing, then the ordination should take place. But in every province the ratification of what is done should be left to the Metropolitan.[10]

It seems obvious that the purpose of this canon was to insure that those who succeeded the apostles, separated as they might be by great distances, would not, in the words of Rufinus, be "giving out different doctrines to the people they invited to believe in Christ." Given the fact that the church, prior to the return of its Lord, manifests within its own ranks the conflict between this age and the age to come, its unity and identity require the presence of people in authority who understand correctly the grammar that is to shape Christian speech and action. Prior to the age in which God is all in all, it is possible to misspeak and misact. Like it or not, those assembled at Nicea insisted on the need to place in positions of authority people whom accomplished speakers recognized as also being accomplished.

Nicene Christianity does more than provide a grammar for right Christian discourse. It suggests also the need for a form of governance capable of protecting and furthering right usage. Nicene Christianity suggests, in short, that the future of a new ecumenism cannot focus on the grammar of Christian belief and practice to the exclusion of an order that serves to insure that the ordinary speech of the church does not lapse into some form of Christian pidgin or, worse yet, become another language altogether. This statement does not imply that the future unity and identity of the church requires a three-fold ministry of bishop, priest, and deacon. It implies only that Nicene Christianity prods us to ask one another what form or forms of order best serve to ensure that in teaching and preaching we are not "giving out different doctrines to the people [who are] invited to believe in Christ."

At some future conference, it would be useful to ask what relevance the fourth canon has for us, the children of the Nicene Council. This question from the old ecumenism cannot be ignored, but it can be put in a different way. If we all become as little children, and if we give up the attempt to be parents one to another, we can ask afresh how, given the spots and wrinkles that now so disfigure Christ's body, we are to maintain a common form of speech and life. This is a question that once more places all the churches "on all fours" one with another. It presents a concern that necessarily arises among all people who claim a common token or badge of identity.

There is no better way of stating this concern and bringing these remarks to a close than by citing the last words of the synodal letter issued by the bishops assembled at Constantinople. Having settled who were to be bishops in those dioceses contested by the Arians, they said this:

> Thus since among us there is agreement in the faith and Christian charity has been established, we shall cease to use the phrase condemned by the apostles, I am of Paul and I of Apollos and I of Cephas, and all appearing as Christ's, who in us is not divided, by God's grace we will keep the body of the church unrent, and will boldly stand at the judgment seat of the Lord.[11]

Would that it were the case that the churches came to the point of being able to say, "among us there is agreement in the faith and Christian charity has been established." Would that it were the case that Christians ceased using the phrases of party spirit condemned by the apostles, "I am of Paul and I of Apollos." Most of all, would that it were the case that, having done all we can to mend the tears in Christ's body, we could at the end "boldy stand at the judgment seat of the Lord."

The essays collected in this volume, when taken as a whole, suggest that according to the Council of Nicene agreement in the faith, the establishment of charity, and the unity that these jointly constitute require a certain sort of "co-presence" within the life of the church. The rule of faith expressed in the creeds; the practice of a form of life rooted in humility, repentance, and charity; and forms of church order capable of protecting and furthering both the rule of faith and the form of life provide the matrix in which the grace of God unifies his people. It was this matrix that shaped the minds and hearts of those gathered at Nicea, and it is this matrix that holds the promise of a new ecumenism.

It is not difficult to see that, at present, discussions of the rule of faith, the Christian life, and the order of the church more often than not take place in separation one from another. So long as this division persists, no ecumenism, be it old or new, holds much promise. Despite the present inadequacies of our efforts, however, there is much reason for hope. Indeed, many of us now recognize our closest theological companions and our closest friends in the Lord across the denominational divides that so mark our history. These friends recognize one another in no small measure because each sees the need to bring these discussions together. This mutual recognition carries the promise of a new ecumenism—one rooted in common repentance, in a common attempt to learn again a common belief and form of life, and in a review of the order of the churches in the light of these concerns.

It is this form of ecumenism that carries promise, and it is this promise that is present in these papers. Their authors represent almost all the major traditions. None of them wishes to leave the tradition that has provided nurture in Christ, but all of them recognize among themselves a unity that lies deeper than these denominational badges. None wishes to start yet another church party—a Nicene party that lies between the spent force of theological liberalism and the dogmatic certainties of its evangelical critics. What they want is to hold up for all a form of belief and life that is rooted in the creed and practice of Nicene Christianity, and so also a form of unity that goes back behind the rending of Christ's body that has produced our present divisions.

1

Our Help Is in the Name of the LORD, the Maker of Heaven and Earth

Scripture and Creed in Ecumenical Trust

Christopher R. Seitz

This essay discusses the exegetical and theological significance of article one of the Nicene Creed. I will set the context (part one), discuss the meaning of the phrase "the maker of heaven and earth" and what was at stake in its selection (part two), discuss the phrase within the context of the entire first line of the creed (part three), and conclude with five reflections on what is still at stake when we use this language in our present context (part four). Much of what I have to say will involve a proper appreciation of God's name and of the relationship between language and truth—or saying what we mean and meaning what we say.

Part One: Setting the Context

I have been much interested in the phrase *the maker of heaven and earth*. If you had a concordance at hand, you would very quickly see that this phrase appears again and again in the Old Testament. It is a fixed formula, and it often appears right next to the divine, personal name, as in "Our help is in the name of the LORD [YHWH], the Maker of heaven and earth" (Ps. 124:8 NIV).

Some time ago this got me thinking that more is at stake in the creed's use of this phrase than a metaphysical declaration about creation, true though that is. The phrase rivots a statement not to an abstract concept, but to a person, Adonai (the LORD, YHWH), the maker of heaven and earth, and that fact ought not be run by too quickly. Moreover, its usage confirms an insight pressed upon us recently by David Yeago, that the creed and Scripture represent a far more natural and happy marriage than some scholars of early church and doctrine have allowed.[1] Creed is more than putting out theological brushfires. It is letting Scripture come to its natural, two-testament expression. Just as the Old Testament leaves its father and mother and cleaves to the New, so the Scriptures cleave to the creed, and the creed to them, and they become one flesh.

I want to dedicate these remarks to my father, Thomas Seitz, and to his father, William Clinton (little did he know) Seitz. My grandfather taught, among other things, doctrine at Bexley Hall. He had a clear influence on my father as priest and teacher. When Genesis speaks of generations, it includes this sort of influencing from one age to the next. "These are the generations of the heavens and the earth" (Gen. 2:4 NIV), or "This is the book of the generations of Adam. When God created man, he made him in the likeness of God. . . . Adam. . . became the father of a son in his own likeness, after his image" (Gen. 5:1–3 RSV). "From generation to generation," as the Old Testament puts it, God's word of instruction goes forth.

I received from my father's library a classic Anglican exposition of the creed by John Pearson.[2] In reviewing it as I brought this address to completion, I was struck at the great learning of the author. I was also struck at the sort of writing that was possible at that time, before the rise of higher biblical criticism and its adoption into the Anglo-Saxon world. (Ironically, it was the same Anglo-Catholic movement that revived interest in Pearson in the mid-nineteenth century that also conceded quite broadly to biblical criticism at the century's end, so for example, the volume of essays published in 1889 as *Lux Mundi*.) Pearson moves from Scripture to fathers to creed in an enormously effective, wide-ranging, and subtle way. The sort of method that Yeago, Frances Young, or Richard Bauckham might now argue for, given the rise of historicism, consists for Pearson as self-evidence.[3]

The other lesson I take away from Pearson, and from my father and his father, is that the work was completed in the context of parish instruction. The book opens with an appreciative address to "the right worshipful and well-beloved parishioners of St Clements, Eastcheap." Pearson is put in mind of Jude's concern for the faith once delivered. Absent from his concern is pride or self-righteousness. Pearson speaks simply of the responsibility before God, as a parish minister, to teach the faith of the church. Here is a model for ministry today.

Pearson says, "If it were so needful (for Jude) and for them to whom he wrote to contend for the first faith, it will appear as needful for me now to follow his writing, and for you to imitate their earnestness, because the reason which he renders, as the cause of that necessity, is now more prevalent than it was at that time, or ever since." Then the quoting Jude (my adaptation of RSV), "For admission has been secretly gained by some . . . ungodly persons who pervert the grace of our God into licentiousness, denying the only Lord God and our Lord Jesus Christ."

In our situation, the difference is that we are not talking about a "secret admission" into the household of God, but of public and proud pronouncement by church leaders. Both Jesus Christ but more deliberately "Our Lord God" have been deconstructed, the latter proclaimed dead, parochial, in need of regendering, reimaging, or replacement.

I recently read the following in a news report of the thirty-first national conference, "God at 2000": "One of the most celebrated speakers was [Marcus] Borg, who advocates a brand of pantheism that rejects notions of a personal God in favor of a broader universal spirit. 'I grew up in a time and place where it was taken for granted that Christianity was the only true religion and Jesus the only way to salvation,' Borg recalled with distaste. 'That's why we had missionaries. . . . I find it literally incredible to think that the God of the whole universe has chosen to be known in only one religious tradition.'"

Compare the remarks of St Augustine.

What are you then, my God—what, but the Lord God? For who is Lord but the Lord? Or who is God save our God? Most high, most excellent, most powerful, most almighty, most merciful, and most just; most hidden, yet most present; most beautiful, and most strong; stable, yet mysterious; unchangeable, yet changing all things; never new, never old; making all things new and bringing age upon the proud, though they know it not; ever working, yet ever at rest; still gathering, yet lacking nothing; sustaining, filling and protecting;

creating, nourishing, and maturing; seeking, yet possessing all things. You love without passion; you are jealous without anxiety; you repent, yet have no sorrow; you are angry, yet serene; change your ways, yet your plans are unchanged; recover what you find, having never lost it; never in need, yet rejoicing in gain; never covetous, yet requiring interest. You receive over and above, that you may owe—yet who has anything that is not yours? You pay debts, owing nothing; remit debts, losing nothing. And what have I now said, my God, my life, my holy joy—what is this I have said?[5]

At least one Trinity conference speaker got it right when she said, "Surely there is no one participating in this conference who really believes that this conference is about God at 2000. This conference is about us at 2000."

There you have it.

By contrast, Pearson settles to have as his task the plain exposition of the words of both the creed for God's own sake and "also the truth thereof, and what efficacy and influence they have in the soul" (a topic ably pursued by Fitz Allison in *The Cruelty of Heresy*).[6] Pearson concludes that his responsibility is "by collection of all, briefly to deliver the sum of every particular faith, so that everyone, when he pronounceth the Creed, may know what he ought to intend, and what he is understood to profess, when he so pronounceth it." I can think of no better statement of purpose than that.

The one inadvertent piece of Christian wisdom at the Trinity conference was supplied by a follower of the faith of Islam: "If you accept that your religion is relative you will not follow it. There must be something of absoluteness within religion. . . . Otherwise, there will just be languages that don't mean anything."

I thank my father for passing on Parson's clear-teaching volume. I especially prize his handwritten notes, which I suspect he made in the context of teaching ordinands, a task that as an examining chaplain it was his responsibility to discharge in the course of parish ministry, now fifty years in the undertaking

Part Two: What Does *Maker of Heaven and Earth* Mean and What Was at Stake in the Phrase's Selection?

> And is it true? And is it true,
> This most tremendous tale of all,
> Seen in a stained-glass window's hue,
> A Baby in an ox's stall?

> The Maker of the stars and sea
> Become a Child on earth for me?
> The Maker of the Heavens and Earth
> Become a Child for all God's worth?[7]

When we say the words, "I believe in one God, the Father Almighty" and then "maker of heaven and earth," we are right to believe we are describing a specific activity of God. God made the heavens and the earth. He made all things visible and invisible, as it says in the creed's restatement of this.

The reference to this activity comes as the very first sentence of Scripture. "In the beginning God created the heavens and the earth" (Gen. 1:1 NIV).

The Old Testament refers to this activity in its own creedlike formulations. God as Creator is the subject of the Psalms of enthronement (Pss. 92–99), and hymns to God as Creator are not uncommon (Pss. 8, 104). Then again, the phrase may appear of itself, as in, "I lift up my eyes to the hills: from whence comes my help? My help comes from the LORD, the Maker of heaven and earth" (Ps. 121:2 NIV; cf. Ps. 134:3). Lengthy descriptions of God as Creator can be found in Job and Deutero-Isaiah. In the long prayer of David at the dedication of the temple, we hear, "Yours, O LORD, are the greatness, the power, the glory, the victory, and the majesty; for all that is in the heavens and on the earth is yours" (1 Chron. 29:11 NRSV), establishing the logic of pantocreator (the Almighty) alongside creation alongside praise of God's name. Paul before the gentile Athenians proclaims, "What therefore you worship as unknown, this I proclaim to you. The God who made the world and everything in it, he is the Lord of heaven and earth" (Acts 17:23–24 NRSV). This is but a modest sample from a large range of usage.

What we see in these examples is the description of God as the one who, amid various other activities, created the heavens and the earth. More than this, we would be right to say this is a special activity of God. As such, it sits alongside other such special activities. For example, the solemn phrase, "I am the LORD who brought you out of Egypt" is notable for its frequency in the Old Testament. So too, "The LORD, the LORD, compassionate and merciful." Phrases like this are repeated and reused until their rough edges are worn off. They are moved from being episodic statements of an activity, making or bringing out or having compassion, and begin taking on an appositive or predicative character. So, in a context of Psalm petition, and not the act of creation itself, we hear "Our help is in the name of the LORD, the Maker of heaven and earth," or "May the LORD bless you from Zion, the Maker of heaven and earth," (Ps. 124:8, 134:3 NIV).

The activities to which such phrases refer are irreplaceable and non-universaliable. They are single events whose doer, whose author or agent, has no substitute. Deutero-Isaiah makes explicit what is everywhere assumed: "For thus says the LORD, who created the heavens (he is God!), who formed the earth and made it; . . . I am the LORD, and there is no other" (Isa. 45:18 NRSV). No one else brought Israel out of Egypt. No one else is gracious and compassionate. No one else created the heavens and the earth. Just this agent and no other agent can be connected to an activity men later will speak about independently of him when they speak of creation, the making of the universe, and all created matter, some visible and some invisible. We now talk about an activity and use various names for it—creation, evolution, cosmology—without using God's name; our words are detached from his sovereignty into rival modes of rationalism.

There can be no doubt that swirling about at Nicea were various rival understandings of God and creation. Was God by himself or were there demigods? Did one god create a good heavenly or spiritual reality and another an earthly or carnal realm? That this discussion took place is undeniable, and the statements of the creed live and have their being within a climate where they are statements canceling out rivals. They are counterfactuals, the saying of "no" to alternatives.

The Old Testament also presents a world where rival understandings of the word god exist, together with rival views of a single deity's or several deities' relationship to the created order. Yet the primary mode of speech on this matter in the Old Testament is not argumentative or persuasive but declarative. In the sentence to which we have just referred, it is important to take account of the order, "I am the LORD, who brought you out of Egypt, you shall have no other gods before me." The LORD's existence and sovereignty are not conclusions to be drawn after one assesses alternatives. We know about creation or deliverance or compassion only because the one God demonstrates these, speaks them forth, and gives us speech in return to refer to him. God speaks his word, and he fulfils what he says, faithfully. In this way he establishes his sole lordship, from which we learn that he is Lord, he alone, the Maker of heaven and earth.

So if we ask what was at stake at Nicea, in the very first instance it was the declaration that the God and Father Almighty of the Lord Jesus was this named LORD and none other. Jesus is not related to godness. Nor is

Jesus known independently of the LORD's speech in Israel, which accords or figures his coming. This properly named LORD gave the name above every name, his own name, to Jesus, that at his name every knee would bow to the glory of the Father. "Our help is in the name of the LORD, the Maker of heaven and earth" is a statement in which the two phrases, seek to fill out what can be said in one only partially as is typical of Hebrew poetry. This might be called an Old Testament version of *homoousia*. The name *Adonai* is "of one being" with *maker of heaven and earth*. To say *maker of heaven and earth* is to say *The LORD*. It is just as specific a denotation as "he who brought Israel out of Egypt," "he who raised Israel from the dead of dry bones," or "he who raised Jesus from the dead." Jenson treats this matter with great clarity.[8]

When Paul says to the Athenians in Acts 17 that the unknown god is the Lord of heaven and earth, he is not in the first instance arguing something about creation on the basis of common assumptions. Rather, he is asserting that the Maker of heaven and earth is the sole Lord, is the LORD who brought Israel out of Egypt, is the Lord who has appointed one to judge the earth. Paul's reference to God's making all nations from one man and determining generations and boundaries finds its source in Genesis 1–11 alone, where the one God speaks these matters forth.

To be sure, among the many, many gods Paul was sickened by seeing at Athens, one was likely in charge of the realm of heaven and another of the realm of earth, and so his statement was canceling out some false and idolatrous things. But his was not a statement about the character of creation as an independent matter that the Athenians were in the dark about (which they were) and needed to be corrected about (which they did). In the first instance, Paul was stipulating that the Lord of heaven and earth was not the summation of all the other gods (a high god) or an alternative with a more compelling account of creation (a better god), but was an unknown and unknowable God, without his own speaking or sending, without his own self-declaration. Paul was virtually enacting the logic of Isaiah 45 at Athens. Isaiah reads "They [the nations] will make suppication to you, saying, 'God is with you alone, and there is no other. . . Truly, you are a God who hides himself, O God of Israel, the Savior'" (Isa. 45:1415 NRSV). Paul announces, "What therefore you worship as unknown, this I proclaim to you" (Acts 17:23 NRSV), filling Isaiah's promise to its fullest measure.

In sum, the phrase maker of heaven and earth functions to point explicitly to the named God of Israel, about whom certain understandings of creation and sovereignty can be known only by reading these, not from nature itself with something called unaided reason—but from the Old Testament's account of the Creator, who rules by his word and his name in Israel, and by his sovereign mystery, his almighty rule, over the nations and in creation, shutting the mouth while opening the eyes of that grateful gentile Job.

Part Three: "Maker of Heaven and Earth" and Article One as a Whole

The first thing to note is that "maker of heaven and earth" exists within a bundle of expressions that speak of God. It is the fourth in a series; "one God," "the Father," "Almighty," and only then "maker of heaven and earth."

Two parenthetical notes: in the seventeenth-century exposition of Pearson, the judgment was made to treat God as Father and God as Almighty as separate while also discussing their meaning conjoined as "the Father Almighty." This is right. Second, we note in passing that the final phrase of the first article of the creed, "and of all things visible and invisible," is a virtual restatement of "maker of heaven and earth"; it does not seek to say anything different.[9] A separate treatment of *of all things visible and invisible* could imply that *Maker of heaven and earth* needed greater precision, which it does not. Each is a virtual restatement of the other, as the history of the creeds shows. Colossians 1:16 is only making clear root understandings from the Scriptures, correlated with the revelation in Christ.

For the phrase "I believe in one God," we look, of course, to the foundational language of the decalogue, "you shall have no other god," which follows directly upon the solemn self-declaration, "I am the LORD your God who brought you out of Egypt." The reflexes of this phrase in the Old and New Testament are too numerous to list. Consider only, "And this is life eternal, that they might know thee the only true God" (John 17:3 KJV); or, "Thou shalt worship the Lord thy God, and him only shalt thou serve" (Matt. 4:10 KJV). These are, in turn, based upon the logic of Deuternomy 4, "Hear, O Israel: The LORD our God is one LORD." "No one can serve two masters" (Matt. 6:24 NRSV), and Tertullian in *Against Marcion* puts it thus, "If God is not one, He is not."[10]

In this context it is important that Christians rightly grasp that God was known in Israel by his personal name, "the name above every name." Based upon a process already at work in the Old Testament, the name is rendered from Hebrew *Adonai* into Greek *kyrios,* "the Lord," but specifying a personal name and not a mere title. This name God gave to Jesus, so that at the name of Jesus, every knee should bow. He did not transfer an office only (lordship); he transferred his name, of himself. As David Yeago has pointed out, this confession from Philippians 2, heard in conjunction with Isaiah 45, establishes the pivotal judgement of Christian Scripture, which will give rise to the judgment of *homoousia,* even while the conceptual systems may and do differ (handing over a name and saying "of one substance or being").

So, God's name is not a phoneme known by those he has elected and withheld from others. Exodus tells us God's name is the disclosure of God's faithfulness in time, by speech in promise and fulfillment: "You shall know that I am who I am when I demonstrate the sovereignty of my promise and self" is the gist of Exodus 3–15. "I am who I am" is God's history and identity, his *ehyeh aser ehyeh* when he says it and *Adonai* when his people say it back or the nations confess it. As such, God's name encloses a particular history with a particular people, providing them with particular memories and particular understandings of their future in God's time. God's name declares a specific identity with a providential purpose. "He who brought Israel out of Egypt" is he who made the heavens and the earth is he who has sworn by himself: to him shall every knee bow and every tongue confess a solemn oath, to the ends of the earth (Isa. 45:22–25). This is the one who is as he is, in revelation to his people.

To believe in one God and no other god is to believe in this God, whose name is spoken not only by a particular people in recollection and promise, but also by those who now, having been enclosed in a covenant of blood, name Jesus Christ Lord (*kyrios*) to the glory of his Father. Barth once said that Christian (trinitarian) doctrine "neither is nor claims to be anything else" than an explanatory confirmation of the name, YHWH-*kyrios.*[11]

The Father is somewhat rare language for God in the Old Testament. It would appear to emerge within a specific set of constraints. First, it appeared when multiple connected covenant promises were threatened, including those to Noah, Abraham, Moses, David, and Zion (so Isaiah's final chapters). "But you are our Father, though Abraham does not know us" the prophet says in 63:16. You O LORD, are our Father, our Redeemer from of old is your name" (NIV). In chapter 64 the appeal is more explicitly to God's act of creation. "O LORD, thou art our father; we are the clay, and thou thou our potter" (v. 8 KJV).

Here is the second constraint. The logic of Genesis 1–5 is that as Seth is in the image of Adam, so mortal man and woman are in the image of God. God is not a male deity. He is not human fathering projected upstairs. God is "our Father" when his created and chosen people so cry out in uncreation and rejection. Genesis speaks of "the generations of the heaven, and the earth" in a pregnant phrase (2:4 NRSV) and then tells of Adam being formed from the earth by God, who is Father in something of the way Adam is father to Seth. "The title of Father is given unto divers persons or things, and for several reasons unto the same God," Pearson writes. Then, quoting Genesis 2:4, he comments, "So that the creation or production of anything by which it is, and before was not, is a kind of generation, and consequently the creator or producer of it a kind of Father."[12] Moving from this basis in Genesis, he can commend Job 38:28, "Hath not the rain a father?" (KJV) alongside Malachi 2:10, "Have we not all one father? Hath not one God created us?" (KJV) en route to 1 Corinthians 8:6, "to us there is but one God, the Father, of whom are all things" (KJV). The proximity to creedal confession is obvious.

God is "our Father" who is "ours" outside Israel when his son teaches us so to pray. When we do so, our unelection and estrangement, in the language of Ephesians our "without God in the world" status (2:12 NRSV) is eternally and providentially altered, in accordance with the promise of those same Scriptures in which God's name was named and known and praised. God is "the Father," and because of Jesus restorative work as the new Adam, begotten not made, "our Father in heaven, hallowed be his name."

The Almighty is yet a further gloss, or virtual metonym, for the name that is to be hallowed (*Adonai*). "Thus says Adonai, the LORD of hosts, I am the first and I am the last; besides me there is no god" (Isa. 44:6 NRSV). As though reflecting on Genesis, "I form light and create darkness, I make weal and create woe; I Adonai do all these things" (45:7 NRSV). Almighty over creation, over time, over holiness and moral order. We know that as the divine name began to recede in use (probably out of fear of misuse by Gentiles "brought near"), metonyms we deployed to refer to God. So *Almighty* (*ha'-olam*), to which, for example, the predications of David's prayer would logically point: "Yours, O LORD, are the greatness and the power and the glory and the victory and the majesty, and so on). So, too, the psalmist's simpler, "Our help is in the name of the Lord, the Maker of heaven and earth" (124:8 NIV). Father, Almighty, Maker of heaven and earth, each in its own way bespeaks the divine and sacred name.

Part Four: What Does "I Believe in the Maker of Heaven and Earth" Mean Today?

Jesus makes no sense without the Father, without the prior "I believe in one God, the Maker of heaven and earth." Childs puts it thus, "The faith of the Christian church is not built upon Jesus of Nazareth who had a Jew-ish background, but its faith is directed to God, the God of Israel, Creator of the world, the Father of our Lord Jesus Christ."[13] James Barr states, "It is an illusory position to think of ourselves as in a position where the New Testament is clear, is known, and is accepted, and where from this secure position we start out to explore the much more doubtful and dangerous ter-ritory of the Old Testament. . . . In so far as a position is Christian, it is related to the Old Testament from the beginning."[14] From the standpoint of the New Testament, Lee Keck states, "the point is that no one can deal with Jesus of Nazareth without confronting the question of God, because his concentration on God and his kingdom is what was constitutive of Jesus."[15]

Three challenges must be resisted: the pursuit of a true Jesus behind the witness, to be called after the fashion of our day "the historical Jesus"; the reduction of a doctrine of God to the *beneficia Christi* (so, for example, Melanchthon in Barth's estimate); and the measuring of the work of Christ according to a virtue or religious asset he brings, especially as this is to be contrasted with the assets and virtues of the Old Testament or Judaism.

I have written at length on items one and three, so wish here only to high-light two, the problem of our understanding of God being fundamentally related to Christ's benefits as received by us.

A recent expositor misses the mark badly when he states, "We do not start, save in long retrospect, with article one of the church's creeds: 'I believe in God the Father.' Rather, our starting point is article two: 'I believe in Jesus Christ, his only son our Lord.' This is an unfortunate distinction, and the problem is compounded when the declaration is made that 'theology is unable to start from God as the creator of the universe.' Then, issue is taken with Barth (and, one might also say, with Augustine, Thomas, Calvin, and a list too long to begin) in a sweeping conclusion: 'Barth did not start with Jesus. He started with the electing or sovereign God who said "Let there be light!" and there was light (Gen. 1:3). He started with God's electing choice in general rather than God's grace in Christ in particular. Barth's God was too removed, too other. This is because we live here!"[16]

Obviously a Christian apologetic must make strategic decisions. But I think we would have to conclude: what is at issue is not Barth's God, but God as he is portrayed in Scripture and in creed, as the starting point from which condescension and enclosure gain their logic in salvation. When the first line of the creed can be called a "long retrospect," we must consider whether the logic of Nicea is being renegotiated in the name of a diagnosis of culture, well-intended, which is itself mistaken.

Let us stay with the matter of the removed or "too other" God. The problem here is to do with matters associated with so-called natural theology. If one were to assume that we begin with vague apprehensions of godness such as these are supplied by nature, God could indeed be viewed as detached or remote (so Locke, Kant). But just as surely he or she could well become too proximate, too naturally derived. Such was the schizophrenia of late antiquity that Athens had an unknown god ranged alongside gods of every description, regulating this or that aspect of the material world.

The otherness or remoteness of God lacks precision in this formulation. God's otherness (or holiness in the lexicon of the Old Testament) is not to do with natural theology, but turns on election and God's own essential character as holy. God is not remote in Israel; he comes as judge! Moses sees him face to face. He speaks his word. Because he has chosen Israel, he enforces his will directly with her. Israel has been told. "Have you not known?!" could not be said with more urgency.

The nations stand in another relationship. Israel insists God governs them in ways they do not know (Cyrus) or in ways they come to learn in judgment (so Sodom, so the nations in Amos 1–2, so Sennacherib in Isaiah 37) or awe (so Job). Here is a remoteness, of sorts, in nature: an estrangement from God without the Creator laying direct claim to us in his son, his servant Israel in whom he is well pleased.

It is not possible to speak of Jesus as this Savior without speaking of the God who sent him. This is the whole force of the creed's logic and order. There is no Jesus Christ apart from the prior electing, creating "Maker of heaven and earth." There is no "for me" that can be said before first is said, "the Maker of the stars and sea became this child on earth."

The creed is not lacking in its affirmation of the witness of the entirety of the Old Testament's presentation of God. Neither is it a "long retrospect." Instead, it is a pithy, telegraphic recapitulation, that focuses on God's self and identity so as to lay claim to the complete sweep of Israel's witness. "One God, the Father Almighty, the Maker of heaven and earth"—these phrases intend to comprehend the vast range of Old Testament witness in law, prophecy, wisdom, and praise.

Kendall Soulen has recently worried about what he regards as omissions in the Christian creeds and in Christian dogmatic theology: "Following the creeds, countless works of Christian theology set forth the dogmatic content of Christian belief almost wholly without reference to God's way with

Israel. The first and largest part of the Bible possesses no doctrinal locus of its own, nor is it often materially decisive for any other locus." And, "Indeed the background can be completely omitted from an account of the Christian faith without thereby disturbing the overarching logic of salvation history. This omission is reflected in virtually every historic confession of Christian faith from the Creeds of Nicea and Constantinople to the Augsburg confession and beyond" ("The First Scottish Confession [1560]" being a recent exception).[17]

But as von Campenhausen has stated (paraphrased by Childs), "the problem of the early church was not what to do with the Old Testament in the light of the gospel, which was Luther's concern, but rather the reverse. In the light of the Jewish scriptures which were acknowledged to be the true oracles of God, how were Christians to understand the good news of Jesus Christ?"[18] What this means theologically is that the Old Testament presentation of God is the fixed point with which the creed seeks to correlate the church's understanding of Christ and the Holy Spirit. It does not belabor the point by listing the mighty acts of God in the Old Testament; to do so would suggest that a defense or apologetic was required. The phrases *one God, Father Almighty and Maker of heaven and earth* unequivocally point to this God, who was known in the Old Testament. The very lack of expansion is testimony to the givenness of this witness from the bosom of Israel, such that the stock phrases function to encapsulate the whole.

It is another thing, rightly I believe, to worry with Soulen about the church's present confusion on this front. The correction does not come from filling out lacunae in the creed, however, which do not in fact exist. The correction comes from making clearer what the language means.

The insistence on the rootedness of this description of God in the Old Testament must guard against another tendency, however. The God of the Old Testament has fully identified himself with Jesus Christ. He does not continue to exercise some separate, untamable, unpredictable rule prior to, and perduring after, what he has made clear in Jesus. The New Testament does not introduce great parenthesis outside which God retains an unruly and undomesticatable authority. The mystery and sovereignty of God the Maker of heaven and earth are guarded precisely as these attributes are true of Christ, who raises the dead and walks on water, and of the Holy Spirit, who blows as he will—not over against them. The creed does not seek to isolate the Father so as to ensure his majesty. It points us to the God of Israel and asks us to see in his life with the world as shown there that which comes to expression in complete terms in his Son. To speak of the Old Testament as Christian Scripture and not as Hebrew Bible is not an offense to Judaism, which takes this same literature and hears it through the testimony of tradition, just as Christians hear it in conjunction with the testimony of a second testament. Stressing the Jewishness of God by reinstating his name or enumerating his Israel-specific life untouched by his condescension in his Son makes sense neither for Jew nor Christian.

Again, Childs puts it succinctly in his review of Brueggemann's recent Old Testament theological exposition,

> By juxtaposing Israel's core testimony with his so-called counter-testimony, Brueggemann sees the task of interpretation to be a never-ending activity of negotiating between conflicting voices. There is never a final testimony, but every interpretation is described as provisional and shaped by shifting "socio-ecclesial-political-economic contexts" within the process of disputation (p. 711). The result is the God of Israel is both gracious and merciless, truthful and deceptive, powerful and impotent which is constitutive of the very nature of this deity.[19]

> In spite of Brueggemann's constant reference to the "Jewishness of the Old Testament," the irony emerging from his description of God is one that no serious religious Jew can tolerate. Israel's faith in God rests on Torah, covenant, and eternal promise, which are nonnegotiable because of the truth of God's Word. The stability of God in relation to his people sets Israel's faith apart from all the arbitrariness and confusion of paganism. Of course, there remain continuous threats, demonic terros, and persistent evil, but these do not alter God's unswerving commitment to the patriarchs. Israel continues to suffer because of its confession that God has not, and will not, change toward his people in spite of experiencing life on the very edge of distinction.[20]

> Precisely being able to turn from their gods to the true God occasioned the joy, with which the apostles' gentile converts . . . received the word. In the act of faith, gentile believers recognize themselves as those who have worshipped or might have worshipped Moloch the baby-killer or Astarte the universal whore or *Deutsches Blut* or the Free Market or the Dialectic of History or the Metaphor of our gender or ethnic ressentiment, and on through an endless list of tyrants. Only a naiveté impossible for the apostolic church, which fully inhabited the religious maelstrom of late antiquity, can think that religion as such is a good thing or that gods are necessarily beneficent.[21]

Jenson makes several points here, but I want to focus on two in conclusion.

We are living in a time of religious naiveté. Culture's claim "that we all worship the same god" points to the issue at stake. If God is not one, he is either many or he is not (to quote Tertullian). To say that God is one is not to say he resides in a Jesus of past history or somewhere behind or above the language about him in the Scriptures of Israel. God cannot be worshiped through a veil of imperfect language about him. That is naive, and here antiquity was far more honest. It spoke of an unknown god but was unable to maintain such a stoic courage, and so filled shrines with gods with names and specific language known to be about them and them alone.

Pearson is right to say that a speaker of the creed should expect to know "what he ought to intend, and what he is understood to profess, when he so pronounceth it." This claim about language is not one Pearson is importing to the creed. It belongs to the Scriptures' most fundamental claim about creation that our language can reliably and specifically name God, address God, and speak of him as he is truly.

Out of the babel of religious talk, "You shall worship the Lord your God and him only shall you serve" sounded the only true alternative. God is one and his creation can speak of him because he has given it to be so, not because we need it or desire it. "I believe in one God, the Father Almighty, the Maker of heaven and earth" is language God has given us to use so we can call upon him and know that he knows himself to be addressed. In so doing, we move into a personal relationship to him, akin to what it meant for Israel to call on his name in their day and to guard the name against all common use, vain speculation, or "god-talk." To be brought into this relationship is, as Jenson puts it, what occasioned the joy of the first apostles.

> Ah, Lord, Who hast created all,
> How hast Thou made Thee weak and small,
> That Thou must choose Thy infant bed
> Where ass and ox but lately fed![22]

Christian talk about God begins with his holiness, his oneness, his majesty in creation, his speech in Israel in order to understand the depth of his mercy and kindness toward us in Christ. It begins with his holiness because this is where he begins, in his eternal life with the Son and the Spirit.

Christians are brought near in Christ to learn the extent of his love and of our estrangement, in one fell swoop. To share his name and self with us, to make us new again in him, requires the bestowal of his holiness, the character that P. T. Forsyth has described as "the eternal moral power which must do, and do, till it sees itself everywhere,"[23] giving us speech to say back to him, "I believe in one God, the Father Almighty Maker of heaven and earth."

A fitting conclusion is Augustine's opening prayer in *Confessions:*

> Grant me, Lord, to know and understand which of these is most important, to call on you or to praise you. Or again, to know you or to call on you. For who can call on you without knowing you? For he who does not know you may call on you as other than you are. . . . Let me seek you Lord by calling on you, and call on you believing in you as you have been proclaimed to us. My faith calls on you Lord, the faith you have given me.

2

And in One Lord, Jesus Christ . . . Begotten, Not Made

Colin Gunton

The Perennial Problem: Arianism

Arianism was perhaps the twentieth century's favorite heresy, and it is among the most appealing of them all. It teaches that in his being Jesus Christ is in some way less than fully divine, and it appears to have support from Scripture. There have been numerous recent studies of Arius himself, and they include attempts to defend him on various grounds.[1] I believe that they fail, but that does not affect the position I want to develop, which is that one can construe Arianism as a perennial type of approach to Christian doctrine, just as one can similarly construe Gnosticism, even if Irenaeus was wrong in detail about the particular teachings of his various opponents. Certain heresies are archetypal as attractive solutions to difficulties that are intrinsic to the faith and will therefore continue to appear in every generation. Various symptoms of the particular disease with which we are concerned can be identified, the best-known being found in the Arian slogan "there was when he was not," that the Son, the second person of the Trinity, has an origin that is in some way posterior to that of God the Father. The ontological aspects—considerations to do with God's being—are theologically crucial, for corresponding to a reduction of the Son's eternity there is one of his ontological status. In some marked respect he is less truly divine than God the Father. The error of this is that it detracts from his saving significance, for if he is not fully divine, his capacity to be the savior from sin and death is called into question. Against Arianism was directed the doctrine of the eternal begottenness of the Son: that God the Son's being the Son of the Father was not a temporal process, as is the case with all instances of created fatherhood, but is eternal.

A reduction in Jesus Christ's saving significance is precisely what Arius's present-day representatives want, for implicit in much modernist critique of ancient theology is the supposition that we do not really require saving because in some sense we are intrinsically able to save ourselves, in some way we are already implicitly or potentially divine. That is why the fate of Christianity in the modern Western world depends upon a secure hold on the Nicene inheritance. Without it, just as ancient Christianity would have disappeared, had Arius conquered, into the mass of ancient religiosity, so today the church would likewise become just one version of modern body, mind, and spirit paganism—as some no doubt wish it to become. It is at this place that study of antiquity profits us, for it is precisely where modern thought contains a restoration of certain ancient philosophical assumptions that it is driven to Arianism.

I will begin a discussion of the ancient evidence with the work of an influential, in my view disastrously influential, Anglican theologian of an earlier generation (indeed, my predecessor but one in the chair that I occupy). It is to Maurice Wiles's credit that, even if he comes to the wrong conclusion on its basis, his setting out of the early development is clear and scholarly.[2] All true scholarship is on the side of the angels, even if we ultimately conclude on its basis that something from the past has to be rejected. For the fact is, as Wiles has shown, that there were two aspects of the development of the doctrine of the eternal generation of the Son of God, which, far from serving to undermine the heresy, were actually fraught with Arian threat. "In the first place the original use of the concept of generation to describe the relation of the first two persons of the Trinity was not very closely linked to an understanding of them as Father and Son." The tendency of the apologists to prefer the word *Logos* to *Son* is a symptom of the first of our problems, for, although Wiles does not note this, it introduces a tendency to depersonalize the relationship, preferring, that is to say, rational to personal categories in expounding the relationship between the Father and the Son. If that is an oversimplification, a clearer view of the problem is given by the kind of appeal to Scripture that was used to support the apologists' case.

Proverbs 8:25 (NIV), "before the mountains were settled in place, before the hills, I was given birth," was, as Wiles notes, "of primary importance."[3] Not only is this full of Arian possibilities—there manifestly was when wisdom was not—but its dominance also dangerously limits both the range and the type of the Old Testament evidence that can be called upon. This is a question to which we must return. Another aspect of the same set of problems raised by the apologists is that the orientation of the discussion was to the eternal Trinity at the expense of the revealed or economic. Our topic has to do with the eternal Trinity—with whom the Father and Son are eternally, and what their relationship may be. But once the conception breaks free from the economy, from what happens in time, the dangers of abstraction present themselves in full force. And that takes us to the second set of problems raised by the early development and noted by Wiles.

For this we move into a later century, to the contribution of Origen of Alexandria, who is much praised even by orthodox historians of dogma for his development of the doctrine of the eternal generation of the Son. The price that was paid, however, is that Origen's primary defense of the doctrine lies in an a priori appeal to divine immutability, almost always a bad form of argument (rather like the "he must have . . ." appeal so popular among modern biographers who wish to impose their own interpretation of their subjects, and particularly to speculate about their sexuality in the absence of evidence). In like manner, Origen is really interested not in the evidence of the relation between the Father and the Son as it is revealed in the biblical narrative, but in what "must be" the case. In the crucial section of his *On First Principles,* he defines "the only-begotten Son of God" as "God's wisdom hypostatically existing."[4] He continues: "And can anyone who has learned to regard God with feelings of reverence suppose or believe that God the Father ever existed . . . without begetting this wisdom?"[5] As Wiles shows, however, this kind of argument offered assistance to Arians in the respect that it failed to guarantee the uniqueness of the Son, but only established his eternity. Origen's other a priori appeal, to God's omnipotence, led him to suppose that not only the Logos but also the creation—or an aspect of it—was eternal.[6] Notice by contrast the emphatic language of the creed, which might have been developed to counter it: "in *one* Lord Jesus Christ."

This consideration raises for us another question to which we must give attention: the nature of the language we are using. To say that Jesus Christ is begotten is to use a metaphor, for clearly, whatever else is the case with his being begotten in time in the womb of Mary, he is not there eternally begotten. To say that God the Father is the negation of this—that he is unbegotten—is to contrast the ways of being of the Father and the Son, their intratrinitarian. It is to specify an intratrinitarian difference, and it remains metaphorical in the respect that its use is transferred from the finite to the infinite realm. It was, however, the further and also metaphorical use of the term *unbegotten* that muddied the waters. G. L. Prestige, to whose scholarship Wiles makes appeal, points out that Clement of Alexandria and Origen use the word originally meaning unbegotten (*agennētos*) "in the sense of 'absolute,' implying eternity, causation, and transcendence of finite limitations."[7] He is, however, far too optimistic in supposing that the development represents a gain both in precision and theology. To use *unbegotten* to characterize the relation of creator and creation confuses two concepts that, as Athanasius well knew, must be distinguished in this context. One pairing, unbegotten-begotten, is best used, as we have seen, to conceive the relation between the Father and the Son; while the other, uncreated-created, to conceive that between God and the world. If the two are confused, we shall be faced with confusions of the kind we observed to arise in the case of Origen's development. Our creedal expression—begotten not made—makes it clear that the Father-Son relation must be understood in the framework of the first pairing, unbegotten-begotten. This is because we are here concerned with the relation between eternal persons, whereas the latter pairing is concerned with the relation between eternal creator and the creation, which is not eternal. To use *unbegotten* of the creator rather than of God the Father runs the risk of confusing the issue.

Why is this so? We saw that Arianism raises two related problems. The first is that God the Son is in some way less eternal than God the Father; the second that he is also in some way less fully divine. It is possible to affirm, as we have seen, that the Son is eternally begotten, and still to deny that he is unique. It can happen when the first of the two pairings we have met is confused with the second. Against that we have to say first that the Son is eternally begotten, which is to say that he not only is the product of the Father's eternal love but also in some way defines that love. To ask who God is is to receive the answer that he is the one who is the love of Father and Son in the Spirit—though for now we must leave on one side the third person of the Trinity. On the other hand, to ask what the creation is is to invite, Christianly, a significantly different answer. The creation, like the Son, is the product of God's eternal love, but it does not form part of that love's definition. To be God, this God cannot but be both Father and Son (at least); he does not similarly have to be creator. Our concept is needed to ensure, in a way that Origen did not, that the Son belongs necessarily to our understanding of the being of God. To see how this is to be understood, we must return to some of the questions so perceptively raised but wrongly answered by Professor Wiles.

The Biblical Center

First we must ask the question of what kind of justification for our creedal confession is given by, or can be sought from, Scripture. It is apparent to anyone reading Athanasius's diatribes against the Arians that what is at stake is not which texts from Scripture are used, but the way in which they are used. Between Arians and Athanasians lies a matter of theological hermeneutics—of what is Scripture made? The lesson for our purposes is that proof texting is not enough, and it must be acknowledged that there is some doubt as to whether Scripture supports the creedal confession directly or without great labor. We have seen already that an appeal to Proverbs 8 is highly dangerous, because whatever wisdom is in that place, it is not coeternal with God. The same may even be said—though admittedly far more questionably—of appeal to the prologue of John's Gospel. There is some dispute about the meaning of *monogenēs* in John 1:18 and whether it supports the kind of absolute identification of Jesus with the eternal Son of God that the creed affirms. It seems to me fairly obvious that it does, and that it clearly connotes something special, even unique. As one commentator argues, it is related to the word *agapētos*, used of Jesus at crucial times of his ministry, specifically his baptism and transfiguration.[8] But that suggests, at the very least, that we must go beyond any single proof text or texts and examine the broader context in which it must be understood, that of Scripture as a whole.

The function of the crucial episodes of baptism and transfiguration in the Gospels is clear. At baptism, Jesus' sonship is affirmed by the Father through the Spirit. During his ministry, this affirmation is tested first through temptations and trials of various kinds and then specifically at Caesarea Philippi in the further temptation, mediated to Jesus through Peter, not to go through with the specific responsibilities of sonship that have been imposed on him by his Father. Peter, like the devil in the wilderness, suggests that Jesus can be Son other than through the way of sacrifice. The reiterated *agapētos* at the transfiguration confirms and reinforces the original designation. Jesus' decision to go unarmed into the realm of the enemy is ratified by his Father. Similarly, at the death of Jesus—the fulfillment of his earthly calling—as it is described in Mark's Gospel, the words of the centurion place further confirmation on the lips of a Gentile. But the words in the Greek remain ambiguous, as are John's if we really wish to be skeptical. "Surely this man was—*a*—Son of God"? (Mark 15:39). Even here, therefore, the texts do not of themselves provide the uniqueness that we need, so we must proceed to examine something more of the character of the sonship that is presented in these and other passages.

One key to this phase of the inquiry is to be found in the fact that a crucial deficiency of Origen's defense of the eternal begottenness of the Son is its lack of appeal to Jesus, in whom he is not really very interested.[9] Indeed, we have to confess that many of the church fathers do not concern themselves overmuch with the fact indicated by his name, that he is a Jew, the roots of whose meaning are to be found only in the Old Testament. It is as faithful Israel that Jesus works out his sonship in a recapitulation of Israel's story, beginning, as we have seen, with a new wilderness temptation, a new testing in which this time a faithful sonship is realized, raising a cry of affirmation even from the lips of the Gentile observing the end of the ordeal. This Son is faithful and obedient, learning obedience in what he suffers as a man. We may not construe our creedal confession of his eternal sonship apart from this. Yet on the other hand, neither may we understand him simply as a man, for his sonship is not so limited. To develop the wider dimensions, we must return to Israel. Robert Jenson has recently reminded us of the centrality of Israel's sonship in the Old Testament:

> We see the way in which the narrative identification of God by his involvement with Israel displays a mutuality of *personae* whose differentiating relations are between God and Israel *and* somehow between God and God. . . . God is identified *with* Israel in that he is identified *as* a participant *in* Israel's story with him.
>
> Having seen these structures, we may then also note that prophets could explicitly evoke the Lord's relation to Israel as a relation of father to son, although their use of this language is rare.[10]

What we learn from this is something of the interaction of the eternal and the temporal already with Israel. Everything that takes place here is, indeed, the work of the eternal God, but because it is not achieved apart from Israel, neither can the being of Israel's God be construed without it. But there is a complication.

Israel may be the son of God, but not so eternally as the way in which our creed affirms of Jesus,[11] so we have to end this appeal to Scripture by saying something of what here is new also. We return to John 1:18 (NRSV), where "no one has ever seen God" almost certainly contains a reference to God's words to Moses in Exodus 33:20 (NRSV): "you cannot see my face; for no one shall see me and live." With this Israelite, things are decisively different. The *monogenēs* Son of God *exēgēsato,* exegeted, the Father—set him forth in time. That is surely part of the burden of John's Gospel as a whole: that those who see Jesus and are later educated into his story by the Holy Spirit *have seen* the Father. "Long ago God spoke to our ancestors in many and various ways by the prophets, but in these last days"—and observe the eschatological note which is so often absent from the later patristic treatments, though not from Irenaeus—"he has spoken to us by a Son," writes the author to the Hebrews. And this is a Son to fulfill, indeed, but also to exceed anything seen or spoken by the prophets: "whom he appointed heir of all things, through whom he created the worlds" (Heb. 1:1–2 NRSV). Paul had earlier engaged in a similar, and surely related, contrast of Jesus and Moses, speaking as he does of "the light of the knowledge of the glory of God in the face of Christ" (2 Cor. 4:6 NRSV).

The burden of all this is that we must extend our notion of Jesus' sonship to include more engagement with the relation between Jesus and his Father as it is worked out in the time of his ministry. Jesus is not only obedient Israel, but the eternal Son of God become, in Luther's words, the proper man. The relation between Jesus and the Father who affirms his sonship is also a relation between God and God, and this taking place of God in time is to be found in the verbs that describe what happened. Central are those that indicate sending and sacrifice: that God the Father sends and gives up his Son for the sins of the world (Gal. 4:4; Rom. 8:32). Perhaps most suggestive here is the placing in parallel, in Philippians 2, of the divine sending and the obedience of the second Adam. The one who was in the form of God both emptied himself to human estate and was obedient to death on the cross. The verbs express both a divine and a human obedience, whose meanings are inseparable. But theologically that is the source of problems as much as of solution, and that takes us to the second set of questions raised by Wiles's analysis. If the eternal Son is only given in and with time, by what right do we abstract or project to eternity and speak of one who is eternally begotten? And what is the meaning of the metaphor in which the relation of Father and Son is expressed?

From Economy to Theology

Scripture, to recapitulate, gives us across a broad range of its witness the foundation for our creedal confession, but it does not yet give us the fullness of the Nicene affirmation. All the texts we have adduced can be read in an Arian sense if we are determined enough, as some of our contemporaries appear to be. God may be in the verbs, because it is in and by them that time and eternity are given together, but the verbs remain temporal, lodged in time, and it does not of itself follow that from them we can read an eternal begottenness. We have a foundation but need to build upon it theologically if we are to move from economy to theology. A similar point can be made by saying that much of the language we have encountered could be given a subordinationist interpretation, that is, one that continues to hold that Jesus, even as Son, is subordinate in being to God the Father, and so in some way is less truly God than he.[12] We must here concede that there is a sense in which the Son is indeed subordinate to the Father. As we have seen, he is Son as he is sent, given, obedient; as he is, in a certain respect, though certainly not in others, passive.[13] It is in his suffering that his effective action lies. Two questions have to be pursued. First, could he not have done all the things attributed to him while remaining less than fully divine? Second do we need to move from economy to theology, from time to eternity? Much recent trinitarian writing has argued that we do not really need a doctrine of the immanent Trinity.[14] Do we, likewise, not need a doctrine of the eternal begottenness of the Son?

The first question has been answered definitively by Athanasius, and the shape of his answer will enable us to answer the second also. Much of his argument in *Against the Arians* tends, to be sure, to be rather a priori and to appeal too much to proof texts. But its achievement is in showing beyond all peradventure that Jesus could not have done all the things attributed to him had he been less than fully divine. Underlying everything is, it seems to me, an assurance based not on a priori questions about what Jesus could have done, but on what he did in fact do. Athanasius has a deep sense of human sinfulness and the fallenness of the whole creation, and this derives from his prior conviction that what has in fact happened can only be the work of one who is fully God. It is here that the theology of *On the Incarnation of the Word* is in many ways more helpful to our case than the polemics of the later work. Athanasius believes that Jesus Christ is the mediator of creation returning to his creation to restore the created order to its maker and so enable it to fulfill its original purpose. In turn, that founds his belief in the eternal divinity of the Son, and, accordingly, his later defense of the doctrine of eternal begottenness. The real basis of our creedal confession is to be found in what God has in fact achieved through the life, death, and resurrection of his Son, the one through whom he created and upholds the world.

For Athanasius,

> transgression of the commandment was turning them (human beings) back to their natural state, so that just as they have had their being out of nothing, so also, as might be expected, they might look for corruption into nothing in the course of time.[15]

The return to nothingness that was the natural result of sin could be prevented only by an act of grace of the original creator:

> Now, if there were merely a misdemeanour in question, and not a consequent corruption, repentance were well enough. But if, when transgression had once gained a start, men became involved in that corruption which was their nature . . . what further step was needed? or what was required for such grace and such recall, but the Word of God, which had also at the beginning made everything out of nought?[16]

The chief reason for the move from economy to theology, from what happened to an account of the being of the eternal God whose economy it is, is Athanasius's conviction, which was that of Irenaeus also, that the Son of God is mediator not only of redemption but of creation also. Perhaps here, at the risk of complicating matters, I should pause to say something about Athanasius's awareness of a matter that has been with us from the beginning: the metaphorical nature of the language that is being used. "The divine generation must not be compared to the nature of men, nor the Son considered to be part of God."[17] This is part and parcel of his recognition that it is one thing to be Creator, another to be creature. His firm hold on the distinction enables him, as is well known, to distinguish also between God's being and his will, that which God is and that which he does freely in relation to that which is not himself. There is a case for saying that the very distinction between Creator and creation became possible only because of Christology, and, indeed, the very Christology that was sketched in the previous section. Because the action of the man Jesus is also so unself-consciously identified in Scripture as also the action of God, it carries in itself connotations of God's freedom over against the world. It was such an interpretation of Scripture that gave Irenaeus his cutting edge and authority against the Gnostics who were Gnostic because they confused the creature with the Creator. This is our safeguard against Arianism also. In making the Son of God a hybrid, something between the Creator and the created, Arians offend against the absolute rule, that it is one thing to be God, another to be a creature. That paradox is here twofold: first that by putting this man, and this man alone, on the side of the Creator we maintain the integrity of the creation; and we can do it while remaining true to a confession of his full humanity.

How can this be? The key must be found in the words of the confession we are considering: *Jesus Christ*, not *Logos* or even *Son*, but Jesus of Nazareth who is also the Christ of God, the one Lord. What claim are we making? Essentially, that all of God's action, whether in creation or in the redirection of that creation gone astray, is achieved by Jesus Christ. As we have seen, there is a tendency in the tradition to play down the "Jesus" part of the action, but we cannot do that if we are to be true to the biblical places we have visited. The only begotten Son is also the lamb who takes away the sin of the world. The one who is the object of the worship of heaven in Revelation is the lamb bearing the marks of slaughter upon him. It is not a Logos with no relation to Jesus whom we confess, but "one Lord, Jesus Christ . . . begotten, not made." Jesus of Nazareth, the one who was begotten in time, is also and at the same time the one who is eternally begotten. But what is the meaning of that "at the same time"? Here is the place at which our categories simply fail to encompass the mystery, for we have to say two things that appear to be contradictory: that he is Son quite apart from and in advance of being Jesus of Nazareth—for Jesus of Nazareth has a begetting in time—and yet he is not Son apart from being Jesus.

Irenaeus puts this as well as it can be put:

> [God's] only-begotten Word, who is always present with the human race, united to and mingled with His own creation, according to the Father's pleasure, and who became flesh, is Himself Jesus Christ our Lord, who did also suffer for us, and arose again on our behalf, and who will come again in the glory of His Father, to raise up all flesh.[18]

Notice that there is an identity statement—"God's only-begotten Word . . . is . . . Jesus Christ"—alongside one of historical action—"united to and mingled with His own creation." Everything depends on how we hold the two in tension. Here we face a twin peril. On the one hand, as we have seen, we play down the human Jesus' part in all this; on the other, we project this

Jesus into eternity and make no distinction at all between time and eternity, leaving ourselves once again only the economy.

Something on the Point of It All

Why do we need thus to stretch our categories to the breaking point? The reason is that if we are to speak truly of the God we confess, we must make Jesus Christ in some way intrinsic to his being, and that requires insisting that he is eternally begotten. This involves holding to the traditional practice of understanding the persons of the Trinity in terms of their relations of origin, of where so to speak, they come from within the being of the triune Godhead.[19] Wolfhart Pannenberg is perhaps the most respectable of recent theologians to have questioned the theological adequacy of the practice.

> When scripture bears witness to the active relations of the Son and Spirit to the Father, it is not good enough to treat these as not constitutive for their identify and in this respect to look only at the relations of begetting and proceeding (or breathing), viewing solely the relations of origin, which lead from the Father to the Son and Spirit, as applicable to the constitution of the persons.[20]

While agreeing with the first half of that contention—that we have to take into account the biblical characterization of the actions of the persons—I wish to deny the second. It seems to me that, in general, the church fathers were right to concentrate their account of the biblical relations in the so-called relations of origin. For the purposes of referring to the distinctive *tropoi hyparxeōs* of the persons of the immanent Trinity, they serve very well. Indeed, to introduce the economic actions into a definition of the eternal being of the persons is to muddy the water by confusing—as distinct from distinguishing—the relation of the economic and immanent Trinities. The following theses are designed to demonstrate the point.

The purpose of developing a notion of the eternal Son of God is that it enables us to speak of one who is God in a different way from God the Father. The point is often enough made, especially in recent theology, that too great a stress on the indistinguishability of the actions of God *ad extra* leads to the effective redundancy of the doctrine of the Trinity. The solution to that problem is not to be found in post-Rahnerian programs to collapse the immanent Trinity into the economic, but rather to show in what ways the Father, Son, and Spirit are to be distinguished in the mode of their actions in the world. The distinguishing mark of the Son's action in the world is that he is sent by, given by, and obeys the Father even at the cost of his life, not heteronomously as being *merely* commanded, but as realizing his obedience in the freedom of the Spirit who maintains him in truth by maintaining him in right relation to his Father.

The point of the notion of Jesus Christ's eternal begottenness is that it enables us to characterize the kind of relationship that subsists between the two persons we have so far considered. It also enables us to do justice to the undoubtedly subordinationist elements of the biblical record that we have noticed: the Son is sent, is given, obeys, and, indeed, expresses his eternal sonship in temporal or economic subordination. His eternal Sonship is the other side of this agency. Pannenberg is right,[21] it seems to me, in seeking to retain the distinctive subjecthood of the Son, but wrong in basing it in his self-distinction from the Father. That attributes to the Son an autonomous initiative that he simply does not have. His proper human autonomy derives rather from the freedom, given by the Spirit, to be the kind of subordinate Son that he is. This is what justifies the church fathers in limiting their descriptions of the intratrinitarian relation to relations of origin in the way that they do. To say that the Son is eternally begotten is to point to a particular kind of personal relation, which is like that between a created father and son but must be construed only on the basis of what happened in the conception, birth, ministry, death, resurrection, and ascension, all realized in and by the Spirit of God, of the actual man Jesus of Nazareth.

All this means that we cannot do justice to the notion of eternal begottenness without some attention to the doctrine of the Spirit also. One of the many good reasons for rejecting the doctrine of the *filioque* is that in the economy the Son is also the gift of the Spirit, who is the one by whose agency the Father begets Jesus in time, empowers his ministry, and raises him from the dead. To speak of the Spirit's work also in terms of self-distinction, as Pannenberg does,[22] gives the Trinity a tritheistic air, for the Spirit is himself only as one of the two hands of the Father, his eschatological power and energy, albeit a distinctive concrete particular, a person.[23] We should beware of mere projection, but can at least ask whether it is right to suggest that because the Spirit is the agent of the begetting of Jesus in the womb of Mary, he is also the agent of his eternal begottenness. The Son is the kind of eternal Son that he is by virtue of the way (*tropos*) in which he is related to the Father in the Spirit in the eternal triune love. In view of the fact that there is nothing that is not at once and in different ways the act of the whole Trinity, something like it needs to be said. It might be rather near to Augustine's doctrine of the Spirit as the bond of love, but I hope that it says more than that, particularly about the Spirit's being the focus of God's movement outward. The Trinity locked up in itself, to use Rahner's characterization of much post-Augustinian trinitarianism, by conceiving the Spirit as the closure of an inward-turning circle, militates against a link between the Spirit's being in eternity and his action in the world.[24] In the gospel stories, accordingly, we must conceive the Spirit as the one who indeed maintains the Son in truth as the particular human being that he is: the only one who, after the fall, is enabled to be in true relation to God the Father and so truly human.

We thus achieve a trinitarian perichoresis. The Father who begets and the Son who is begotten are together one God in the *koinōnia* of the Spirit. They are one because the Son and the Spirit are, in a sense, though as God, subordinate in the eternal *taxis* as they are in the economy. But in another sense they are not subordinate, for without his Son and Spirit, God would not be God. So Athanasius states "for, whereas the Father always is, so what is proper to his essence must always be; and this is his Word and His Wisdom."[25] It follows that the distinctive personhood of each—their being each what they are and not someone else—derives first from the constituting action of the Father, but also from the responsive action of the Son and the particularizing action of the Spirit. Accordingly, in both the mutuality and reciprocity, but also the distinctive particularity of the three persons, consists the eternal love of the one God. In other words, it is thus possible to maintain an Eastern—and scriptural—sense of the monarchy of the Father without succumbing to an ontological hierarchy that renders the Son and the Spirit as less than fully divine.

Why, finally, do we bother with all this? Both because it is true and because our salvation hangs upon it. The second part of the answer is second because it is secondary, because if the creedal confession is not true, we are still in our sins, and the assumption of Christian theology is that we are not—not that we do not sin, but that because of Christ our sins no longer define who and what we are. And so a final word about truth. I have asserted once or twice that in saying that Jesus Christ is begotten we are using a metaphor. In popular parlance—and we must remember that the word *metaphor* is often used metaphorically these days to refer to things other than linguistic change—to say that something is metaphorical is to say that it cannot really be true. The truth, however, is quite the opposite. Just as for Kierkegaard nothing important—nothing, that is, that concerns our relation to eternity—can be said without paradox, so it is also with metaphor. Nothing truly interesting, and certainly nothing interesting about the relation between God and the world, can be said without some kind of metaphor. And that takes us back to the place where we began. It is the Arians who are the literalists, who will not allow language to be stretched to speak of eternity. Polanus, the late-sixteenth-century Calvinist, put it thus: "what the Fathers say, that the Father begat the Son of His essence, is to be taken metaphorically, because he did not do so outside of his essence . . . as the Arians once used to say."[26] Because he, the Word become flesh, is the truth, it follows that created things, and that includes our words, can also be true; and that is one reason why we must continue to work at our theology.

3

Being of One Substance with the Father

Alan Torrance

"Of One Being with the Father"

At the very heart of the Creed of Nicea and the Nicene Creed (which emerged over fifty years later) stand the affirmation that Jesus Christ is "God from God, Light from Light, true God from true God, begotten, not made, of one Being (*homoousios*) with the Father," and that "through him all things were made." The intention is clear—to affirm with unambiguous clarity that the One whom we meet in the person of Jesus is none other than God— God come not merely *in* a human being but *as human*.[1]

What is at stake here is not simply a matter of doctrinal propriety, but nothing less than the very possibility of warranted Christian God-talk, not to mention the essential ground of salvation. Without this decisive affirmation, not only is it questionable whether the Christian church would have continued to exist (as Harnack famously observed), but much more importantly, whether its existence is justified at all! Intrinsic to the very raison d'être of the church is the recognition that Jesus is not simply a good example, an inspired prophet, a liberative presence, a symbol of fulfilled existence, or a person with spiritual insight, but rather, the very presence of God identifying with humanity, revealing himself to humanity and uniting human-ity with himself in a reconciling act of pure and unanticipatable grace.

Put simply, if I did not believe I could affirm what is being affirmed in the *homoousion*, I would cease to be a Christian forthwith; I would resign from the church, from my vocation as a theological teacher, and go and do something useful!

† † †

If affirmation of the *homoousion* defines the faith of the church catholic, one could be forgiven for thinking at times that the lowest common denom-inator of much modern theology is a common desire to reject it.

The tone of much contemporary dismissal of the *homoousion* is that of Adolf von Harnack, who argued that the Nicene doctrine of the incarna-tion was the result of a Hellenizing process through which Greek meta-physical concepts and categories were imposed inappropriately on Chris-tian faith. The implication was that the christological claims of the New Testament should be regarded as essentially "functional" rather than "onto-logical." Indeed, the last two hundred years have witnessed the widespread desire exemplified in Albrecht Ritschl to get behind such "metaphysical" claims to the "simple" faith of the New Testament.

Over the last thirty years, however, this claim has taken on a new life in the charge that the *homoousion* exemplifies not only the Hellenization of Christianity but the Eurocentricization of Christianity by binding it to exclusive European thought forms that are no longer appropriate in a "post-Eurocentric," multicultural, multiethnic, and multilingual world—a world characterized by diverse and disparate spiritual and philosophical homes. Consequently, a new generation of "indigenous" and "contextual" Chris-tologies have emerged, many of which have little interest in affirming the *homoousion*. Their concern is, rather, to reinterpret Jesus' significance in the light of the spiritualities and conceptualities characteristic of their specific contexts. Notable examples of such an approach have been found emerging in southern and eastern Asia, from within the very different contexts of Sri Lanka, India, China, the oppressed workers (*minjung*) of South Korea, and the peasant farmers of Japan and Thailand; in Australian "indigenous the-ologies" Australasian and in North America. I have even found the terms used (horrifyingly!) of Scottish theology.[2] The irony of the situation illus-trated in these contexts is precisely how unindigenous the self-conscious, identity-driven search for an indigenous theology is. This worldwide fash-ion is clearly conditioned by the archetypically Western concern with "identity," together with psychotherapeutic categories of self-affirmation. What this suggests is that the self-conscious search for an indigenous theology is too often the betrayal of the unself-conscious hard-nosed engagement with the question of what can be affirmed truthfully about God and God's engagement with human beings in all their diversity. I like to think that the only things deserving of the term *Scottish theology* were forms of theological engagement that were distinctive precisely because they refused to be fashion-driven but steadfastly focused on the truth question. Decades later, historians may look back and see an approach that was distinctive and admirable, and it might be described as Scottish or New Zealand theology—a description that its authors never sought or intended! The redeemed in Matthew 25 are recognized as those driven by proper concerns in ways entirely lacking in self-consciousness: "Lord when did we see you hungry or thirsty or a stranger or needing clothes." One might add, "and those pursuing theological truth for truth's sake will ask, 'Lord, when were we doing indigenous theology?'"

A second quasicontextual critique of a different but related kind has emerged in recent feminist debates, which have viewed the affirmation of the *homoousios* as serving to divinize the male—in short, it served not only the Hellenization of Christianity or, given a wider horizon, the Eurocentricization (or, now, anthropocentricization!) of theology, but its androcentricization. As Elisabeth Moltmann-Wendel has asked, how it is it possible that the identification of God with a male human being could be liberating for any more than 50 percent of the human race? Mary Daly famously insisted that if God is male, then male is God. Affirming that the incarnate Son is *homoousios to patri*, it is supposed, served ultimately to elevate maleness—and the life and practice of the church has enshrined the elevation of maleness ever since. As a result, the tendency of contemporary feminist theologians (Elizabeth Johnson, Rosemary Radford Ruether, Elizabeth Schüssler Fiorenza, and others) has been to advocate "theologies from below," sidestepping the incarnational affirmations characteristic of the Nicene tradition in order that God-talk can be allowed to unfold from women's experiences and spiritualities.

Finally, there are those who simply cannot perceive the relevance of such seemingly abstract affirmations. There is a widespread supposition that the really significant issues of the day concern ethics, poverty, ecological concerns, and a universal hunger for spirituality. These concerns, it is assumed, simply displace the need to mess about with obscure metaphysical and ontological debates. Here the *homoousion* is not so much denied as ignored, and assumed to be irrelevant.

Underlying and enforcing these trends, however, is the (Eurocentric, male!) Enlightenment-driven suspicion of the *homoousion* that has haunted Christian theology since the eighteenth century. This has been compounded by the writings of David Friedrich Strauss, Rudolf Bultmann, and, more recently, the influential (if unimpressive) collection of essays edited by John Hick, *The Myth of God Incarnate*,[3] in which a group of influential biblical scholars and theologians argued that it was time to recognize that the doctrine of the incarnation was a piece of mythology more appropriate to the thought patterns of ancient civilization than to those of contemporary society. What emerged in its wake were myriad interpretations of the incarnation not only as myth but as symbol, metaphor, story, fable, parable, saga, and so on.[4] The underlying supposition throughout is that Christian doctrine should free itself from the "mythological" projection inherent in affirming that the incarnate "Son is God from God . . . true God from true God, of one Being with the Father," *homoousios to patri*.

In the context of all of this, it is of critical importance to note that the concern to distinguish theology from mythology is by no means new—this question lay at the heart of the Nicene debates over the *homoousion*. Indeed, it was precisely Athanasius's profound conceptual clarity that led him and the Nicene Council to affirm it as the cotter pin of Christian doctrine and the necessary ground of the very possibility of Christian God-talk. In order to appreciate this, we need to rehearse briefly what the debate was about.

The Debate between Athanasius and Arius

At the heart of Arius's approach stood a foundational dichotomy between God and the world. God was identified as "that which has no cause or source outside itself," and the world as being that which does. To be confused about this distinction was to commit a fundamental philosophical mistake, namely, to undermine the absolute qualitative difference between God and that which is not God. As Alasdair Heron points out, this supposition became wedded, in Arius's mind, to a confusion between two similar but entirely different Greek concepts, that is, between the word *gennētos*, which means "begotten," and *genetos*, which means "has come into being." As a result, Arius believed that to describe the Son as *gennētos* (begotten) involved his being *genetos*, that is, his having come into being. If he had come into being, he could not be eternal and thus could not be God.[5]

Consequently, Arius sought to drive home the dichotomy between God the Father and the Son by insisting that there was never a time when the Father did not exist, but that there *was* a time when the Son did not exist: "The Son has a beginning, but God is without beginning."[6] Consequently, he argued, the Son neither was nor could be "of one Being" with the Father but was *created* by him. For Arius, therefore, the Son was not God but belonged to the contingent, creaturely realm. The Son was a creature, albeit the "first creature" (*prōton ktisma*). Created first, he was the one through whom everything *else* was created,[7] but emphatically *not* the one through whom *all* things were created. The effect of Arius's own argument was to deprive himself of any warrant for making even the claims he made.

As we all know, the debates surrounding Nicea were stormy, political, and politicized. At stake, however, were theological questions of crucial importance, the ramifications of which were perceived by Athanasius with remarkable clarity and profundity. So how is it that such a seemingly abstruse metaphysical dispute could be of such decisive significance? And why was the struggle between the Nicene fathers and Aruis over the word *homoousios* so unavoidable? What mattered was not the word itself (indeed, Athanasius uses it only once in his *Contra Arianos*, which is his most extensive response to Arius),[8] but what it affirmed, which was quite simply that in the person of the Son the reality of God himself is present with us and for us. But what did the *homoousion* safeguard that was not equally preserved by Arius's interpretation of the Son as the "first creature"? Heron answers this as follows:

> To this eminently reasonable question Athanasius had a single shattering answer. What was missing in Arius' entire scheme was, quite simply, God himself. True, he was there—after a fashion. He was there, but he was silent, remote in the infinity of his utter transcendence, acting only through the intermediacy of the Son or Word, between whose being and his own, Arius drew such a sharp distinction. The God in whom Arius believed had no direct contact with his creation; he was for ever and by definition insulated and isolated from it in the absolute serenity of an unchanging and unmoving perfection. God himself neither creates nor redeems it; he is involved with it only at second hand.

What lay at the heart of the debate was the same issue that has haunted Christian doctrine right through to the present day, namely, the basic and fundamental incompatibility between the God of the biblical witness and the Hellenized God of Arianism. As Athanasius saw with such clarity, the

biblical affirmations about Jesus are entirely devoid of theological significance unless they refer to a God who is present and who acts in and for that
same world he created. The Christian faith lives and breathes from the recognition, through the Spirit, that Jesus is Immanuel, the one in whom we meet
the fullness of the Godhead dwelling bodily, giving himself to us to be known
and understood and loved, the redemptive presence of the one through
whom and for whom all things were created. For Athanasius, therefore, the
incarnation constitutes the "hinge" between God and humanity—the *topos*
and *skopos* (locus and focus) of God's involvement with humanity. Without
it our God-talk loses its ground and its warrant and necessarily dissolves
into mere and unwarranted projections, into the transcendent "beyond" of
the self-understandings of creatures who are quite simply and literally *agnōsis'*
(without knowledge)—ignorant of that to which they pretend to refer. If
God is not self-giving to be spoken of by creatures as Word within the contingent order, "theology" can amount to no more than confused mythological speculation of a kind that, as Athanasius sees, only "insanity" (*mania*)
could identify with veridical God-talk.[9] In short, for Athanasius, Arianism,
under the pressure of its Hellenistic suppositions, dismissed a priori the very
possibility that God could identify himself with human history and thus
the very ground of the Christian faith. Any statements whatsoever about
God's relationship to the contingent order must be regarded, on their own
terms, as unwarranted, ungrounded, and lacking any Logos rooted in the
divine realm.

Heron again offers a neat summary of the situation:

> If one takes seriously Arius' conception of the divine being, it is hard to see
> how anyone could know anything about God at all. By a curious irony, on
> which Athanasius was not slow to remark, Arius seemed to possess a good
> deal of privileged information. But where had he got it from? Athanasius was
> in no doubt about the source: the Arians had fabricated this concept of the
> divine being out of their own minds, thus making their own intellects the
> measure of ultimate reality, and assigning to Christ, the Word-made-flesh,
> the place which their minds could make for him.[10]

For Athanasius, it is the fact that Jesus is the eternal Word of God made
flesh that constitutes the ground of Christian God-talk. Jesus mediates
knowledge of God because he is Immanuel. If he were not, then it would
be entirely unclear how, ultimately, the Son would be relevant for God-talk
at all.

A Problem

Such an account, however, is not adequate in itself—indeed, it poses a fundamental problem! To affirm that Jesus is "of one Being with the Father" does not of itself solve the problem of epistemic access to the Godhead. Two conditions are required for knowledge of God to be mediated by Jesus. First, the being of God must be identified with him, and second, it must be *recognized* to be so. Without the latter condition, the incarnation simply does not succeed in facilitating knowledge of God. The incarnation of God as Jesus would no more be an event of communication than if God had become incarnate as a fish in some mountain stream!

This, of course, was not lost on Athanasius, who was clear that the New Testament bears witness not only to God's identification with humanity in Jesus, but also, simultaneously, to God's presence with humanity in the person of the Holy Spirit, who gives us the eyes to perceive who Jesus is. As becomes unambiguously clear in his *Letters to Serapion*, affirming the *homoousion* of the incarnate Word was inextricably bound up with affirming the *homoousion* of the Holy Spirit—a point insufficiently appreciated vis-à-vis the theological assessment of incarnational claims. The transforming presence of the Holy Spirit who is "of one Being with the Father" is the necessary subjective condition for the recognition of Jesus as the incarnate Word. There is, in short, an essentially and irreducibly *trinitarian* structure to the faith of the church. If God is not present as the Holy Spirit in and with the "mind" of the church, then there is no possibility of that "mind" recognizing or being informed by the presence with humanity of God the Son— "flesh and blood" does not, cannot, and will not reveal this in and of itself! (Here one might mention the woeful failure of New Testament scholars to appreciate this simple point. The commitment to "methodological naturalism" in New Testament research will invariably and necessarily fail to endorse the incarnation. There are no circumstances whatsoever under which the search for the historical Jesus, which brackets out the pneumatological condition of recognition, could discover the Incarnate One! That is intrinsic to the New Testament message as we have it in the Gospels, as well as in the Johannine and Pauline writings.)

In *Contra Arianos*, Athanasius speaks a great deal about the importance of the reference of our concepts as what is accessed by the mind (*phronema*) of the church—the church's *dianoia*, as Young argues in *Biblical Exegesis and the Formation of Christian Culure*.[11]

Arius's view, however, simply does not allow for any such *dianoia*.[12] As Athanasius sees with such clarity, Arius's God-talk (*theologein*) is itself no more than the projection of mere opinion (*epinoiai*) into the beyond, and that is not *theologein*, but, rather, *mythologein*. It is Arius, and not Athanasius, therefore, who is the mythologizer—and his failure to distinguish between his own mythological projections and theology constitutes nothing less than a form of mania—the kind of insanity that claims identification with the divine for one's own subjective ponderings!

Paul argued that we are *echthroi tē dianoia*—alienated, or hostile, in our ability to think through to (*dianoein*) the nature and purposes of God. Consequently, a transformation of our *noein* is required for there to be veridical *dianoein*. It is in and through the reconciliation of our *noein* that *theologein* (God-talk) can take place. It is where there is veridical recognition of God's free, creative presence with us as the incarnate Logos that *theologein* becomes possible. That is where human understanding and speech penetrates through to the reality of God. The very possibility of theology is thus given in and with an event of participation by the Spirit *en Christō*, in the incarnate Son's knowledge of the Father, when that mind that was in Christ Jesus (together with all its epistemic affiliations) is realized *in us* by grace. God-talk is thus the privilege of the reconciled body of Christ as it is given to share, as John's Gospel suggests, in the *rhemata* (the language games) that the Father gives us in the Son by the Spirit. In sum, God is known, spoken of, and communicated within and through an all-embracing event of reconciled, semantic participation in the divine life.

The Relationship between Jesus and God's Creative and Salvific Purpose

So far, we have focused on the *homoousion* as the essential warrant for Christian God-talk, but its significance is considerably more wide-ranging than that. The debate between Athanasius and Arianism in all its forms has profound ramifications for the interpretation of God's relationship to creation and, indeed, for the whole grammar of salvation. It is to these questions we must now turn.

Clearly, the synoptic accounts of Jesus' healing and restoring presence identify him with the creative agency of God—an implication formulated more explicitly in the Johannine and Pauline accounts. Just as in the event of creation God imposed form on the forces of chaos, so Jesus exercised parallel power over those same symbols of chaos—calming the storm, driving out evil spirits, delivering people from physical and spiritual dysfunction. The implication was that Jesus is the redemptive presence of God reconciling an alienated creation to God and recapitulating God's purposes for it.

None of these claims has any theological significance whatsoever without the recognition that in the person of the Logos we meet the concrete and creative presence of God himself, that same agency without which nothing at all would exist. In radical contrast to this, however, for Arius and his disciples (disciples prevalent in contemporary theology!), we do not (and cannot) meet the Creator in the person of the Word because, in the final analysis, Jesus himself is simply another creature and object of God's creative activity—and, as such, is required emphatically *not* to be confused with God.

The problems with the Arian approach are further compounded when we come to focus more specifically on the soteriological question. Again, central to the Judaeo-Christian tradition is the recognition that only God can redeem his people. This is because sin is perceived as a violation against God—that is, against the Creator and his purposes—perpetrated by his creatures. To the extent that sin is sin against God (and not merely some problem internal to creation), only God can be the agent of reconciliation and forgiveness. The implication is that the created order has neither the right nor the ability (given its alienated state) either to reconcile or to restore itself. It is precisely for this reason that, as Paul emphasized, God comes in Christ to reconcile the world to himself. As Gustaf Aulén has stressed, salvation is the work of God from beginning to end.

In stark contrast to this, Arius's description of Jesus as "savior" suggests that salvation is nothing more than a minor adjustment internal to the contingent order. Salvation is something that one creature performs in relation to others. The implication is that God is not the object of sin and that God is not the one sinned against. Indeed, given that God is neither the subject nor the agent of any such process, the implication is that there is no sense whatsoever that God is offended by sin or that God should be involved in dealing with the problem. Put simply, God is entirely uninvolved in the business of reconciliation and redemption.

To summarize, for Arius and those who stand in his tradition, the gulf that exists between God and creation is axiomatic—an essential presupposition of Hellenistic thought. In stark contrast to this, however, for Athanasius, the only separation between the Creator and his creation is that generated from the human side by sin—an alienation that God determined to overcome in Jesus.[13]

What becomes unambiguously clear from the debates over the *homoou-sion*, therefore, is that, far from being Hellenizers of the gospel, Athanasius and the Council of Nicea set out to affirm its content precisely *over and against* Hellenistic disjunctions between the divine and the contingent, between the eternal and the spatiotemporal, between mind and body, and between the intelligible and the sensible realms. For Athanasius, Christian faith was grounded in recognizing God to be a God of grace, thoroughly and profoundly involved in and committed to the world he had created—a God whose purpose from the beginning of all things was to bring creatures into dynamic communion with himself and to adopt us as daughters and sons in Christ. The contrast between this God and the remote, metaphysically transcendent Monad of Arianism could hardly be more stark! What this suggests is that the *homoousion* debate poses us with the clearest either-or in the history of theology and the church—an either-or that relates to the very ground of our faith.

Tragically, so much modern theology perpetuates the Arian tendency to assume an Hellenistic dichotomy between the divine and the contingent orders. The inclination to operate on the basis of a priori assumptions as to the actuality, possibility, and boundaries of God's engagement with the contingent order have been at least as influential in modern theological debates as they were in the heresies of the fourth century. The fundamental question at issue throughout the history of the interpretation of Jesus in Christian doctrine concerns not only whether God is involved—or is capable of involvement—in the contingent order, but whether the Gospel narratives and the New Testament writings actually refer to God and provide warrant for God-talk *of any kind whatsoever*. Either God is there as the subject and agent of the whole drama or God is not, in which case all our exegesis (all our *hermeneuein*) is theologically nothing more than *mythologein*. If God is not there, then, as Athanasius saw, there is no sense whatsoever in which the incarnate Word serves to deliver us from *agnōsis* and the mythological projection onto the transcendent of whatever philosophical or cultural or personal epistemic affiliations we might find ourselves adopting.

To reiterate, what is at stake here is not the word *homoousion*, but that to which it refers—what those at Nicea were seeking to affirm when they used it. The challenge that Nicea issues to modernity, to postmodernity, and to the various forms of context-driven theologies is whether, if they reject the *homoousion*, they can provide an alternative justification for Christian theological statements that possesses anything of the coherence, rigor, and cogency associated with the profound affirmations of the Nicene Creed.

The Humanity of Jesus

So far, we have sought to consider the strengths of the Nicene affirmation of Jesus' divinity. It is also the case that the Nicene tradition would unintentionally open the door to some problematic tendencies. An unfortunate consequence of the Nicene debates was the emergence of a one-sidedness in christological interpretation. In his classic study *The Place of Christ in Liturgical Prayer*, Josef Jungmann explores the distorting impact that fear of Arianism had on the interpretation of the significance of Jesus for Christian worship.[14] Concern to avoid any Arian diminishing of the divinity of Christ led the church to emphasize the divinity of Jesus to the detriment of the all-important stress on his humanity. Jesus was therefore seen to be an object of prayer and worship, but with the result that recognition of his role as the agent and mediator of prayer and worship suffered. Prayers were directed *to* Christ rather than *through* Christ, with a loss of emphasis on the priesthood of Jesus—the recognition that he prays with and for his people as our intercessor (cf. John 17 and Rom. 8), as our human advocate and the priest of our confession, to use the language of the author of Hebrews. Whereas the Council of Nicea emphasized that in Christ we have God coming to humanity *as God* (what T. F. Torrance refers to as the *anhypostatic* or God-humanward movement), their integral and attendant emphasis that the incarnation simultaneously denotes the incarnate Son's presentation, *as our fellow human,* of humanity to the Father (the *enhypostatic* or human-Godward movement) was weakened. Without this twofold movement the essential grammar of the New Testament, namely, that Jesus represents both God's coming to humanity as God and God's reconciliation and representation of humanity to himself as human *(*as the *eschatos Adam,* the true human, the Second Adam), is lost.

In short, fear of an Arian denigration of the divinity of Christ opened the door to the church's failure to take sufficiently seriously the full humanity of Christ. Whereas the church had wrestled with Arian tendencies, it also had to wrestle with the opposite tendency—albeit a related one— namely, "Apollinarianism." Like Arius, Apollinaris also failed to hold together the divinity and humanity of Christ, but took a different turn. He suggested that the eternal Logos expropriated the human soul of Jesus in such a way that any "human source of initiative" (to borrow a phrase from G. T. D. Angel) was replaced by God. The mind of Christ was identified with the eternal Logos and was not therefore to be regarded as human. The effect of this was to suggest, on the one hand, that the human life of Jesus was something of a charade and, on the other, that human beings do not have a fully human saviour, advocate, representative, or priest and that the temptations and suffering of Jesus were not ultimately human at all. Jesus ceased, on this account, to be one who in every respect has suffered and been tempted as we are (cf. Heb. 4:15; 5:7–8). The soteriological implications of Apollinarianism, moreover, were equally clear. If the unassumed is the unredeemed, then God has not redeemed the human mind in Christ. It is thus impossible for human beings either to have "that mind which was in Christ Jesus" or, indeed, to participate in his knowledge of the Father—because his knowledge of the Father is not a human knowledge. The effect of Apollinarianism was thus to reintroduce the Hellenistic dichotomy between mind and body, between the divine and the human. In parallel with Arianism, therefore, it undermined the Irenaean dictum that the Son took "what was ours" (our full humanity) and redeemed it in toto, that we might have what is his, namely, participation *as human beings* in the divine life.[15]

Although condemned, an Apollinarian tendency tinged with the fear of Arianism has had a profoundly unhappy influence on the grammar of Christian worship. If worship denotes the full and all-embracing response of humanity to the loving faithfulness of God, it is not something that sinful human beings are capable of offering. The logic of the gospel, however, is that the faithful human response of gratitude to God—that all-embracing correspondence to God's unconditional faithfulness that is required of us (as this includes worship and "worth-ship")—is provided *by God* on behalf of humanity in Jesus. He alone offers that true human response, that faith and faithfulness, that worship and *koinōnia,* that humankind cannot offer. In other words, God provides for us by grace the amen to God and God's purpose required of us. This is offered by Jesus *as human* standing in our place as our kinsman-redeemer, as the Second Adam. And this same risen and ascended Lord now comes creating and sustaining his body, uniting us with himself by the Spirit so that we come to live in the light of the response that he has offered on our behalf and continues to offer as our High Priest. The existence of the body of Christ, the new humanity, is thus characterized by Paul as participation "in Christ"—a phrase that he uses over 150 times! Worship, conceived in this all-embracing manner, requires to be seen in the first instance not as something that human beings provide in and of ourselves, but as something that Jesus fulfills on our behalf. Both worship and ethics, conceived as lived gratitude, are to be regarded, therefore, as the gift of participating by the Spirit in *his* life of worship and communion with the Father.

When fear of Arianism, combined with Apollinarianism, played down the humanity of Jesus, its effect was to undermine this vision of the full extent of the grace of God. As a result, worship came to be conceived as a "task" that human beings are expected to perform in relation to Jesus rather than the gift of participating in *his* humanity, in *his* risen life, and in *his* continuing priest-hood. The impact on the history of the church was that worship became a "legal" obligation placed on humanity rather than the "filial" gift of partici-pating in the divine life—that which lies at the very heart of the gospel.[16]

This means, quite simply, that the essential grammar of the Christian faith, of its God-talk and of its life, requires that the *homoousion* be affirmed of both the incarnate Son *and* the Holy Spirit. It possesses an irreducibly trinitarian structure. At the same time, the incarnation must also be described in terms of a further twofold *homoousion*. The incarnate Son is of one being with the Father but also of one being (by grace) with an alienated and sin-ful humanity.

Mythological projection was not Athanasius's problem; it is the problem of his Arian detractors, who can be found in all ages. As to the question of whether we are warranted in appealing to God-talk in repudiating sexism, racism, the abuse of our environment, and, indeed, any ethical agenda what-soever, unless we can say truthfully (*alēthos*) that we have grounds to affirm that God is actively concerned with the forms of alienation, oppression, and exploitation characteristic of our contemporary world, and that God, more-over, seeks to reconcile and deliver humanity from these, then God-talk has nothing to offer our engagement with any of these issues and becomes entirely irrelevant and inappropriate in discussing them. In stark contrast, however, to affirm the *homoousion* is not only to claim permission to make theological statements on these fronts, it is to recognize that we are required (apodictically commanded!) to oppose all forms of oppression, marginal-ization, anti-Semitism, racism, sexism, and the exploitation of creation. In the one in whom there is neither Jew nor Gentile, black nor white, male nor female we have nothing less than the one for whom and through all things were created, the one who seeks to reconcile them. We have light from light, the very being and presence of God.

4

By Whom All Things Were Made

Trinitarian Theology of Creation as the Basis for a Person-Friendly Cosmology

J. Augustine Di Noia, O.P.

W

e are the product of 15 billion years of an expanding, evolving universe and 3 billion years of an ineluctable evolution from primitive living organisms to the most complex entity known to exist, the human brain. But that evolutionary path was not a straight and narrow one."[1]

The path, scientists generally agree, goes back about 15 billion years: it was then that the universe erupted in an explosion called the Big Bang, and it has been expanding and cooling ever since. Working backward to the moment of this eruption, scientists have attempted to map the first three minutes after the Big Bang occurred in order to explain the background for the gradual emergence of the conditions necessary for the formation of atoms about three hundred thousand years later, the condensation of galaxies and stars about 1 billion years later, and the formation of planets about 10 billion years later. Recent observations of the behavior of supernovas tend to confirm the Big Bang theory and to point, somewhat unexpectedly, to an accelerating rate of cosmic expansion in which a balance between inflationary and contracting forces will be maintained.

In our own solar system and on Earth, which were formed about 4.5 billion years ago, the conditions have been favorable to the emergence of life.

While there is little consensus among scientists about how the origin of this first microscopic life is to be explained, they generally agree that the first organism dwelt on this planet about 3.5 to 4 million years ago.[2] They are virtually certain that all living organisms have descended from this first organism.[3] This represents a considerable development since Charles Darwin first advanced his account of the evolution of species more than one hundred years ago. Although Darwinian and neo-Darwinian versions of evolutionary theory have been subjected to vigorous criticism, particularly with regard to the role of natural selection in evolution, converging evidence from many studies in the physical and biological sciences furnishes mounting support for the evolutionary hypothesis.[4] Among scientists there is controversy over the pace and mechanisms of evolution but not over the general explanatory efficacy of evolutionary theory.

Set within this broad history of biogenesis, the story of human origins is extremely complex and is regularly revised on the basis of new discoveries.[5] While there is considerable disagreement among scientists over the interpretation of the prehuman (and, indeed, prehominid) fossil record, lines of evidence in physical anthropology and molecular biology combine to make a convincing (but by no means universally accepted) case for the origin of the human species in Africa at about forty thousand years ago in a humanoid population descended from a common genetic lineage. Over the next thirty thousand years, modern humans spread from Africa to Asia and beyond. However it is to be explained, the decisive factor in human origins was a continually increasing brain size culminating in that of *Homo sapiens*, "which is acknowledged to be a feat of fantastic difficulty, the most spectacular enterprise of life since its origin, a unique instrument of as many as one billion nerve cells, . . . a network of incredibly complex neural circuits."[6] Furthermore, with the development of the brain, the nature and rate of evolution were permanently altered: when the uniquely human factors of consciousness, intentionality, freedom, and creativity were introduced, biological evolution was recast as cultural and social evolution.[7]

By Whom All Things Were Made

"By whom all things were made"? Indeed yes. To be sure, it may have been easier to comprehend and maintain this affirmation of the Nicene Creed when the universe was a cozier place and our position within it more secure. Nonetheless, ours is a moment when the Nicene confession must continue to define the contours of Christian faith, and it is urgently relevant to address a cosmology and an account of human origins that has permanently dispelled the coziness of the universe. The immense age and unimaginable vastness of the universe have made it increasingly difficult to paint a significant niche for human persons in the big picture. Indeed, far from viewing the universe as centered on the flourishing of human persons, some environmentalists seem to regard us as interlopers and spoilers. In these circumstances, religious communities, like those of Buddhism, that affirm the radical impersonality of the universe and whatever lies beyond it, are at an apologetic advantage in comparison with Christian communities.

We need to recover and articulate the Christian understanding of the cosmos as a person-friendly place. A trinitarian theology of creation is essential to—indeed, requires and entails—this recovery and reaffirmation. Central to this project is what Colin Gunton has termed a "theology of relatedness."[8] This vast, ancient, and seemingly impersonal universe exists for one reason alone: because of the divine desire to share the communion of trinitarian life with persons who are not God.

Before proceeding to consider the contemporary relevance of this clause of the second article, let us briefly review what the clause affirms and what has been at stake in this affirmation.

What does the clause affirm?

The clause draws directly upon a scriptural idiom. "In the beginning was the Word . . . and the Word was God . . . all things were made through him, and without him was not anything made that was made" (John 1:1–3 RSV). God created everything by the eternal Word. In him, "all things were created, in heaven and on earth . . . all things were created through him and for him. He is before all things, and in him all things hold together" (Col. 1:16–17 RSV). The Triune God created the world. As St. Irenaeus says, "he made all things by himself, that is by his Word and his Spirit."[9] Although the third article of the Nicene Creed is to be covered by other writers in this volume, we should note here that the Catechism takes the phrase "giver of life" to affirm the part of the Holy Spirit in creation—*Veni Creator Spiritus*. Creation is a free, personal act of the Blessed Trinity, operating through Word and Wisdom.

What was at stake?

The question of what was at stake is more fully discussed in Alan Torrance's chapter. We may note briefly here that the Arian notion, as summarized by J. N. D. Kelly, entailed the view that "the created order could not bear the weight of the direct action of the increate and eternal God."[10] As Jaroslav Pelikan puts it: "Only he who had created the universe could save man, and . . . to do either or both of these he himself had to be divine and not a creature."[11]

What is at stake now?

Addressing the topic of evolution recently, Pope John Paul II stated that "new knowledge leads to the recognition of the theory of evolution as more than a hypothesis. It is indeed remarkable that this theory has been progressively accepted by researchers following a series of discoveries in various fields of knowledge." In view of this growing consensus among scientists, Pope John Paul went on to state that the concern of the Church with the question of evolution focuses particularly on "the conception of man," who, as created in the image of God, "cannot be subordinated as a pure means or instrument either to the species or to society." Created in the image of God, each person is capable of forming relationships of communion with other persons and with the Triune God. Pope John Paul encouraged philosophers and theologians to continue to collaborate with scientists in addressing the questions that scientific studies of human origins raise about human beings within the perspective of God's plan."[12] What is at stake now in the Nicene confession that all things were made in Christ can be stated simply: the history of the evolving universe since the moment of creation can be seen in its complete reality only in the light of faith, as a *personal history of the engagement of the Triune God with creaturely persons.*

The truth that human persons are created by God in the image of the Triune God illumines all aspects of the concrete human reality. It provides the indispensable foundation for the dialogue between science and theology about the origins of the universe and the place of human persons within the universe.

The new ecumenism furnishes the resources to approach this dialogue with science about the place of human beings in the universe confident that because the God who created the world also created the human desire and capacity to know this world, scientific truth and divine truth cannot be in opposition (cf. *Fides et Ratio*). Scientific inquiry is itself an exercise of the dominion and stewardship of human persons created in the image of the Triune God. To be sure, in the conversation between science and theology, there is always the possibility that particular scientific questions might challenge and even oppose the affirmations of the faith. But both scientists and theologians have increasingly recognized that the relationship between science and theology should be viewed as one of neither permanent conflict nor mutual irrelevance, but rather as one of dialogue and, where appropriate, integration.[13]

It is important to take advantage of the new recognition of the possibilities afforded by dialogue between science and theology. Christian theology in this new ecumenical moment cannot be satisfied with a situation in which scientific and religious understandings are regarded as either contradictory or irrelevant to one another. For one thing, the great Catholic tradition insists on the complementarity of faith and reason, and on the possibility that inquiries undertaken in science and under faith can be mutually illuminating. In addition, the present atmosphere is quite favorable for positive dialogue between scientists and theologians. A growing number of scientists regard developments in biology and astrophysics as opening the way to a more fruitful kind of dialogue with theologians than might have been possible even in the recent past. Theologians for their part are challenged to keep abreast of these developments and to consider both their implications for the Christian understanding of creation and the light which Christian faith throws on accumulating scientific discoveries about cosmic and evolutionary history. We cannot withdraw from this discussion, leaving it to a variety of New Age strategies that seek "salvation" through the cultivation of spiritual powers in an otherwise closed universe. Speaking from within my own tradition, I should note that the Catholic theology of creation approaches the dialogue with the science of evolution and the origins of the universe with considerable experience and resources. In particular, there is a long tradition of biblical exegesis of the first books of Genesis that has generally sought to keep pace with developing scientific understandings of the world.[14] I believe that these resources are accessible to many Christian traditions. In general, while Catholic theologians and philosophers have been critical of the materialistic and naturalistic positions that some scientists and intellectuals have thought evolutionary theory to entail, faith in the doctrine of creation has been seen as generally open to the idea of evolution. It is significant that Catholic theologians have not on the whole espoused the systematic opposition to evolutionary theory that has emerged in some Christian circles under the rubric of "creation-science."[15] Notwithstanding the tentative character of scientific understanding of the universe, it remains true that emerging theories of evolution and the origin of the universe possess particular theological interest and relevance for the doctrines of the creation *ex nihilo* and the creation of human beings in the image of God.[16]

The Cosmos as the Place of Personal Communion

The Nicene confession that all things were made through Christ teaches us that the cosmos is the stage upon which the Triune God enacts a great drama of communion by sharing the divine life of the Father, Son, and Holy Spirit with persons who are not God.

Human beings are created in the *image of God*. This likeness to God in nature is the basis for a likeness to God in grace. Human persons are created in the image of God in order to become partakers of the divine nature (2 Peter 1:3–4) and thus to share in the communion of trinitarian life and in the divine dominion of the created universe. At the heart of the divine act of creation is the divine desire to make room for created persons in the communion of the uncreated Persons of the Blessed Trinity through adoptive participation in Christ. What is more, the common ancestry and natural unity of the human race are the basis for a unity in grace of redeemed human persons under the headship of the New Adam, the ecclesial communion of human persons united with one another and with the uncreated Father, Son, and Holy Spirit. Through the eyes of faith, then, the likeness to the divine nature that is enjoyed by spiritual creatures endowed with intellect and will turns out to be a likeness to the divine Trinity enjoyed by created persons who, in grace, know and love the Father, Son, and Holy Spirit, and one another in them. The likeness of human beings to God rests not only in their possession of intellectual capacity, but even more in their vocation, as Pope John Paul II has said, "to enter into a relationship of knowledge and love with God himself, a relationship which will find its complete fulfillment beyond time."[17]

Human beings are *created* in the image of God. The gift of natural life is the basis for the gift of the life of grace (cf. *Evangelium Vitae)*. Where the central truth concerns a person acting freely, it is impossible to speak of a necessity or an imperative to create, and it is, in the end, inappropriate to speak of the Creator as a force, or energy, or ground. Creation *ex nihilo* is the action of a transcendent *personal* agent, acting freely and intentionally, with a view toward the all-encompassing purposes of personal engagement. The history of the doctrine of the origin of human beings is guided by the determination to secure and maintain the revealed truth of this fundamentally relational or personalistic understanding of God and of human nature. The exclusion of pantheism and panentheism in the doctrine of creation, and of emanationism and traducianism in the doctrine of the creation of human beings, can be interpreted at root as a way of protecting this revealed truth. The doctrine of the immediate or special creation of each human soul, which is central to the present discussion, must be viewed in this light: it not only addresses the ontological discontinuity between matter and spirit, but it also establishes the basis for a divine intimacy that embraces every single human person from the first moment of existence.[18]

A properly trinitarian theology of creation, such as the Nicene confession warrants, entails a singular affirmation of the truly personal character of creation and its order toward a personal creature who is fashioned as the *imago dei* and who responds not to a ground, force, or energy, but to a personal creator. The Nicene confession teaches us that the existing universe is the setting for a radically personal drama in which the Triune Creator calls out of nothingness those to whom he then calls out in love. Here lies the profound meaning of the words of *Gaudium et Spes:* "Man is the only creature on earth that God has wanted for his own sake" (24). Created in God's image, human beings assume a place of stewardship and dominion in the physical universe. Under the guidance of divine providence and acknowledging the sacred character of the created order, the human race reshapes the natural order and becomes itself an agent in the evolution of the universe. The physical and ontological structures that support the possibility of the personal engagement in and with the Triune God, as well as the role of stewardship and dominion under God, on the part of creaturely persons can be the object of study in science and philosophy. In the light of faith, the history of the evolving universe is a history of the Triune God's engagement with created humanity.

It is within this perspective that, while rejecting all reductionistic accounts of human persons, Christian theology in the ecumencial vein must consider scientific accounts of the origins of the universe and of evolution and human origins. Catholic theologians recognize that scientific reasoning concerning evolution and the origin of the universe does not in the main directly conflict with the doctrine of creation.

Trinitarian *Creatio Ex Nihilo*

Granting the hypothetical and tentative character of theories concerning cosmic history—particularly the Big Bang theory and the anthropic principle—and of theories concerning the origin of human life, theologians can well ask whether recent theories in fact lend a certain support to, or at least do not conflict with, the doctrines of the *imago dei* and the *creatio ex nihilo*.[19]

The Big Bang theory can be construed as supplying indirect support for the doctrine of *creatio ex nihilo* insofar as it can be said that "there is nothing scientifically or philosophically inadmissible about the supposition of an absolute beginning."[20] To be sure, it must be recognized that Catholic theology has generally held that the knowledge that the universe has an absolute beginning in time is given only by the divine revelation of creation and is thus knowable only by faith. Because the Big Bang theory does not exclude the possibility of an antecedent stage of matter, it can only be asked whether the theory appears to provide *indirect* support for the doctrine of *creatio ex nihilo:* "if an absolute cosmic beginning *did* occur, it could look something like the horizon-event described in the Big Bang theory."[21]

Continuing Trinitarian Action

A properly trinitarian account of divine causality in creation understands that as universal transcendent personal agent the Triune God, in his Word and Wisdom, is not only the cause of existence but also the cause of causes.[22] This agency is utterly unique: there are no natural analogs for it. For this reason, divine causality can never be seen to be at the same level or in competition with created causes, whether they act necessarily, contingently, or freely. God's action does not displace or supplant the activity of creaturely causes; rather, he enables creaturely causes to act according to their natures and, nonetheless, to bring about the ends he intends.[23]

Two implications of this account of divine agency are fundamental to the perspective that Nicene Christianity affords when it ponders current scientific understandings of cosmic history and human origins. First, the traditional distinction between primary and secondary causality entails that the Triune God as primary cause (absolutely speaking) makes use of secondary or subordinate causes in bringing about the states of affairs he intends.[24] Second, "the creator of the world can act beyond the causal powers granted to created things . . . and thus both bring about particular effects in the world and preserve the immanent structures of nature."[25]

According to this account of divine agency at work in a plan exhibiting divine Word and Wisdom, it in no way detracts from the doctrine of the *creatio ex nihilo* to affirm that in freely willing to create and conserve the universe the Triune God wills to activate and to sustain in act all those secondary causes whose activity contributes to the unfolding of the law-governed natural order that he intends to produce. It is entirely in accord with the divine wisdom that God should will that through the activity of natural causes operating both necessarily and contingently there should gradually arise those conditions required for the emergence and support of living organisms, and, furthermore, for their reproduction and differentiation. While scientists have generally insisted that the purposiveness of these developments cannot be *scientifically* established, they are increasingly ready, as we have seen, to acknowledge that these developments have de facto favored the emergence and flourishing of life.

Within the broad areas of agreement concerning the origin of the universe and the evolution of human life, many unresolved and disputed questions continue to stimulate inquiry and research and to provoke controversy among scientists. One question of particular interest to theology of creation concerns the so-called anthropic principle.[26] Granted that, as is generally agreed, the universe evolved in the direction of increasing complexity, and that steadily developing physical conditions favored the emergence of life, and in particular of human life, still scientists ask whether these developments can be regarded as purposive and thus directed to the emergence of human life as such, as the anthropic principle is understood to maintain. While it is generally agreed that the sequence, timing, duration, and nature of these cosmic developments exhibit a definite degree of fine-tuning favorable to the subsequent emergence of life, the significance of these developments is much disputed. The already-mentioned discovery of the accelerating rate of cosmic expansion and the resultant "cosmological constant" has been seen by some scientists (e.g., Stephen Hawking) as unlikely to be susceptible of a nonanthropic explanation and by others (e.g., John Polkinghorne) as confirming the relevance of anthropic reasoning, if not of the anthropic principle itself. Additional support for anthropic reasoning comes from what has recently been called the "rare Earth" hypothesis, which argues that while simple life may be widespread in the universe, the conditions for complex life, such as are instantiated in our solar and terrestrial world, are extremely rare.[27]

Despite the tentative character of these findings, Catholic theologians can ask whether anthropic lines of reasoning in scientific accounts of cosmic history can be construed as consistent with teleological lines of affirmation entailed by faith in divine creation and divine providence. Such questions are suggested by the Christian conviction that in the providential design of creation the Triune God intended to make a place for human beings not only in the universe, but also, and ultimately, in his own trinitarian life.

At the same time, this account of divine agency involves the affirmation that particular actions of the Triune God bring about effects that transcend the capacity of created agents operating according to their natures. The appeal to divine causality to account for genuinely *causal* gaps as distinct from merely *explanatory* gaps does not involve a reversion to the rightly discredited physicotheology that inserted divine agency to fill in the "gaps" in human scientific understanding (thus giving rise to the so-called God of the gaps).[28]

But both in a scientific perspective and certainly in a theological perspective, the structures of the world can be seen as open to divine action in directly causing events in the world. Thus, it must be recognized that the emergence of the first members of the human species, whether as individuals or in populations, represents an event that is not susceptible of a purely natural explanation and that can appropriately be attributed by faith to divine intervention.[29] Acting indirectly through causal chains operating from the beginning of cosmic history, God prepared the way for what Pope John Paul II has called "an ontological leap . . . the moment of transition to the spiritual."[30] Although scientific investigation of evolution can observe and perhaps eventually chart with precision the developments that led to the threshold of this "transition to the spiritual," theologians ask whether the event itself can be explained entirely by appeal to the operation of natural causes. Scientific understandings of human origins must be complemented by philosophical and theological reflection. Philosophy can study the distinctive spiritual conditions of human consciousness, freedom, and creativity and thus account for the ontological discontinuity between matter and spirit. But it falls to theology to locate this account of the special creation of the human soul within the overarching plan of the Triune God to share the communion of trinitarian life with human persons who are created out of nothing in the image and likeness of God, and who, in his name and according to his plan, exercise a creative stewardship and dominion over the physical universe.

Scientific understandings of the origins of the universe and of human life must be viewed in the light of Nicene faith—that is, a robustly trinitarian faith—to offset their tendency to conceive these processes in entirely deterministic and impersonal terms with which only Buddhism or New Age religiosities will feel at home. The Nicene confession—whose relevance must be fully recovered in the new ecumenism—sees the evolving universe since the moment of creation as a personal history of the engagement of the Father, Son, and Holy Spirit with creaturely persons. We must never settle for less.

5

For Us . . . He Was Made Man

Robert W. Jenson

The second article of our creed begins with confession of the one Lord Jesus. The inserted theological propositions against the Arians follow. Then "for us . . . he was made man" is the first part of a narrative unpacking of the confession of Jesus as Lord.

The passage makes a circle, though our politically correct current translation obscures this. The Greek text begins, of course, *"ton di' hymas tous anthrōpous"* and ends, *"enanthrōpēsanta."* These phrases must now, I suppose, be translated with something like "who for the sake of us human persons was made a human person." The circularity is of some importance, which will come out later. I will proceed phrase by phrase.

"For us. . . ." The incarnation is *"for"* a specifiable set of things, "us human persons." The incarnation here narrated is necessarily unique, there being only one Lord Jesus, the Christ of Israel, and it has a unique telos, the good of a particular set of creatures. There is thus no way around the scandal of particularity, as it is fashionable to call it. Not only is there just the one Son to be incarnate, there is just the one set of creatures for whom he does this— though who counts as a member of this set, as an *anthrōpos*, is another matter, which I am delighted not to have to take up. However, the boundaries of that class are finally to be delineated with the question, "Do you mean to say that all this agitation on God's part is for the benefit of just this little group on just this little planet or set of planets?" The creedal answer is "Yes, that is just what we mean to say."

But my citation was elliptical. The creed, of course, reads "For us humans and for our salvation." Those are two phrases, with an explicit "and" between. The first makes us simply, as human creatures, the telos of incarnation; the second makes the telos be our rescue from something, and at this point we are permitted to assume that this something is at least in part sin. What is the relation of the two phrases?

The matter has been debated throughout the history of the church: Would the Son have been made man for our good, under the rubric of the first phrase, even if we had needed no saving as specified in the second phrase? Or if there had been no need of rescue, would there then have been no Son named Jesus, no man of sorrows?

Is the fact of our needing to be saved from something already given with our existence, so that the two phrases are linked? One need not be Hegel or Tillich to think this; one can be Karl Barth, who taught that saving us belongs to the purpose for which God creates us, not in a systematic way or by any sort of implication, but just as an *historical* coherence within God's act of decision.

I go with the Franciscans and the Easter night liturgy and Barth. I find it biblically inconceivable that the incarnation should be a repair operation. The *felix culpa* of Easter night is dangerous to be sure. If we treat it as part of a system to explain the behavior of God, it leads straight to unbelief or blasphemy. But that is no reason not to pray it, because such danger is a general character of Christian faith; every one of its chief affirmations and practices teeters over some abyss or other.

If then we say—as I do—that the incarnation is not an adventitious incident in the divine life, we must take our two phrases together in a specific way. Is it simply for us that the Son is man? Yes. Can we then construe an unfallen humanity, for whom the Son might have been more painlessly man? No. The import of the first clause demands the second. As Luther put it in his manual for parents and church-school teachers, "God has created us precisely to redeem us."

Perhaps, however, some of you will find yourselves compelled to follow the Dominicans rather than the Franciscans in this matter, the infralapsarian Calvinists rather than the supralapsarians. It is not a point on which knock-down arguments are available, and you and I may live together in confessional peace. In what we nevertheless should agree about there is enough to astound us.

If God's only Son, true God from true God and all the rest of it, becomes and is incarnate *for* us, this says that creaturely circumstances are the occasion of an event in the life of God. If we attend to the maxim that in God doing and being are not different—though their identity is conceptually impenetrable—then the fact that God's Son is incarnate for us says that creaturely circumstances are involved in what it means for God to be God. This is no doubt contingently so. Undoubtedly we must say that God could have been God altogether without us; but this changes nothing, because God is himself the one absolute contingency.

It would, I think, make a great difference in the preaching and liturgy of the churches, and in any instruction that may take place, if they made more of the drastic ontological difference between this God of the creed and the usual God of Western Enlightenment and coordinated pietism. In the usual homiletic or pedagogic presentation, God appears first as a deistic something or other up there, and then suddenly as totally taken up in accepting us and partaking in similar sentimental exercises. To the contrary, the God of the creed is utterly before and behind us, just so to involve our good before and after any pitiable needs of our own. He is a God to whom "for us humans and for our salvation" belongs to his own grasp of his own deity, and just thereby has its immense weight.

Most of this passage is then an account of what it is that God does for us and our salvation, an account, that is, of his becoming and being a human person for us. Immediately we are confronted with another ancient choice between two ways of reading the text, and again one that has divided theologians and even confessional groups throughout the church's history.

If we *start* our reflection with "came down from heaven" and with the observation that this comes before "became incarnate . . . and was made man" so that there is a sort of linear metaphysical narrative, our reading of the creed will easily track with much of our usual language about "preexistence." Before the Virgin conceived, there was a not-yet incarnate divine Son who was, at that point, located in heaven and not on earth. Then later the *theanthrōpos* came into existence on earth.

But on this reading the Son's identity as a man threatens to become unthinkable. This story of an eternal Son who at first is *not* man, and then later on is, imposes severe difficulties. The immediate suggestion of the creed's text, read this way, would be that the eternal Son was turned into a man, a notion whose impossibility for biblical faith was seen almost from the start. The alternative seems to be that there are two entities, even if only in abstract potentiality in the one case, the Son and the man, and then their *otherwise* to be conceptualized identity. But when theology has started with the notions of an entity on the creator's side of the Bible's great divide and of an entity on the creature side, even if you dutifully register the point that the latter never actually exists for itself, the identity of the two has proven impossible to think, and not in the sense in which the mystery of incarnation ought to be impossible to think, just in the ordinary sense that all attempts to state the fact of the matter lead to incoherent positions.

Moreover, even if we could finally say—by whatever desperate means— that the two entities, the Son who was in eternity and the man Jesus who was not, are now joined into one actual identity, the problem would smite us from the other side, from the side of that "now," for what can be the meaning of talk about a situation before the existence of the *theanthrōpos?* One who is true God from true God cannot simply be an eternal entity but must be eternity itself, for God falls within no genus, and *eternal* does not modify him like an adjective. Now if eternity as such was born of the Virgin, if eternity as such has a birth, what sense can it make to speak of anything in any way before that birth?

So we try the other way of reading. If we simply start with the fact of the incarnate Logos, of the man Jesus who is the Son, some things become much easier. We avoid the just-recited conceptual knots. We can take intended comfort from the noted circularity of our passage. Most important, we can then more easily sustain a soteriological insight that was effortlessly entertained by Irenaeus, but for which Cyril and Maximus and Luther had to fight within themselves—and there fought tenaciously—that the protagonist of the Gospels' story is, in Chalcedon's phrase, always "one and the same"; that whether the Gospels depict him doing divine things, like saving creatures, or human things, like being born of a woman or dying on a cross, it is always the same doer. The creed, after all, begins with the unitary identification of "one Lord, Jesus Christ," of which identification our passage is simply a narrative explication.

But this reading too has its difficulties. If there is just this one, the *theanthrōpos,* who or what comes down from heaven to be made man? And what are we to make of the Johannine prologue's seemingly clear narrative sequence, which talks of the Logos for thirteen verses before it comes to "and the Logos became flesh and dwelt among us?"

A conceptually coherent answer to these last questions can, I think, be given. Irenaeus did it, (see Douglas Farrow's writings) and maybe Athanasius did it, and Barth did it, and so—in my judgment—have I. But answering these questions requires a major effort of revisionary metaphysics, which I have discovered that many find pressing reasons not to follow. Who knows? One of those reasons may be good.

Throughout the history of the church, theologians and confessions have been divided between these two readings. Which set of advantages do we want to exploit and which set of attendant difficulties are we willing to hoist? We have had Alexandrians versus Antiochenes, the neo-Chalcedonian East versus the Leonine West. Within the East, we have had the Monophysite East versus what they at least thought was the position of the Chalcedonian East. Within the West, we have had Lutherans versus Reformed. Now we have dialogue consensus of the Orthodox with the Monophysites versus dialogue consensus of the same parties with Rome, and we have dialogue consensus of Rome with the monophysites and of Rome with the Orthdox, in each of which dialogues Rome and the Orthodox have taken quite different positions. The split seems to be there whenever the christological task is taken seriously.

I must return to going phrase by phrase. The following is, in the first instance intended simply as a commentary on the text. It is done, however, in some slight hope of contributing to a transcending of the ancient alternative just named, though I will not take time to make that explicit.

The Son "came down from heaven." So where is heaven?

The words *came down* of course suggest that heaven is a region up there someplace, and that is undoubtedly the *Vorstellung,* the maieutic picture, in most of Scripture. It has always seemed to me that here is one place where Bultmann had a point. Within the parameters of any premodern cosmology, there was in fact nothing absurd about the notion of going up to reach God's throne within his creation, but after Copernicus and Newton it is not possible to think of space in the way required to locate heaven "up" there.

Copernican and Newtonian space is homogeneous. No matter how far up you go—which now just means away from wherever you happen to be—space gets no more refined, no more crystalline, no more suited for God's dwelling. There simply is no place out there that is candidate to be heaven.

Nor is it any use trying to evade the problem by saying that *up* is a metaphor or some other trope and leaving it at that. With all due acknowledgment that language is pervasively metaphorical and so forth down the litany of late-modern platitudes, at some point we have to say what a metaphor or nest of metaphors is *for,* if we are not to float off into the mists of endless variety.

If we are to confess it as our faith, as something for which we would die, that the Son came from heaven or went back there, we had best have some concept of what is supposed to have happened. The ancients did. When they said "up there," this was intended as straightforward topography: they *looked* up there. The gods were visible as the host of heaven. After Israel had debunked that notion, Jews and Christians looked up at the firmament, just on the other side of which the Lord had his created place. Finally, within the Ptolemaic mapping, they looked toward the outermost celestial sphere, which in its purity provided admirably for heaven. We happen to know none of these mappings is right. Our "demythologizing" may not be of the same sort as Bultmann's, but some sort is obviously required.

It does seem to me that Karl Barth has made the necessary first point. After all, we speak of heaven in the first place because Scripture does, so we need to start by asking not *where* heaven is, but *what* heaven is in Scripture. As Scripture speaks of it, heaven is part of creation, God's pied-à-terre within his creation. The fathers had it precisely right: God's own place is just God himself, heaven is his created throne, as earth is his footstool.

Now if we ask *how* heaven is a part of creation, Barth says that heaven is any starting point in creation from which God moves through creation toward us; it is wherever in creation God has taken residence in order to come to us within creation, in order that his coming to us shall be an inner-creaturely event. Barth's suggestion is not quite so drastic a demythologizing as it may first appear.

On closer inspection, the biblical *Vorstellungen* are not in fact unilaterally devoted to "up." We should attend, for example, to parallel constructions in which the Lord's riding heaven's storms—up there—and his riding the temple's cherubim throne—over there or in there—are the same thing; or to the passages in which the Lord's speaking to Israel from heaven and his speaking from the fire and storm on the mountain are conflated; or to the chronicler's version of Solomon's prayer dedicating the temple, where worshipers' prayers to the Lord emphatically above are to be directed not up but in whatever geographical direction the temple lies.

So we can, I think, go with Barth, so far as he himself goes, but his account needs to be supplemented in one decisive way. Barth seems to think that heaven is the border and limit of anywhere at all in creation, in such fashion that heaven itself is located everywhere and nowhere. But in Scripture, heaven has "gates," that is, stipulable places in creation that specifically locate that boundary from which the Lord moves toward us. No doubt the firmament, through a door into which the seer John looked, was one such gate. But Bethel, geographically marked by Jacob's stone, was a gate of heaven, and then the temple was the gate of heaven. For Christians, the gate is the body of Christ, that is, the church is the gate for the world, and the Eucharist is the gate for the church.

We have finally to say, I suggest, that heaven is located in space precisely and only by its gates. What is on the other side of those gates is also in creation, but it is not in another piece of space. That is, heaven is not in creation's present tense. Consider what John the Seer saw when the firmament-gate of heaven opened and he was permitted to look through. What he saw was "what must take place after this": he saw the future, as the Spirit anticipates it for and in God's triune life.

Heaven is a mode of God's final kingdom, which is the future of creation. For God also this is truly future and is not simply dissolved into a timeless present. But because God as Spirit is fully God for and with the Father and Son, God's future is not unavailable to him; indeed it is present in his life as an agent of that life. Just as the kingdom will be created reality, it is creation also in its present availability to God and can then, in turn, be the part of creation in which God chooses to dwell for us and from which he comes to us. It is in that God will take the saints into his own life, that in him they are now active.

So from whence did Christ come to us? From heaven; indeed, that is, from the eschatological future as this is available to God. And his gate from heaven into our present age was the womb of the Virgin. Through it he entered from the future of his arrival to judge the living and the dead and to take his church with him into God. There is only one advent of the Messiah, and from that advent, the Lord, through the womb of the Virgin, entered the world that is then to be ended.

Here we must, I think, ask what difference it makes that there is heaven and that the Lord came from there.

That there is heaven means that the future is a real part of creation, insofar as creation is accommodated by God and so is temporally and spatially shaped to the movements of the triune life. Modernity has, of course, been obsessed by futurity, but what that has meant for modernity itself is an obsession with what simply is not yet. Therefore, the all-determining future has appeared to modernity either as waiting to be made by us, or as simply the void. The good word of the gospel at this juncture is that it is neither. That the future is in its own way, as future, not a mere vacancy is a good word because what comes from there is Jesus.

Of course, the creed has the obverse first in mind. What difference does it make that our "one Lord" comes from heaven and not from someplace else? That the Lord comes to us from heaven means that he comes to us from our own future as creatures. He does not come as a stranger; he is indeed strange to us, but in the same way as my future is always strange to me yet nevertheless is my own future and recognized as such when it arrives. He does not come unmediated from the place God is for himself, which coming we could never abide, but from the place where God is for us.

Our next phrase is that the incarnation is "by the power of the Holy Spirit," of whom we have already been speaking. We should not here read the Greek genitive as if it had the separative force that sometimes accompanies the English word *of.* The Spirit does not exactly "have" power; he *is* power, the agent of God's future to shape God's own life and so the power of God's future to shape us.

In the singular and absolute contingency of God, a specific future is decided to be God's future. The personal agency of that future is the Spirit, who opens the Father and the Son to it. Given what God's future is, a perfect kingdom, a community of fulfilled and fulfilling love, the Spirit is the one who frees the Father and Son for each other, so that their mutuality is not that of source and emanation, of first and second instance of something, but of Father and Son, Speaker and Word, so that their mutuality can be love.

Now—the incarnation happens in the sphere of this agency, the agency of God's futurity to himself. That is, the incarnation happens within the absolute possibility that is the final reality of historical being. Because there is the Spirit, anything can happen—what does happen is determined by the faithfulness of God within his eternal decision for himself. An event is intelligible insofar as it has place within some coherent set of events, and some events are intelligible only within the set of all events, as these are drawn into coherence by the Spirit as the power of the end of all events. The incarnation can happen because God is God the Spirit. The Son comes toward us in creation, through the gate of the Virgin's womb, from that last future of which the Spirit is the power. The Spirit impels the Son into our age through the Virgin's *fiat mihi.*

There is an error to be avoided here. There has been much talk lately of "Spirit Christology." Sometimes the notion seems to be that the Spirit is the power by which the divine Son and the man Jesus are one. This is a short road to heresy, for there needs no such third power at this point; one does not need to fasten together what is not separated in the first place. The starting point of right Christology is—as I have been insisting—not the existence or potential existence of two entities, the Son and a human nature. The right starting point of Christology is the concrete fact of the protagonist of the Gospels; talk of different "natures" is a second-level analytical abstraction. What the Spirit does is to be the possibility of an event such as the birth of Jesus.

The one Lord's coming is an incarnation, an enfleshment. *Flesh,* (*sarx*) is a notoriously multivalent word in the New Testament's milieu. It can simply mean the finitude of created living things: there is the Creator and there is flesh—the one endures and the other does not. It can mean the creature in rebellion against the Creator, as in the famous Pauline warfare between the Spirit and the flesh. And in the late-antique milieu, it sometimes meant an aspect or even part of the human creature; whether it ever has this meaning in the New Testament is disputed.

Through much of the pre-Nicene or pre-Chalcedonian use of *flesh* in Christology, the matter is not as clear as we might wish it to be. This led to doctrines of incarnation that make one think of clothing the Son or Logos with animate meat and bone. We need to be very strict in interpreting "became incarnate" from "and was made man." We can go the other way around only if we are very clear about the biblical sense of *flesh*.

If we *are* clear about all that, then this clause, of course, says something tremendous. It says that the "one Lord Jesus Christ," the protagonist of the Gospels, the second identity of God, is a creature, "grass" over against the Creator, sustained only so long as the Lord lets his Spirit hover, and liable like the rest of us to wither when he withdraws the Spirit. We may say that the force of this phrase, as another phrase than "was made man," is antidocetic. A superman is always conceivable. The Lord who actually came is heir to all that the flesh is heir to and is not a super-anything. In this phrase lies the connection of the first event in the creedal article's remarkable biography of the Lord, his birth, with the second event, his death.

It is "of the Virgin Mary" that the Son is incarnate, to be man. The Son has a mother; there exists a *theotokos.* Mary became pregnant, gestated, and gave birth, and the one whom she gestated and gave birth to was the sole and solitary person of the Son of God. She gave birth to one hypostasis of the Trinity. You may contrast that with what is preached and taught in the mainline churches, which can plausibly be described as a sustained effort to evade this scandal.

God the Son really has a mother who does not need to be a goddess to achieve this. That is what the creed here gives us to contemplate. It is precisely the reality of the Son's humanity that is first thrust at us. As the Son has an executioner, so he has a mother. And indeed, one aspect of the mother's and the executioner's appearance in immediate juxtaposition is the ancient correlation of womb and tomb as marks of mortality. It has been the open or concealed goal of each successive Christian heresy to shield Western antiquity's native concept of deity from the import of biblical narrative about God, that is, to protect deity from contamination by temporality's slings and arrows, above all from women's wombs or the tombs women tended. The creed, in its abbreviated recital of the gospel story, rebukes all such evasions in the most in-your-face fashion possible, by naming only these very two. And the point of at least the birth reference is clear: one who has a human mother is a human, and if this is the Son of God, then this human and the Son of God are, in the phrase of the good part of Chalcedon, "the same one."

The *theotokos*, taken seriously, blows all naive constructions of God's relation to time, whether they are of eternity as an infinitely extended version of the line of created time, or as a merely timeless point. What, we may want to ask, of the Son before Mary's pregnancy? But if the one Mary bore is the eternal Son, there can be no before. This seems problematic to us only because, even though we know better, our *Vorstellung* of eternity is still of a line extended indefinitely backward and forward. The more crude result of this is talk about a time before creation, which Augustine derided, or about a time after the *parousia*, which is perhaps not so well renounced. The insight demanded here is that the birth of the Son from Mary requires avoidance of this *Vorstellung*.

What we must learn is that created time does not encompass God's life, but that this does not mean God has no time, that he is timeless. Rather, the truth is that God's time, which we call eternity, accommodates created time within itself. In this encompassing, there is a spiral by which the birth of the Son eternally and his birth from Mary are not events separated on a merely linear timeline.

We must note that this is the Virgin Mary. By the time of the Creed's composition, *Virgin* was, of course, a title evoking the place of Mary in the church's liturgical and devotional life. Some theologians have said such things as "Holy Mary, Mother of God, pray for us sinners," and some have decidedly not. Some have an icon of Mary where they worship, and some assuredly do not. I note only that the creed assumes that Mary has some role in the life of faith.

The soteriological and metaphysical—not chronological—outcome of this passage is "and was made man." There is one who is simultaneously one of us and *unus ex trinitate*. His is either only inasmuch as he is both; he does the things of his divine reality through his life as a man and does the things of his human reality through his life as one of the Trinity. That is the saving fact, though it would not be were this one not the crucified and risen one of the next creedal sections.

I want to end by considering an important question: So what? I rely on a greater authority than my own, that the Reverend Father Brown, G. K. Chesterton's detective priest. I cite a word from the collection *The Incredulity of Father Brown*, addressed to one of his young modern friends: "It's drowning all your . . . rationalism and skepticism, it's coming in like a sea; and the name of it is superstition. . . . It's the first effect of not believing in God that you lose your common sense and can't see things as they are. [So] a dog is an omen, and a cat is a mystery." Modernity will be afflicted by "all the menagerie of polytheism; dog Anubis and great green-eyed Pasht and all the holy howling bulls of Bashan, reeling back to the bestial gods of the beginning, . . . and all because you are frightened of four words, 'He was made man.'"

To see that Father Brown was right in his prediction, you need only browse any bookstore or note what Amazon.com thinks you might be interested in because you once ordered a book about of theology. We late moderns and postmoderns do not inhabit a secularized world; quite the contrary. The West now lays open before the church's mission in much the same condition as in the days when the missionaries had to cut down its sacred oaks and prove their case by combat with demons. The chief mode of damnation from which the mission has now to rescue our sisters and brothers is superstition, the fear of nameless and named powers that are neither Creator nor creature, that project our wants on infinity without ever quite getting them there, and from which middle position they haunt us dreadfully.

There is in the world of religion only one offering that, on the one hand, presents us with God as no sort of extension or projection of ourselves or other creatures, that offers no handle for "great green-eyed Pasht" or the male or female divinities projected by our fears, but yet on the other hand does not abandon us in finitude. The protagonist of the Gospels is always "one and the same" protagonist, one and the same concrete and active subject, whether doing God-things or human-things. Where *he* is, God therefore is very much available among us. But just so, the difference between God and creature is made inescapable, for no one but God could suffer as did Jesus, and no one but a creature could be enthroned as was he.

6

Crucified Also for Us under Pontius Pilate

Six Propositions on the Preaching of the Cross

David S. Yeago

On Good Friday, the congregation in which I worship venerates the cross on which Jesus died and, like Christian congregations throughout the world, cries out:

> Behold the life-giving cross on which was hung the salvation of the whole world. Oh come, let us worship him.
> We adore you, O Christ, and we bless you. By your holy cross you have redeemed the world.[1]

The task of this chapter is to explicate this faith of the church, as it is summarized in the Nicene Creed: the one Lord Jesus Christ "was crucified also for us under Pontius Pilate; he suffered death and was buried."

About this creedal affirmation in its own setting, it is possible to be relatively brief. The confession of Jesus' crucifixion, passion, and burial is notably terse and unadorned compared with the preceding sections that deal with his coessential deity and incarnation. The reason for this brevity is simple: these phrases are not present in the Nicene Creed in response to any specific controversy of the day, but have been received from the earlier creedal traditions that underlie the Nicene-Constantinopolitan text. That is to say, the clauses before us have as their original context the confession of the faith at baptism and the three-article creeds that developed in the early centuries as the instrument of that confession.

Against that background, our phrases have the force of a compact reference to the apostolic *paradosis,* the message handed down to the church by the apostles as it is summarized, for example, in 1 Corinthians 15:1–4 (NRSV):

> Now I would remind you, brothers and sisters, of the good news that I proclaimed to you, which you in turn received, in which also you stand, through which also you are being saved, if you hold firmly to the message that I proclaimed to you—unless you have come to believe in vain. For I handed on to you as of first importance what I in turn had received: that Christ died for our sins in accordance with the scriptures, and that he was buried, and that he was raised on the third day in accordance with the scriptures.

The creed's affirmation that Jesus Christ "was crucified also for us under Pontius Pilate; . . . suffered death and was buried" constitutes in effect an affirmation of this apostolic witness, an undertaking to "hold firmly" to the apostolic proclamation of the cross. The creed's contribution to the exposition of the apostolic witness is largely indirect; by placing this reference to the apostolic preaching amidst its great trinitarian and christological affirmations, the creed "makes absolutely clear that the one who was crucified, suffered, and was buried was none other than the eternal Son of God who became a human being."[2]

My task, however, is not only to discuss the creedal affirmation in its historical setting, but also to bring it into our setting, to explicate its bearing on the life of the church today. This turns out to be a difficult assignment both because of the depth of the mystery and for contextual reasons. The mainline church tradition to which I belong is nowadays deeply ambiguous about the cross, and that ambiguity lies somewhere near the heart of the manifold confusions that presently bedevil us.[3] Mainline Christians today live uneasily amidst the rubble of the old doctrine of penal substitution, according to which Jesus was the divinely provided substitute who endured in our place the infinite punishment that God's justice must impose on our sin. This teaching we have on the whole rejected for reasons both good and bad, and I share that rejection, I hope for the good reasons and not the bad ones.[4] Yet there is no wide consensus among us on what the cross *does* mean if it does not mean *that*. Or rather, what consensus there is fails abysmally to do justice to the faith of the church that by his holy cross Jesus Christ has redeemed the world.

Here I propose to blunder in assertively and set forth six propositions about what it means to proclaim the cross of Jesus Christ as the redemption of the world, in fidelity to the apostolic witness. While all the issues I shall address have long and interesting histories in modern academic theology, I will ignore most of that and speak directly to the task of Christian proclamation, which I would interpret broadly to include every form of articulate witness to Christ. I hope that these propositions add up to a framework for proclaiming and expounding the faith of the church today; perhaps the propositions themselves could serve as a sort of checklist even for those who would develop them differently in each case.

Proposition One: In Jesus' death on the cross, God has acted to redeem the world and renew human life.

This first proposition speaks directly to the major loss that has accompanied the collapse of the penal doctrine in mainline church traditions—the loss of the sense of the cross as divine action that changes things. It would be fair to say that most preachers in mainline churches today describe the significance of the cross in revelatory terms. The cross manifests vividly some general truth or state of affairs that we could not know, or would not find easy to believe, without it. "God is on the side of victims"—just look at the cross, where God's beloved Son himself became a victim. "God is with us no matter what"—just look at the cross, where God was present in the very depths of pain and loss. "Nothing we can do will turn God away from us"—just look at the cross, where God the Son endured the extremity of human abuse and yet did not turn away.

None of these accounts is exactly false; each can be developed with genuine profundity, yet something is missing from all of them. Each finds the good news of the cross in some claim that could be true, though it might not be known, even without the cross. The cross figures in such preaching as the manifestation of a principle that is universally valid, not as an act whose power is universally transformative. It may indeed be essential to our salvation that the principle be made known to us with a certain kind of depth and power, and in that sense the cross can be said to be a saving event. But this surely falls short of St. Paul's celebration of the death of Jesus on the cross as God's act reconciling his enemies to himself (Rom. 5:8–10; 2 Cor. 5:14–21), the righteous deed that has brought about righteousness and life in place of judgment and death (Rom. 5:17).

This way of construing the cross has two important and lamentable consequences. Hermeneutically, it has promoted what I call the evanescence of Jesus in contemporary preaching. Because the role of Jesus is to make known a principle or a divine attitude that can be described in nonchristological terms, then it follows that proclaiming the meaning of Jesus requires us to move beyond his particularity to the appropriate level of generality at which that meaning can be apprehended. In other words, we start with the particular man Jesus and disentangle from the contingencies of his story some general affirmation of divine presence or acceptance or solidarity, which becomes the real good news, the real message. Jesus evanesces; his particularity blurs and dissolves to reveal the "meaning" of which he is but the vehicle.

Much contemporary preaching thus sidesteps the figure of Jesus, quite effortlessly and probably unconsciously, by the second or third paragraph of the sermon, sometimes even sooner.[5] The odd outcome is that though we seem to have more preaching on the gospel lessons than ever before, we have at the same time less discourse that is actually about Jesus than we did in the days of forty-five minute expositions of Paul. The contemporary pulpit proclaims forgiveness, acceptance, wholeness, liberation, and a host of other desirable things, but it seems very seldom to bring good news whose content is actually Jesus Christ.[6]

The second problem is deeply connected with this. The gospel thus preached is invariably a gospel of affirmation, not transformation. It reassures us but does not make anything happen. The cross of Jesus is proclaimed as the token of our assurance that God is with us "no matter what," a divine presence that enables us to cope with things as they are but does not change anything and therefore in the end reconciles us to things as they are. We have no plausible working exegesis of Paul's audacious pronouncement: "So if anyone is in Christ, there is a new creation: everything old has passed away; see, everything has become new!" (2 Cor. 5:17 NRSV). We tend rather to say: "If anyone is in Christ, there is a new interpretation: everything remains the same, but we feel quite differently about it."

It is depressing to record that the decisive critique of this sort of preaching, which is still the default practice in mainline churches, was written as long ago as 1909 by the great Peter Taylor Forsyth. As we have not yet absorbed his warning, it seems appropriate to repeat it:

If God were all sympathy, if His divine power lay chiefly in His ability to infuse Himself with superhuman intimacy of feeling into the most unspeakable tangles and crises of human life, then also He would be less than God, and we should have no more than what might be called a monism of heart. . . . God's participation in man's affairs is much more than that of a fellow-sufferer on a divine scale, whose love can rise only to a painless sympathy with pain. He not only perfectly understands our case and our problem, but he has morally, actively, finally solved it.[7]

This, then, is the first issue with which the preaching of the cross must come to terms: How is this death, the death of Jesus on the cross, in its unity with the resurrection, not only the expression of God's attitude but also the act of God's power, not only the sign of God's solidarity with our plight but also the active engagement of his mercy to resolve that plight? How do the dying and rising of Jesus not only manifest God's constant attitude but also constitute a new creation, a new reality, into which we may somehow enter? How does the death of Jesus on the cross not only reassure the world but also redeem it? This brings us to my second proposition.

Proposition Two: In Jesus' death on the cross, on account of the hypostatic union, divine love acts in a human way and human acts have divine force.

Here I would simply call attention to the relevance of the ecumenical christological dogma. That dogma, as the work of St. Cyril of Alexandria makes clear, is really a formal description of the narrative structure of the second article of the Nicene Creed.[8] In Jesus Christ we have to do with a single hypostasis or subject, a single someone, to whom Holy Scripture ascribes two natures, two complete and irreducibly distinct sets of properties. This subject, this someone, is the one who was born of the Father before all ages, God from God, Light from Light. For us and for our salvation, this same one made his own what is ours, and as he is one being with the Father from eternity, so he came voluntarily to be of one being with us as well. As St. Cyril says:

We confess that he is the Son, begotten of God the Father, and Only-begotten God; and although according to his own nature he was not liable to suffering, yet he suffered for us in the flesh according to the Scriptures, and although impassible, yet in his crucified body he made his own the sufferings of his own flesh.[9]

The doctrine of the two natures in one person, or hypostasis, simply describes this movement of mercy, this *kenōsis*, in which the one who shares all that the Father is incomprehensibly undertakes to share all that we are as well.

The unity of the divine and the human is thus simply Jesus himself, the incarnate Son, this particular someone to whom Peter could point and say: "You are the Son of the living God." The two natures are not united on the plane of nature, producing some third thing neither divine nor human. They are united in the concrete particularity of Jesus' person and agency, and their unity is displayed in the singular texture of his words and deeds, the distinctive character of the way things go in his story. In this particular person, in this particular life, in this particular story, divine and human, God's reality and our reality are indissolubly and redemptively one.

The hermeneutical implications of this doctrine were worked out most clearly by St. Maximus the Confessor in his account of the interpenetration (*perichōrēsis*) of the two natures in the unity of Jesus' person and life.[10] According to St. Maximus, we cannot interpret the gospel story as though the two natures were two bins into which the various actions and episodes of Jesus' life are to be sorted—this bit divine, this bit human, and so on. The two natures remain distinguishable in thought, but in the action of the story their energies are inseparably joined. "In neither of those [natures] of which he was the hypostasis does he work in separation from the other, but rather he confirms each through the other."[11] The incarnate Son of God does divine things in a human way, in irreducible unity with his human living and suffering; he likewise does human things in a divine way, so that in the freedom of divine love he realizes human existence in an unheard-of mode, through human acts of limitless significance and consequence.

We will not understand this doctrine as the early church did until we learn to use it as an interpretive tool, a guide to grasping the force and implications of the gospel story. Taken as such, it has important bearing on the task of proclaiming the death of Jesus as the divine act constituting a new creation. He does divine things in a human way: divine love intervenes for our redemption in a concrete identity with the human devotion of the crucified Jesus. He also does human things in a divine way: in its unity with the divine love, the human obedience of the Crucified has overcome sin, death, and the devil.

In St. Maximus's terms, in the passion for the Father's reign that over-comes Jesus' fear in the Garden of Gethsemane, we see human will and desire "formed and moved" by divine love, so that the human faithfulness of Jesus, to the point of death, *is* the concrete engagement of divine love with the sin of the world. It is precisely this fidelity, achieved against the grain of fear and horror, within the frailty of the flesh that the Son of God has truly made his own, that redeems the world.[12]

The world is redeemed not simply by a divine love up in heaven, a distant benevolence that wishes us well, nor even an abstract but sympathetic divine solidarity near at hand; we are saved inseparably by a particular human love, by the human love of a still-young Jew of first-century Palestine who endured a terrible death rather than accept less for his people and for the world than the Father designed. We do not encounter the divine love that redeems the world otherwise than in the form of this singular human love: the two natures are indivisible and inseparable. For all time, under all circumstances, and for all people, to be embraced by the redemptive love of God is to come under the rule of Jesus the Messiah, to be grasped by the zeal of Jesus for the Father's kingdom and glory, to fall under the sway of the specific human love depicted and attested in the Gospels.

The interpretive force of the classical Christology of the church, as it is outlined in the Nicene Creed and explicated by the great christological coun-cils from Ephesus to III Constantinople, is therefore to focus our attention on the human particularity of Jesus Christ as the concrete engagement of divine love for the redemption of the world. We do not find the good news by moving beyond the particulars to comforting generalities that they sup-posedly symbolize; we find the good news insofar as we grasp the singular human faithfulness of Jesus, the particular intentions that inform his "Not my will, but your will be done" in the Garden of Gethsemane. In the end, according to the creed, these particular intentions shall rule over all: "for he shall come again with glory to judge the living and the dead, and his king-dom shall have no end."

Proposition Three: Jesus' death on the cross is the redemption of the world precisely as an event in God's history with Israel.

If we are to place the detail of Jesus' story at the center, we must come to terms, first of all, with the particularity of its setting—not only its geo-graphical setting but also its narrative setting. Holy Scripture presents the career and cross of Jesus to us as an episode—the culminating episode, to be sure—in the story of God and the elect people Israel; Jesus came to the cross by way of a conflict with the rulers of his people over Israel's identity and destiny, and his own role within that destiny. The death of Jesus is proclaimed by St. Paul as the actual accomplishment of the righteousness that was Israel's corporate vocation:

> For God has done what the Torah, weakened by the flesh, could not do: by sending his own Son in the likeness of sinful flesh, and to deal with sin, he condemned sin in the flesh, so that the just requirement of the Torah might be fulfilled in us, who walk not according to the flesh but according to the Spirit (Rom. 8:3–4, NRSV, with my substitution of *Torah* for *law*).

Jesus' death is first and foremost an event in the history of Israel, in the story of a people called to struggle with Torah and walk in righteousness, and so become a light to the nations. The universal significance of Jesus' dying is contained in its significance for Israel: the cross of Jesus redeems the world precisely as it fulfills the specific vocation of Israel.

In this context, I would like to make a plea for a new reception of *Messiah* as the primary soteriological title of Jesus. Jesus is Savior of the world only insofar as he is "King of the Jews," the king promised to Israel. He has redeemed the world on the cross only insofar as by his dying he has accomplished his messianic task.

It is, of course, provocative to highlight such claims today, in the face of a widespread impression that the confession of Jesus as Israel's Messiah is somehow the cause of the Christian anti-Judaism we are rightly struggling to shed. However, this impression is accurate only in the most superficial way, insofar as disagreeing with the Jews about Jesus was clearly the point of departure for the growth of hostility toward them. At any more profound level, though, anti-Judaism actually impedes taking the messianic idea seriously.

The old notion was that because Israel rejected its King, the Messiah in turn rejected Israel and turned away to be the King of a successor people, a Gentile people. But to suppose that the Messiah could be King of a group of Gentiles rather than King of the Jews empties the concept of its content. To uproot the Messiah from Israel is to remove the messianic idea from the whole dense context of prophecy and narrative that gives it force. At the end of this road, the notion of the Messiah becomes an empty vessel for our dream of a cosmic benefactor who will give us what we want and think we need. Indeed, part of the importance of the confession of Jesus as Messiah is that it mandates a complex encounter with Old Testament texts and traditions that impedes the construction of a Christology that is read off of our felt needs and religious aspirations.

The Messiah is first and foremost Israel's King, and the work of the Messiah is first and foremost to purify and vindicate Israel. If Jesus surrendered himself to death specifically as Messiah, and if his self-offering has been affirmed by the Father in the resurrection, then this is first and foremost a promise that God is *not* through with the Jewish people, but holds to his purpose of placing this people at the center of history's consummation. The church does not replace Israel; the church is that *part* of Israel that has received the good news of the enthronement of the Crucified as Lord and Messiah and has found itself launched thereby on a mission to the Gentiles.

The relationship of this part of Israel to "Israel after the flesh," the Jewish kinship group, the community of Abraham's descendants who remain "as regards election . . . beloved, for the sake of their ancestors" (Rom. 11:28 NRSV); the hope of the church for reunion with the Jewish people in the consummation of all things; and the problem, never wholly resolved through twenty centuries, of domesticating a largely Gentile population within the community of Israel's Messiah are all matters of greatest importance that cannot be taken up here. But one point at least must be made very briefly about the implications of the confession of Jesus as Messiah for the preaching of the cross.

The Messiah is a King, the ruler of a people. If Jesus redeemed the world *as Messiah*, then the outcome of his dying must be corporate and community-grounding. He has "freed us from our sins by his blood, and made us to be a kingdom, priests serving his God and Father" (Rev. 1:5–6 NRSV). If the dying of Jesus on the cross is to be proclaimed as a *messianic* deed, then it must have a *public* outcome. His death does not merely provide a mechanism by which individuals can clear their guilt and find access to God, nor a symbolic assurance of God's therapeutic presence in the midst of our stress and sorrow. Enthroned on the cross, Jesus the Messiah makes his own crucified body the core and center of a new kind of human community, a renewed Israel, an Israel bound to God in a renewed and eschatologically consummated covenant. In this consummated covenant, the destiny of Israel to be the core and center of a universal renewal of the whole human family is at last being fulfilled: "Nations shall come to your light, and kings to the brightness of your dawn" (Isa. 60:3 NRSV).

Proposition Four: In his death on the cross, Jesus Christ has acted for us as God's true covenant-partner, and in so doing has brought into being the new humanity in which we hope to share.

This thesis maintains, first of all, that Jesus Christ has *acted* for us on the cross, and this is itself a point that needs exposition. The enormous power of the idea of victimization in our culture has led much contemporary preaching to a one-sided presentation of Jesus as victim, as one buffeted and battered as we are by violence and betrayal. Jesus is taken to symbolize God's solidarity and healing presence with all victims. Jesus is therefore in a certain sense a symbol for *me,* for me in my victimhood, whether at the hands of specific others or simply amidst the pressures of life.

That this line of thought starts from a truth cannot be denied, nor, of course, would I belittle the reality of victimization and suffering. Nonetheless, this sort of preaching is dangerous, not least to genuine victims. There is a fine but decisive line between *acknowledging* victims as those who have suffered wrong and *defining* persons as victims whose very identity then comes to be constituted by the constrictions of possibility imposed upon them by their oppressors. When Jesus becomes a simple symbol of the self in its affliction, the power of the symbol presses toward the definition of persons by victimization. This is, I think, the core of truth in contemporary feminist criticism of the cross: if our message is simply that God loves victims, that God is specially present in the midst of victimization, then we have come a bit too close to saying that a victim is a good thing to be.[13]

There is, however, an opposite but equally threatening danger in such preaching. The simple proclamation of God's solidarity with victims places no critical controls on the way in which the victim is validated. When the message is simply, "If you are a victim, God is on your side," the identification of oneself as victim becomes a ticket to power and perhaps also to vengeance. Indeed, in a community dominated by such preaching of the cross, public discourse easily devolves into a power struggle carried on through competing claims to victimhood, in the midst of which real victims are easily pushed aside and ignored. I well recall that just after my own denomination was formed an ecclesiastical offical agreed with those who objected that our denominational structures were divisive and abusive of persons, but continued: "Yes, yes, but don't you know that the treasure always comes in earthen vessels?" In other words, the very dysfunction of the institution gives it authority, and its managers become God-favored victims precisely insofar as they are criticized by those whom the institution has demeaned and ignored.

The way to avoid these alternate catastrophes is to reject from the beginning the depiction of the crucified Jesus as a symbol of the victimized and suffering self. It is true that Jesus on the cross joins suffering humanity in suffering and victimization and death, but in so doing he does not simply become a symbol of the self in its suffering. On the contrary, the world is redeemed because this other person, Jesus specifically, in his irreducible particularity, submits by his own act to death on a cross, and thereby does for us what we cannot do for ourselves. The world is redeemed by the dying of someone *other* than you or me. And it is precisely insofar as his death is his, unique to him, irreducibly other than your death or mine, that his death redeems the world. It is this particular death with its unique subject, Jesus of Nazareth, in its singular placement within a particular narrative context that, precisely in its particularity, is the world's redemption.

Of course, when the crucified Jesus is presented as a symbol of the suffering self, all such particularity becomes an obstacle to proclamation; everything about Jesus' suffering and death that makes it different from ours must be discounted if we are to get at its saving significance. But the narrative form of the Gospels suggests otherwise, as does the very wording of the Nicene creed: "Crucified also for us under Pontius Pilate." It has often been pointed out that "under Pontius Pilate" grounds the Christian gospel in history, but it also has particularizing force: it is that particular death, the death of Jesus under Pontius Pilate, that is "for us" and redeems us.

Furthermore, Jesus' death is redemptive only insofar as it is action as well as passion, undertaken as well as undergone. The widespread depiction of Jesus as symbolic victim has led to an almost complete forgetfulness of what the old Protestant scholastics called the "active obedience" of Christ. The world is redeemed not only by what was done to Christ, but by his distinctive agency; as St. Maximus put it, by the singular way in which human agency is "formed and moved" by divine love and freedom in his human career. The passive suffering of the cross is indeed redemptive only as it is accepted and endured as the final test and unsurpassable realization of Jesus' distinctive way of being human.

In this active obedience that culminates in the cross, Jesus has fulfilled in his own person, on Israel's behalf, the vocation of Israel as a covenant people. The vocation of Israel is to live in a distinctive kind of communion and covenant partnership with God, practicing righteousness and bringing forth praise as "a priestly kingdom and a holy nation" (Ex. 19:6 NRSV). In this way, Israel is to become a light to the nations so the Gentiles will say, "Let us go up to Zion and learn their ways and walk their paths, for God is with them."[14]

The mission of the Messiah, the God-anointed King, is to take responsibility for Israel and bring about the fulfillment of Israel's vocation. Jesus' pursuit of that mission, as narrated in the Synoptic Gospels, comes to a peak in Gethsemane with the prayer, "Not what I want, but what you want." What "God wants" here is not God's arbitrary whim, but the divine purpose invoked in the Lord's Prayer: "Your will be accomplished on earth as it is in heaven." Jesus puts that divine purpose before his own will, though the burden it lays on him is crushing, though it means his own apparent failure and certain death. His very flesh, his concrete bodily being, is handed over without reserve to the fulfillment of the Father's purpose, the inauguration of his reign.

In this faithfulness, the Messiah himself becomes the covenant partner God has summoned Israel to be.[15] On the cross, covenant faithfulness is fully realized on this earth and in actual human flesh; righteousness is thereby made fully and concretely actual in the world in a superabundant and definitive way. In the wake of the cross, righteousness is no longer simply a norm, an impossible ideal with merely regulative force. Righteousness is a fact, a thing achieved, something actual. It has become actual in the righteous deed of Jesus Christ (Rom. 5:18), in his obedience even to the point of death on the cross, in his giving of himself to God.

If the crucified Jesus were simply God's sustaining presence with the afflicted and overstressed, then the cross would have no constitutive reference to any prescriptive will of God, but only to a therapeutic will. But if we take seriously the relation of the active obedience of Jesus to his vocation as Messiah, then behind the cross stands divine calling and commandment. Israel is called to be a priestly people, a holy nation, and in this vocation lies the "glory and honor" (Ps. 8:5 NRSV) with which God intends to crown the whole human race. It is this vocation that Jesus Christ has fulfilled by his holy cross.

In other words, we cannot understand the cross as the redemption of the world except in the context of God's will that his creature be a certain way—the context, that is, of his law. While it is not possible to pursue all the questions this raises, it should at least be noted that we cannot proclaim the cross according to the apostolic witness without also proclaiming God's commandment, his Torah, his insistent will for human creatures.

Proposition Five: Jesus Christ by his death on the cross opens our future in such a way that he simultaneously deals with our sin.

Jesus crucified constitutes in himself the new humanity, the new and transformed mode of human existence in covenant with God, in which we all may hope to share. But this by itself does not adequately account for the full reality of Jesus' reconciling work. He does not only live and die in perfect covenant partnership with the Father; his living and, above all, his dying take the form of confrontation with evil, and consequently his faithfulness to the Father is consummated amidst pain and terror and abandonment.

The confession that Jesus died "for our sins" (1 Cor. 15:3 NRSV) is at the heart of the apostolic tradition on which the church is founded; no responsible account of the *pro nobis,* the "for us" of the creed, can bypass it. But why was it necessary for our sin to be dealt with by the pain and suffering of the cross? From ancient times the question has arisen, "Why could God not simply have declared amnesty?"

The short answer to this question is that God tried amnesty and it failed. After all, Jesus came on the scene in the Gospels as the embodied pardon of God. His coming meant that amnesty was declared, the lost were welcomed, and sinners were received at the eschatological banquet table. In the gospel narrative, these things precede Jesus' death on the cross, and there is no indication that they are only conditional on subsequent events. But if Jesus could announce God's forgiveness before his passion, what is added by his death on the cross? What do we need besides pardon?

In the gospel story, I would suggest, the problem is not that God demands compensation as a condition of forgiveness; rather, the problem is that there is "no one home" to *receive* his forgiveness. The free gift of communion with God enclosed in Jesus' proclamation of forgiveness found no adequate response, no corporate or individual subject capable of entering fully and finally into the renewed covenant partnership that Jesus offered. "Jerusalem, Jerusalem, the city that kills the prophets and stones those who are sent to it! How often have I desired to gather your children together as a hen gathers her brood under her wings, *and you were not willing!*" (Matt. 23:37 NRSV).

What becomes visible in Jesus' ministry is that God's forgiveness does not simply have amnesty in view, but also covenant and communion; it is not so much a matter of letting us off punishment as of gathering us in to covenant life. Perhaps God could simply forego the exaction of consequences for the offense of sin, but this would not advance his purpose of communion. The exigencies of intrahuman forgiveness point in the same direction:

simply to forego vengeance against those who have wronged us is not yet to restore fellowship with them. The genuine renewal of communion requires a cleansing and clearing out of the relational space, so to speak, between the offender and the offended, beginning with truthfulness and acknowledgment of the reality of what has occurred.

Our current habit is to regard this as a need primarily of the injured, a need on the part of victims for acknowledgment of what they have suffered. But in another sense, the need lies even more heavily and objectively on the part of the offender. The wrongdoer *needs* to "make things right," not in order to escape punishment but in order to recover the dignity without which one cannot take part with others in a common enterprise or a common life. The need in question here is not merely psychological, though studies of the psychology of shame may illumine it in spite of themselves. The need for dignity, for honor, is not merely the need to *feel* a certain way, but the need to *be* a certain way, to have a kind of substance, a kind of "weight," *(kabod, gravitas)* without which we cannot hold up and bear our part in the exchanges of common life.

To say that Jesus, by his suffering and dying, dealt with sin (cf. Rom. 8:3, NRSV) is to say that in his death there took place for all humankind that cleansing and clearing out of the relational space between God and sinful humankind that is necessary for the restoration of communion and covenant partnership. Jesus on the cross does not join us in sinning, he does not turn from God, but he endures the emptiness and pain and abandonment that are sin's reality. When he cries out "Why have you abandoned me?" he is speaking in our voice, from our place, acknowledging our reality. It is just this acknowledgment of sin's truth, I would suggest, that "deals with sin" and sets things right between God and sinners.

There is this particle of truth in the notion of a compensation for sin required by divine justice: God, who is truth, cannot enter into communion with us on the basis of pretense. The establishment of communion requires judgment because it requires truthfulness. Things must be called by their right names; sin must be exposed as emptiness and decay while God is honored as holy and good precisely in his wrath, his implacable rejection of sin. Only the accomplishment of such truthfulness can clear and cleanse the relational space between God and humankind; only in such truthfulness can sinners stand before God with the dignity of daughters and sons, partners in covenant.

Jesus on the cross is therefore not "paying God back" or being punished for our sins. There is no such invisible transaction going on behind the scenes of the narrative we rehearse each Passiontide. Jesus is doing just what appears in the story: he is being faithful to his Father even to death, and in this way realizing in himself, in his own person, the covenant partnership that is Israel's vocation and God's ultimate purpose for the whole human race. He does so in such fashion that in his story truthfulness is restored between God and humankind; the reality of sin is exposed and judged; God is justified in his wrathful *No* to sin. Anyone who comes under the sway of Christ's righteousness therefore comes into the sphere of this truthfulness; the renewed Israel, the community founded on the righteous deed of the Messiah, is a community constituted in truth, a community therefore of penitence and confession of sin, and *only* so a community of sinners restored to the dignity of priesthood and covenant partnership.

During the course of the twentieth century, most of the Christian churches of the Western world scrambled to abandon their ancient traditions of penitential piety. Doubtless the forms of that piety were genuinely in need of overhaul, but this proposition suggests a considerable irony in the project of getting "beyond" penitentialism to a more "affirming" type of piety. The old penitentialism was rejected in part because it was found to be demeaning; to describe ourselves in constant repetition as "miserable offenders" and the like was, it seemed, to commit ourselves to an unconscionably restricted view of human possibility. But if this analysis has any validity, the penitentialism that acknowledged in the crucified Jesus the truth of *our* condition was the very form of the dignity bestowed on sinners by the mercy of God in Christ.

Abandoning penitence, therefore, we abandon the ground of authentic dignity founded in truth and are left only with "self-esteem," which can be defined as the doomed attempt to found dignity on sheer self-assertion rather than on truth and mutuality. To preach the cross according to the apostolic witness is to know ourselves as "miserable offenders" whom the Messiah Jesus has taken in charge, for whose sake he has acted and suffered. In him our honor is restored precisely and only as the emptiness and wrong of our sin is relentlessly and definitively exposed.

Proposition Six: The salvation achieved on the cross is not separable from the person who was crucified.

According to what has been said so far, Jesus on the cross not only models righteousness for us, he embodies it and realizes it in our place and on our behalf, as our representative, as the King appointed to renew God's people and bring blessing thereby to all nations. Jesus Christ has experienced in his own body the full nullity of our sin; he has endured in his own dereliction and death the divine negation of our sinful form of life; he has in his resurrection received the new beginning on the far side of the divine *No* that can only come from the utter freedom of divine love. In all this he has acted and suffered and triumphed *for us*, restoring us to dignity as God's children and priests, fashioning in his own person a new way of being human in which all people are called to share. In this he has done for us what we could not do for ourselves: he has done what is right in the very teeth of sin's wrong and so has restored the lost world to God.

Therefore, in the New Testament witness, Jesus crucified and risen *is* the new humanity in which we hope to share. The hope given to the human race in his living and dying and rising again is that our own way of being, our mode of existence, will be reformed and conformed to his crucified and risen form. Salvation is existence in Christ and at the same time Christ living in us (Gal. 2:20). In baptism, we clothe ourselves in the Messiah, and so become children of Abraham (Gal. 3:27), and conversely Christ is formed in us (Gal. 4:19). In Romans 6, Paul speaks of this in terms of co-crucifixion, and co-burial. In Colossians the baptized have died and risen with Christ, and this is to determine the concrete shape of their existence: "For you have died, and your life is hidden with Christ in God. When Christ who is your life is revealed, then you also will be revealed with him in glory" (3:3–4 NRSV). In the Gospel of John, Jesus is the vine and his disciples are the branches; they live only as they abide "in" him (John 15:4–6).

The most drastic statement of the point comes, however, when the Johannine Jesus identifies himself as the bread of life and specifies this with a reference to his flesh and blood, his concrete bodily existence:

> I am the living bread that came down from heaven. Whoever eats of this bread will live forever; and the bread that I will give for the life of the world is my flesh. . . . Those who eat my flesh and drink my blood have eternal life, and I will raise them up on the last day; for my flesh is true food and my blood is true drink. Those who eat my flesh and drink my blood abide in me, and I in them (John 6:51, 54–56).[16]

The point seems to be that the salvation that Jesus has won for us is not separable from his person. To share in salvation is to be joined to this particular person, this crucified and risen Jew, precisely *as* a particular person, in his own concrete flesh and blood. Martin Luther develops this point in his sermons on John 6:

He speaks openly, clearly, and plainly of this, so that no one may think that he says it in a dark or hidden way or is using a figure of speech: "I am the bread," a food which has come from heaven. "Whoever eats of me, shall live." Here no one can deny that he is talking about himself, since he says this about himself, that is, about his *person*. Therefore one is to grasp and take hold of the person of Christ with certainty, and not go wandering on other paths. But people are most offended by this, that he says *"I".* Whoever overcomes this offense, has triumphed, for this is the real art and the highest wisdom of faith, if one can only consider and regard this person Christ as God, as his food and bread of eternal life, yes, as his comfort, redeemer, and savior, *for whatever he is, that you obtain with him.* This article makes you a Christian, so that you are called "Christian" from Christ, and you receive your Christian title from *him.*[17]

Luther simply turns on its head the famous dictum of Philipp Melanchthon that "to know Christ is to know his benefits." Salvation cannot be described as an experience of "benefits" in abstraction from the presence of Christ himself: "whatever he is, that you obtain *with him."* The "benefits" that faith receives are consequences of our union with the crucified and risen person of Jesus Christ, who is himself the substance of all blessings.

Therefore when I have him, then I really have it, for he is himself nothing other than sheer righteousness, life, and eternal salvation, and a Lord over death. Christ is without all lack and defect, the eternal life, joy, righteousness, and salvation; this treasure is indeed present, I have it in Christ, for he is the whole thing; in him there is no deficiency and nothing is lacking to him.[18]

Salvation is thus not a sort of product of what Jesus has done that could be separated from Jesus himself. If we think of salvation as a product, a separable outcome, as Western Christians have sometimes tended to do, then Jesus himself will sink into the past with no continuing role to play after he has "acquired" salvation for us. On the contrary, as Paul writes, Christ himself *is* the salvation bestowed on us by God:

It is God's doing that you are in the Messiah Jesus, who has become wisdom for you from God, and righteousness and sanctification and redemption, so that, as it is written, "Let anyone who boasts, boast in the Lord" (1 Cor. 1:30–31, my translation).

The past work of Christ is saving, therefore, because it constitutes him as the saving person, indeed as salvation in person: he himself is, in his singular living and dying, the gift by which our lives are justified and renewed. For us, therefore, salvation involves adherence to this person, union with him, sharing in what is his and in what he is.

The preaching of the cross, therefore, makes sense only within the economy of the Holy Spirit, by whose power he who was crucified is glorified and liberated and, so to speak, set at large. It is by the Holy Spirit that the crucified Christ in his incarnate particularity is set free from the bondage of death to give himself to his people as their food and drink. The preaching of the cross makes sense only as an element in the economy of communion by which the risen Lord in the freedom of the Spirit makes his own crucified and risen person the ground of a new community that is a royal dominion, a community of priests for his God and Father.

In other words, the preaching of the cross makes sense only as a sacramental act, an act that not only tells of Christ but also bestows him on those who hear, drawing all together in him, and thereby founding and nurturing a new kind of community. As Luther put in a sermon of 1532:

> Christ is the food that is set on the table by the mouth of the preacher, for it is placed within the preaching; it is only present in the word and is heard by young, old, learned, ignorant, etc. One receives as much as another throughout the world, as soon as a person believes. . . . All believers eat of the same Christ, and each one receives him whole, and yet Christ still remains whole.[19]

This is only possible by the action of the Spirit, who joins his own action to the witness and celebration of the church, making of these practices loci and instruments of eschatological communion with the crucified and risen Christ.

This last proposition calls us to look critically at a bad legacy of the penal theory. According to that theory, the righteousness of Christ's death is sacrifice because it fulfills the legal conditions on which we may receive blessing from a just God. This suggests that the righteousness of Christ accomplished on the cross is important to us not for its own sake but instrumentally, for the sake of what it gains or earns for us.

This implies that the idea of salvation can be defined apart from Christology as a state of abstract well-being,—"peace," "wholeness," "freedom," "divine favor," or the like—that can be described without reference to Jesus Christ and his cross, to which Christ and his cross are related only extrinsically as means to an end. This way of thinking of Christ and salvation in terms of means and end has survived the collapse of the penal theory and also characterizes much contemporary preaching. Three disasters follow once this move is made.

First, to think of Christ and salvation in terms of means and end gives rise to questions to which no answer ever seems entirely satisfactory: Why precisely *this* means to that end? Why *only* this means to the end? Why would God bestow the blessing of salvation exclusively by way of Christ? Why would there not be many ways to such an abstract sort of salvation if God indeed desires the salvation of all?

Second, this instrumentalization of Christ's righteous dying promotes what I have called the evanescence of Jesus in contemporary preaching. If Christ is a means to the end of human wholeness or peace of mind or what have you, then the natural move will be away from the means to the end. When the goal is sighted, the means loses our attention.

Third, the conception of Christ and salvation in terms of means and end leaves the notion of salvation empty and uncontrolled, ready to be filled by our cravings and anxieties. It becomes very easy then to suppose that we put our trust in Jesus Christ as the helper who will secure what we want rather than as the Lord and Messiah who will unfailingly accomplish the purposes of God.

The way to avoid these outcomes is to refuse from the start to walk the path that leads to them. The crucified Jesus is not a means to an end, a device to achieve some outcome to which he is merely instrumental. The crucified Jesus is himself the end of all God's ways; in his crucified obedience, his realization of covenant partnership, God has achieved the good for which the world was made. There is nothing beyond the crucified Jesus; the resurrection does not mean that Jesus moves on to something beyond his conclusive self-giving on the cross, but rather that in the power of the Spirit the crucified Messiah is exalted to draw all things to himself.[20]

The Christian hope is simply to be included in that good, to bear the image of the crucified Jesus, to be joined with him in his dying to sin and rising to God. The church has nothing else to give and nothing else to promise. Our hope is for the great assembly around the throne of God and the slaughtered Lamb, in which we join by anticipation at the Lord's table. To preach the cross, therefore, is to set forth the crucified Jesus as good of every person, the form of all fulfillment, and the food by which all may live.

Behold the life-giving cross on which was hung the salvation of the whole world. Oh come, let us worship him.[21]

7

The Reality of the Resurrection

Carl E. Braaten

The ecumenical movement has not yet reached its goal; Christianity is still badly divided. However, the deepest divisions are no longer denominational, say, between Catholics and Protestants, Lutherans and Reformed, Evangelical and mainline churches, and so on, although such divisions lamentably still exist and we should not pretend that the ecumenical movement has swept them all away. The deepest fault line appears where faith and unbelief meet *within* the churches, among their theologians, bishops, and pastors. Nowhere is this more evident than in the matter of the resurrection of Jesus.

Prior to the Enlightenment, Christian theologians were not vexed by the question, "Did the resurrection of Jesus really happen?" What Paul said placed the question beyond dispute: "If Christ has not been raised, then our proclamation has been in vain and your faith has been in vain. . . . If Christ has not been raised, your faith is futile and you are still in your sins. . . . If for this life only we have hoped in Christ, we are of all people most to be pitied" (1 Cor. 15:14, 17, 19 NRSV). For many post-Enlightenment Christians, Paul's words no longer seem to settle the matter. For example, A. J. M. Wedderburn, New Testament professor at the University of Munich, concludes that Paul's argument is thoroughly flawed. He writes: "Paul's logic simply cannot hold water today. His rhetoric has led him astray."[1] The title of his book, *Beyond Resurrection,* is also its thesis: The results of modern historical criticism have placed the resurrection of Jesus beyond our capacity to believe that it really happened.

Take another example. Robert W. Funk tells about how he once formulated the proposition that the resurrection was an event in the life of Jesus, then presented it to members of the Jesus Seminar. He writes:

> My proposition was received with hilarity by several Fellows. One suggested that it was an oxymoron. . . . Others alleged that the formulation was meaningless, since we all assume, they said, that Jesus' life ended with his crucifixion and death. I was surprised by this response. I shouldn't have been. After all, John Dominic Crossan has confessed "I do not think that anyone, anywhere, at any time brings dead people back to life." That's fairly blunt. But it squares with what we really know, as distinguished from what many want to believe. Sheehan is even blunter: "Jesus, regardless of where his corpse ended up, is dead and remains dead."[2]

Some years ago I wrote an editorial for *Pro Ecclesia* entitled "Can We Still Be Christians?"[3] It was prompted by Gerd Luedemann's book, *The Resurrection of Jesus*, in which, like Wedderburn, he reconstructs Christian belief apart from the resurrection. That question, "Can we still be Christians?" was originally asked by David Friedrich Strauss after he had dissolved the entire life of the historical Jesus, from the incarnation to the resurrection, into a Christ-myth. Strauss's answer was simply and honestly a brazen "No." Luedemann's answer, exactly opposite, was an emphatic "Yes." We modern Christians, unlike the deluded Christians of earlier times, may not be able to believe that the resurrection is an event that really happened to Jesus, but we can still believe all that is truly essential—Jesus' exemplary life and moral teachings. The resurrection adds nothing that was not already present in the historical Jesus, such as forgiveness of sins, affirmation of life, and experience of eternity here and now. The conclusion of my editorial was that Strauss was right, and Luedemann wrong. Without the confession that God raised Jesus from the dead on the third day, Christianity has mutated into a different religion.

Meanwhile, I have learned that Gerd Luedemann has reconsidered his answer; he has renounced the Christian faith.[4] There is something tragically clarifying about that decision, one that the likes of Bishop John Spong, Marcus Borg, and a host of others lack the insight or courage to make. The motto of the Enlightenment was *"sapere aude!"*—have courage to use your own reason. Luedemann apparently has finally acquired the courage, like Strauss, to reason that there's no point in calling yourself a Christian if you don't believe that God raised Jesus from the dead. The Christian faith stands or falls with the reality of the resurrection, and it's time theologians took the courage to say it to their colleagues who pretend otherwise.

Consider a contrary verdict. Professor Wedderburn tells about an unpublished paper he received from a colleague, J. L. Houlden, entitled "Is the Historical Reliability of the Resurrection Necessary to Christianity?" In this paper, "Houlden comments that when a meeting of British New Testament scholars debated the evidence for and against the resurrection of Jesus in autumn 1991, the dispassionate and restrained character of the discussion and the cheerfulness in the bar afterwards suggested, rather, 'that both unbelief and Christianity can manage very well whatever the historical reliability of the resurrection. Whatever makes Christianity stand or fall, it is not the resurrection.'"[5]

Today, Christian theology is in a life and death struggle to set itself free from the long shadow of death cast by the secular canons of historical reason that have prevailed in post-Enlightenment Protestant theology, from that of G. E. Lessing, Immanuel Kant, and Friedrich Schleiermacher to that of Ernst Troeltsch, Rudolph Bultmann, and the Jesus Seminar. In a deeper sense, the death we are talking about is the "death of God" because the God of Christian faith is the one who raised Jesus from the dead. It is very appropriate that we consider the reality of the resurrection in the context of the trinitarian structure of the whole Christian creed. When the hermeneutical framework of the creed, with its trinitarian and christological dogmas, was set aside as irrelevant to historical inquiry and interpretation, things began to come unglued. History was studied as though God did not exist. The historicity of Jesus' resurrection was debated as a naked fact of the past, as though it could bear any significance one way or another apart from the God whose act it was.

Albert Schweitzer's classic, *The Quest of the Historical Jesus*, eloquently shows how the zeal to be emancipated from church dogma was the engine that drove historical scientific inquiry. "This (christological) dogma," he wrote, "had first to be shattered before scholars could once more go out in quest of the historical Jesus, before they could even grasp the thought of his existence. That the historic Jesus is something different from the Jesus Christ of the doctrine of the Two Natures seems to us now self-evident."[6] Along with the shattering of the dogma came the shattering of the Scriptures as the history of our salvation and the shattering of the coherence of the articles of faith, each of which becomes opaque when isolated as a *ding an sich*.

The Resurrection and the Identity of God

For Christians, the question of the identity of God was given a definitive answer in the event of Jesus' resurrection. Faith in God is not separable from the belief that God raised the crucified Jesus from the dead. We cannot expect other religions to stake their claim to the knowledge of God on the resurrection of Jesus, but we do expect that every theology that merits the name Christian will do so. How is it then that process theology, the one school of thought that boasts of the distinction of being "made in America" (all the others being somehow imports from Europe), produces tomes about a God who looks so different from the one "who gives life to the dead and calls into existence the things that do not exist" (Rom. 4:17). In dismissing the resurrection, Schubert Ogden, one of the majordomos of process theology, confesses that the resurrection of Jesus "would be just as relevant to my salvation as an existing self or person as that the carpenter next door just drove a nail into a two-by-four, or that American technicians have at last been successful in recovering a nose cone that had first been placed in orbit around the earth."[7] Considering that Ogden had a long career as a seminary teacher of future Methodist pastors, can you imagine the joy the gospel according to his theology would bring the faithful on Easter Sunday? Or consider another of the same persuasion, David Griffin, who writes: "Christian faith (as I understand it) is possible apart from belief in Jesus' resurrection in particular and life beyond bodily death in general, and because of the widespread skepticism regarding these traditional beliefs, they should be presented as optional."[8] This explains why so many of us have had a difficult time seeing the resemblance between the God of American process thought and the God of the classical Christian tradition.

Christians believe in God because he raised Jesus from the dead, and they believe in Jesus for the same reason. When Paul spoke to the Athenian philosophers in front of the Areopagus, he did not adjust his telling of the good news about Jesus and the resurrection to fit their metaphysical beliefs. He told them what sounded like babbling nonsense: God will judge the world by Jesus of Nazareth, and this he guaranteed by raising him from the dead. Some scoffed, some believed, same old story then as now, but with this difference: now the scoffers—many of them—are to be found inside the churches, among them Episcopal ministers, seminary professors, and parish pastors.

Jesus said, "No one comes to the Father except through me" (John 14:6). For us this means that we have no way into the heart of God the Father except through his Son and the Spirit whom he sent. If Jesus had not been raised, he might have been vaguely remembered as an unsuccessful leader of a tiny Palestinian sect. At best he would be recognized as a teacher of religion and ethics, like Socrates or Gautama, but not as the Savior. If Jesus had not been raised, his special claim to divine authority to forgive sins would have been discredited by his crucifixion. A new event was needed to confirm Jesus' claim to stand in for God, to do the things that only God can do. Jesus had spoken and acted as though he were on the inside of God's will for the world. His encroachment on the authority of God, as the Jewish leaders felt so keenly, was blasphemy unless his claim was to be legitimated. The resurrection was an act by which God identified himself with the cause of Jesus, vindicating Jesus' claim to represent the kingdom of heaven in his earthly ministry. At the same time, the resurrection was an act of God by which the cause of Jesus could be continued in history and not terminated by humiliation on a criminal's cross. Thus the resurrection is the pivotal point in the story we love to tell about Jesus and his love. From henceforth both God and Jesus will become interchangeable subjects of the same predicates in Christian discourse, in Christian prayer and praise, worship and proclamation.

The Resurrection as Event and Meaning

Two questions about the resurrection of Jesus can be distinguished: Did it really happen? What does it mean? There are two rival theories about how to answer these two questions and how to relate them. The first and traditional theory is that the resurrection is a real event that happened to Jesus and that its meaning is located in its very occurrence. The second theory, steadily gaining ground since the Enlightenment, is that the resurrection is not something that happened to Jesus, so its meaning has to be located elsewhere.

Suppose we grant that the resurrection of Jesus really happened. What kind of event was it? This debate is going on within the framework of Nicene-Chalcedonian Christology. The easiest way to characterize the debate is by using two familiar words: history and eschatology. One side of the debate will urge that the resurrection is indeed a historical event. The name of Wolfhart Pannenberg is typically associated with this position. The other side speaks of the resurrection as an eschatological event. Karl Barth and Rudolf Bultmann, as different as their positions finally came to be developed, are often attached to this eschatological view. But then the plot thickens. Those who stress the historicity of the resurrection divide into two camps. The one, preeminently represented by Pannenberg, maintains that because the resurrection is a historical event, it can be known by historical reason; the other, following someone like Walter Kunneth, who has written one of the most important books on the resurrecction,[9] holds that the resurrection, though an actual event, can be known and confessed by faith alone.

On the other side, Karl Barth and Rudolf Bultmann gave currency to the idea that the resurrection is not an historical event, but rather an eschatological event. Eschatology and history are set in opposition to each other. In his Romans commentary, Barth declared that "the raising of Jesus from the dead is not an event in history. . . . The resurrection is the non-historical relating of the whole historical life of Jesus to its origin in God."[10] Bultmann also referred to the resurrection as "the eschatological event par excellence."[11] In marked contrast to Pannenberg, both placed the resurrection above and beyond the realm of historical investigation as something that can be grasped only by faith. As time moved on, Barth and Bultmann realized that they were not in agreement on the resurrection. Barth feared that for all of Bultmann's talk about Jesus being raised into the kerygma and faith, the resurrection had lost its objective reference to the concrete objectivity of Jesus himself. In his *Church Dogmatics,* Barth wrote realistically of the ontological reality of Jesus Christ who is "risen—bodily, visibly, audibly, perceptibly in the same concrete sense in which he died."[12] Here the later Barth and Pannenberg come full circle to meet each other's chief concern: the resurrection of Jesus is an event of the objective order. But they would still disagree about whether the historian can use the historical critical method to reach a sound judgment on the truth claims of the resurrection narratives. For Barth, no; for Pannenberg, yes. But the difference is not so great as it appears on the surface. When Barth put the resurrection beyond history and therefore outside the historian's field of competence, he was using the term *history* in the way modern secular historians ordinarily use it. Not so Pannenberg. He calls into question the secular understanding of history that a priori exludes God from the picture.

It is useful here to recall Ernst Troeltsch's extremely influential view of history and historical research. He laid down four principles that govern our modern understanding. First, the principle of correlation: history is a closed continuum of interrelated events in a succession of causes and effects. Second, the principle of analogy: all interpretation of history must be based on our human experience of similar events. Third, the principle of probability: in historical research we can only reach judgments with a greater or lesser degree of probability. Fourth, the principle that the only actors on the stage of history are human beings, not gods or demons.[13] Now if we subject the resurrection of Jesus to the test of such axioms, would it qualify as an historical event? Obviously not, because such a thoroughly secular understanding excludes the very idea of God acting in history. If we exclude God from our understanding of historical reality, we will have to find a way to speak about God and the resurrection in other than historical categories. But what these might be is not clear.

I fully agree with Pannenberg that it would be better for Christian theology to exempt itself from a thoroughgoing secular view of history[14] so that God-statements and history-statements are not placed on different tracks, leading to acute epistemological schizophrenia. Christian theology cannot tolerate a split consciousness in which the work of biblical exegetes is done in the everyday world of secular experience, obeying Troeltsch's axioms, and dogmatic theologians take refuge in a sacred asylum of church doctrine or religious experience. God cannot be happy about being made a stranger in the very world that he created and that continues under his providential guidance. The confession that God raised Jesus from the dead is a public truth, not a private opinion.

Barth and Pannenberg are thus in agreement that nothing is more fatal to the Christian faith than to locate the meaning of the resurrection outside its happening. The resurrection is not worth talking about unless it happened, for as an illusion it cannot be the ground of hope and the source of life. From the beginning, Christianity has presupposed the resurrection of Jesus as the ground of its existence. Without the Easter faith there would have been no Christian church, and the New Testament would not have been written. Even the most skeptical scholars admit that. Willi Marxsen is among the most skeptical of German exegetes, but even he is willing to concede that "Easter is the presupposition for the fact that Jesus later became the object of preaching."[15] The consensus is widespread among scholars, conservative and liberal, that for the early Christians the resurrection was an event in space and time and there were men and women with real eyes and ears who witnessed the appearances of the risen Jesus. But what are we moderns to make of all that? Bultmann's postulate has become the mantra of many exegetes and theologians: "An historical fact which involves a resurrection from the dead is utterly inconceivable."[16]

Now, if the resurrection can no longer be thought of as something that really happened to Jesus, the shift of emphasis can move in either of two directions. It can leap forward to the faith of the disciples and the first community of believers (where Bultmann located the meaning of the resurrection), or it can move in the opposite direction, back to the historical Jesus. That is where the emphasis was placed by some of Bultmann's pupils, who started what is called the new quest of the historical Jesus.

No one can deny that the resurrection is meaningful to Bultmann, but it is only meaningful as an eschatological event. Bultmann does speak of the risen Christ, but only in the word of preaching as kerygma, not as the historical Jesus whom God raised from the dead on the third day. In Bultmann's treatment the old Nestorian separation of the two natures of Christ recurs; the historical Jesus and the kerygmatic Christ have been divided. History and eschatology mix like oil and water. For Bultmann, faith and the kerygma are not interested in what happened to Jesus after he died. That is merely an historical question, and history cannot provide the basis and content of Christian faith. Bultmann's pupils, Ernst Kasemann, Gunther Bornkamm, Gerhard Ebeling, and others, protested his disinterest in the Jesus of history and its lack of connection to the Christ-*kerygma* of the early church. They called Bultmann's position Docetism, even Gnosticism, which it is. But they did no better than Bultmann with the resurrection. For them the continuity between the historical Jesus and the kerygmatic Christ is not the resurrection as a real event but faith, the faith of the believer as a reenactment of the faith of Jesus himself. What becomes of the resurrection? It is an expression of the faith of the disciples and of their commitment to continue the cause of Jesus (*Sache Jesu*) after his death. Since the resurrection is a nonevent, it can only evaporate into words, either the words of Jesus before his death or the words of the disciples after his crucifixion.

What Really Happened on Easter Morning?

Can we know what really happened on the morning of Easter? There were no witnesses to the event itself. We have stories of the empty tomb, and we have witnesses to the risen Christ. Do they tell us what kind of event the resurrection was? So far we have only said that we must speak of the resurrection of Jesus as an act of God. Our knowledge of God and the resurrection of Jesus come from the same source, from the Scriptures and the church. We cannot explain the resurrection by using the reductive categories of historical positivism or humanistic psychology, and we see no point in the attempts of the Jesus Seminar to do so. Such procedures only bring people to the unbelief with which they started.

We can offer no theory to explain the resurrection event. What is basic to the Christian hope is that it happened to Jesus and its salvific meaning for us, not *how* it happened. The urge to explain it, however, is not wrong in itself, so long as our motive is to edify the community. Explanation is a dimension of the understanding that faith seeks, so it is one possible task of theology. A necessary step, however, is negative—to prove the inadequacy of theories that diminish the meaning of the resurrection and call into question its full reality.

In our view the resurrection is more than the resuscitation of the physical body dead in the tomb. If it were just that, Jesus would not be unlike Lazarus, who returned to life three days after his death. But Lazarus had to die again; his return to life did not transcend the conditions of this mortal existence. The resurrected body of Jesus is a new kind of body, said Paul; it is a *sōma pneumatikos*, a spiritual body. Yet there is continuity between the old and the new body; it is precisely the earthly mortal body that is transformed into a new mode of being, an immortal spiritual body. We must think of the postresurrection body of Christ as a new kind of body because, in Paul's theology, the body of Christ incorporates an entire community of members through their baptism into his death and resurrection. We see metaphors flying around and stretched to the limit. This new sort of spiritual body will no longer have to die. This is the beginning of something really new. In raising Jesus from the dead, God transformed Jesus into a new mode of reality, appearance, and expression that includes his church, so that as the reigning Lord who goes ahead of us as our forerunner, he is leading his embodied community into the world with the message of a living hope and, through its apostolic mission, directing history toward its future end and consummation.

We cannot know more than the earliest Christians told us on the basis of their experiences. If we do not trust their testimonies, we will not believe that Jesus really rose from the dead. Christ did not appear to them because they believed but in order that they might believe and confess that Jesus is Lord. It is therefore erroneous to interpret the primitive witness to the resurrection as a product of a hallucinating imagination of faith. The appearances of Jesus were the cause of faith, not its product. Paul was not a believer but an enemy when Christ appeared to him.

A lot of ink, both polemical and apologetic, has been spilled over the empty tomb. Does it prove the resurrection? Did someone steal the body? Was the story made up to bolster the faith of the doubting Thomases? I will not rehearse the arguments pro and con here. I only want to say that the arguments advanced by people like Hans F. von Campenhausen and Wolfhart Pannenberg have been sufficiently persuasive that we can accept the stories of the empty tomb in the spirit in which they were written. The tomb was empty because Jesus was raised from the dead. He was no longer bodily there. Photographers could not have taken a picture of him lying in the tomb. I'll settle for what Karl Barth once said on the matter: "Christians do not believe in the empty tomb but in the living Christ," but that does not mean that "we can believe in the living Christ without believing in the empty tomb."[17]

The early Christians did not come to believe in the risen Jesus by their own reason and strength. The Holy Spirit made the reality of the resurrected Christ present in the life of each individual believer and the whole community of faith. Paul says: "If the Spirit of him who raised Jesus from the dead dwells in you, he who raised Christ from the dead will give life to your mortal bodies also through his Spirit that dwells in you" (Rom. 8:11 NRSV).[22] It is important that the identity and work of the Spirit not be collapsed into the person and presence of the risen Christ. Because our confession of the resurrection of Jesus occurs in the context of the trinitarian structure of the Nicene Creed, we affirm the equal dignity of the Spirit alongside the Father and the Son. The Spirit has his own work to do, to make Christ really present and to apply his benefits through the preaching of the gospel and the administration of the sacraments.

Conclusion

We have said there can be no authentic Christianity without belief in the resurrection of Jesus. There can be no greater heresy in the modern church than the outright denial of this article of faith. I recall that during my first year of seminary teaching a bright candidate for ordination was preparing to take the qualifying examination. He was the gem of the entire senior class, bright, athletic, handsome, and well prepared in background studies for theology. He came to me for counsel, as I had been rather candid in sharing my doubts about a lot of things going on in the church. He had a special problem; he did not believe in the resurrection. I tried to persuade him that perhaps he really did, that a few doubts about a detail here or there would only place him in the best of company. Nope; he just flat out did not believe that Jesus was raised from the dead. For him there simply was no living Jesus who appeared to some of his friends and disciples on Easter morning. I gave up. I told him that he could not honestly become a pastor in the Lutheran church, but gave him the names of some churches where it might not matter so much. Later I discovered that the resurrection was a stumbling block for many pastors, regardless of denomination.

In addressing such things as the resurrection Lessing spoke of an "ugly ditch" between eternal truths and historical facts. The ditch has been getting wider and it is becoming impossible to straddle it by theological stunts and linguistic gyrations. If we believe in the resurrection of Jesus in the New Testament sense and in sync with the creed, we can be assured that God himself has crossed that ditch. No longer are suffering and death on one side and eternal life and blessedness on the other.

But we should not exaggerate the problem of the resurrection in our time. Many of the Areopagites could not believe the good news of the resurrection. Perhaps it was no more credible in ancient times than today. The Hellenistic worldview was not amenable to the Easter gospel; it was foolishness then and it will always remain such except for those who see through the eyes of faith. Why do some believe and others don't? We have no answer. Resurrection faith is a gift of the Holy Spirit of God, and it's not something we can generate with all the intelligence, will, and emotion we have at our command. But perhaps we can and should do something about the state of theological education, which remains for the most part undisciplined. When Van Harvey quit teaching at a seminary because he could no longer profess basic Christian beliefs, and instead opted for a religious studies program, that made a lot of sense and exemplified something to be encouraged across the church at all levels of leadership. A good place to start would be to remove bishops from office who relegate the resurrection story to mythological status.

The most telling effect of the loss of resurrection faith in the mainline churches is the collapse of the world missionary movement. All the resurrection narratives are a summons to mission and bestow authority on the apostolic office. The apostles who saw the Lord and believed all became missionaries. The risen Lord commissioned the church to go and tell the gospel to all the nations. The missionary nature of the church from the beginning until now is grounded in the resurrection of the crucified Jesus. In the encounter with the risen Christ, the apostles were authorized and empowered to continue what Jesus began in his earthly ministry. The content of the church's missionary proclamation can be none other than Jesus Christ crucified and risen. If we don't believe in the reality of the risen Lord, there is no compelling commission and no mission. We are off the hook. Missionaries can stay home, and that is exactly what is going on.

How else can we account for the great uncertainty in the churches regarding whether it is imperative to preach the gospel to people of other faiths? Do not all religions say the same thing, only in different idioms? Are not all religions equally salvific? If Jesus is the risen Lord, that makes him different from all other putative messiahs, prophets, and religious founders. There is no need to be mission-minded if we do not believe that Jesus' resurrection is God's unique way of reclaiming the whole world for himself, and that he is the one and only way of salvation for Christians and people of other religions and no religion alike. The very reason for the church's being includes engagement in the mission of Christ to the nations. The church is the only witness and instrument that God has elected to win back the world. He has promised to be with his church to the close of the age, always accompanying his people in the power of his Spirit. When we talk about the resurrection, we are not talking merely about a historical event, of something passé, but we are talking about the present-tense reality of what God is doing through the mission of the church, opening the way for all humankind to inherit the future of eternal life.

8

Confession and Confessions

John Webster

This paper addresses some fundamental theological questions about the nature and function of creeds and confessions in the life of the church. The basic positive claim here is that creeds and confessional formulas properly emerge out of one of the primary and defining activities of the church, the act of confession. In that act, which is constantly to characterize the life of the church, the church binds itself to the gospel. Confession is the act of astonished, fearful, and grateful acknowledgment that the gospel is the one word by which to live and die; in making its confession, the church lifts up its voice to do what it must do—speak with amazement of the goodness and truth of the gospel and the gospel's God. Creeds and confessional formulas exist to promote that act of confession: to goad the church toward it, to shape it, to tie it to the truth, and so to perpetuate the confessional life and activity of the Christian community. In this way, creeds and confessional formulas are the servants of the gospel in the church.

Alongside this positive claim run two polemical points. One, largely implicit, is that when the church tries to do without the offices of these servants of the gospel, it endangers its relation to the gospel. In the same way that the church's life can be threatened by misrule, arbitrariness, or pollution if it neglects canon, sacraments, or order, so also it will be exposed to peril if it attempts to exist without the act of confession and its formalization in creedal texts. The second polemical claim is that the creed is a good servant but a bad master: it assists, but cannot replace, the act of confession. The church, that is, cannot have the creed but somehow bypass the act of confession, for to do so is to convert the event of confession into an achieved formula, graspable without immediate reference to the coming of the Holy Spirit. Whatever else we may say by way of commending the place of the creed in the life of the church, we must not promote the notion that the creed's significance is merely statutory. Creeds serve the confessing community, but cannot of themselves make up the totality of what it means to be such a community.

Both the positive claim and its polemical corollaries rest on a conviction that we need a theological description of creeds and confessional formulas; that is, an account that talks about creeds by talking about God. The creeds must not be naturalized; they must not be depicted merely immanently, as functions of the Christian religious community or tradition considered naturally. Modern critical historical theology has offered a natural history of the creeds, presenting their development as a history of the church's absorption of cultural and philosophical convention and as social tradition. In the case of giants like Baur or Harnack, such natural histories of the creeds had a fundamentally critical intent, demoting the creeds by offering an immanent explanation of their genesis, so that—like canon and order—they no longer encounter the church from outside with a transcendent claim, but are simply an item in its domestic life. More recent attempts to depict the creeds as instruments of community self-description, identity-avowal, social differentiation, or formation and virtue, while they are more alert to the religious functions of creeds, still run the risk of immanence. I suggest, by contrast, that what is required is not a more elaborate natural history, sociology, or cultural geography of the creeds, but a dogmatic depiction. What is required, in other words, is an account of creeds that sees them as features in the landscape of the church, *theologically* considered as that reality of human history transfigured by the Spirit, visible to faith, and therefore to be described spiritually. What is said about the nature and functions of creeds and confessions must be rooted in talk about the Triune God in the economy of salvation, tracing these human texts back to their source in the church's participation in the drama of God's saving self-communication in Christ through the Spirit's power. This is not, of course, to cancel out the natural history of the creeds, any more than to talk of a canon of Holy Scripture is to cancel out the natural history of canonization. It is simply to say that the history of the creeds is part of the history of the church—part, that is, of that sphere of human life invaded and annexed by God and characterized by astonished and chastened hearing of the Word and by grateful and afflicted witness.

Before pressing the claim of the creed as the basis of a renewed ecumenical convergence around some sort of generous orthodoxy, therefore, it is crucial that we put in place a theological account of the act of confession and its creedal instruments. If we fail to do so, what we say will be in the wrong register, and we will fall victim to the shrill juridical and factional hostilities that so often afflict calls for renewed confessionalism. Confession is an act of the church, a spiritual act; it is a matter, therefore, for theological description and judgment.

The Act of Confession

To try to grasp what lies at the heart of the act of confession, we may ponder Paul's statement in 2 Corinthians 9:13 (NASB) concerning the "obedience to your confession of the gospel of Christ." What Paul has to say there forms part of the great flow of his celebration of the abundance of God. To God's abundance, God's open-handedness, there correspond two fundamental acts of the church: material generosity and confession of the gospel. Both acts are echoes of what Paul calls "the surpassing grace of God in you"(v. 14 NASB); both, that is, are brought into being by the limitless lavishness of God that Paul celebrates in the climactic words of the chapter: "Thanks be to God for his indescribable gift!" (v. 15 NASB). It is in this context—the celebration of God's overwhelming generosity—that I suggest we root our understanding of the church's act of confession. Before it is proposition or oath of allegiance, the confession of the church is a cry of acknowledgment of the unstoppable miracle of God's mercy. Confession, we might say by way of definition, is that event in which the speech of the church is arrested, grasped, and transfigured by the self-giving presence of God. To confess is to cry out in acknowledgment of the sheer gratuity of what the gospel declares, that in and as the man Jesus, in the power of the Holy Spirit, God's glory is the glory of his self-giving, his radiant generosity. Very simply, to confess is to indicate "the glory of Christ" (2 Cor. 8:23).

This can be expanded in three directions. First, *the act of confession originates in revelation.* This human act takes its rise in the divine act that is generative of the life of the church in its entirety: God's communicative self-presence, the gracious and saving self-communication of God the Lord.

Revelation is enacted and declared salvation, the open and visible hand of God's mercy. And what revelation generates is the church, the assembly of those called to new life in forgiveness, freedom from sin, and fellowship with God. Confession flows from this electing and life-giving self-manifestation. Confession is not primarily an act of definition; it is, rather, a "thankful, praising, self-committing acceptance of God's self-revelation in Christ."[1] Moreover, this impulse behind the act of confession is, as Paul puts it in 2 Corinthians 9, "surpassing" and "indescribable." It lies wholly beyond our intellectual or spiritual or moral reach. It is not one of the things that we can appropriate and assign a place in our world; in this matter we are not competent. And because God's self-communication is thus permanently disorienting—because it is a movement of God, a gift that cannot be converted into a possession—confession is more a matter of astonishment than an attempt at closure.

Second, therefore, *the act of confession is a responsive, not a spontaneous, act.* Paul calls it an act of obedience, employing a term that connects confession both to submission and to attentive listening. Obedient confession of the gospel of Christ is not first and foremost a proposal on the part of the church; it is an act *of* the church that follows upon an act done *to* the church. As Barth puts it, in making its confession in the creed, "the church bows before that God Whom we did not seek and find—Who rather has sought and found us."[2] Once again, therefore, a thorough description of the church's act of confession must be rooted in a trinitarian account of God's self-manifestation. As Father, Son, and Spirit, God wills, effects, and completes saving fellowship with himself: God alone is its origin, its accomplishment, and its realization. In a real sense, therefore, God alone is the origin, accomplishment, and realization of the act of confession. "Confessions cannot be made; they can only be received as a gift."[3]

Third, accordingly, *the act of confession is an episode in the conflict between God and sin that is at the center of the drama of salvation.* Confession is a countermovement to human wickedness, a countermovement brought about and sustained by the overflow of God's abundance. Sin is, in part, the refusal to confess—the sullen and hard-hearted refusal to acknowledge God's self-gift, failure to respond to God's lavishness by voicing God's praise. Confession refuses these refusals. It is a repentant act, a turning, and therefore a decisive "no" to silence about God or to that murmuring against God that is the response of the wicked to God's generosity. Confession, therefore, is an aspect of the church's holiness. To be holy is to be elect, caught up in God's drastic negation of disorder and unrighteousness, and confession is the first work of the elect as they are separated by God for acknowledgment and praise of God.

In short, "the Community confesses, and it 'exists' in its confessing."[4] The point of stressing this is to highlight how confession is *act* or *event* before it is *document*. Textual formulas are instruments of confession, but they do not in any way render the act of confession superfluous. This point is of considerable importance, not least because we are sometimes tempted to think that confessional formulas represent fixity, that they are a means of settling doctrinal disputes. In one sense, of course, confessional formulas do just that: they articulate dogmatic decisions and so move the life of the church to a new stage that the church cannot repudiate or neglect without redrawing its identity. But the dogmatic decisions the church articulated in confessional formulas cannot simply be thought of as capital in the bank. Confession is a permanently occurring event; the church never reaches a point where the act of obedient confession can be put behind it as something that has been made and can be replaced by a text that will become the icon of the church as confessing community. Properly understood, a confessional formula does not put an end to the act of confession but ensures its persistence. A creed does not ensure the church's safety from interruption—quite the opposite: it exposes the church to the need for an unceasing renewal of confession of the gospel, of hearing, obedience, and acknowledgment of that which the formula indicates.

The Nature of Confessions

With this in mind, we turn to look more closely at the nature of the creeds and confessional formulas that emerge from the act of confession—at confession as text. In propositional form, my suggestion is this: a creed or confessional formula is a public and binding indication of the gospel that is set before us in the scriptural witness, through which the church affirms its allegiance to God, repudiates the falsehood by which the church is threatened, and assembles around the judgment and consolation of the gospel.

First, a creed or confessional formula is a *public and binding indication of the gospel*. I will say a little more about the binding character of creeds a little later; for the present, I want to draw attention to their necessarily public character. "A confession," says Barth, "cannot be spoken *mezzo forte*."[5] That is, a confession or creed is a proclamation, a publication or making known of that which is confessed. To confess is not to reflect, even to reflect theologically; it is to herald the gospel. A confessional formula, therefore, shares the vividness and directness of the act of confession by which it is generated. To confess is to testify—and to testify with a bit of noise.

It's crucial, however, that we realize that this necessarily public character of a creed does not derive from the busy, authoritarian, or loud personalities of the confessors. When that sort of brashness happens—as it often does when calls for a renewed confessionalism are issued—the creed becomes hopelessly distorted because it is the articulation no longer of an act of confession, but merely of pressure group dynamics, of the desire not just to confess the gospel but to win. Unless that temptation is resisted, our confession—however vigorous—will not be obedient confession of the gospel; simply instead it will be the brandishing of a weapon in the church's face. The counter to the temptation is to build into the dynamics of the confession a deep sense of the transcendence of that which we confess. A creed is not a program, a platform, a manifesto to mobilize our forces. It is an amazed cry of witness: "Behold, the Lamb of God who takes away the sin of the world!" (John 1:29 NASB). Confession is attestation, not self-assertion.

Because confession is public attestation, it is inseparable from conflict and affliction. To recite the creed is to enter into revolt against the world and against the church insofar as it has not yet left the world behind. Public confession challenges by setting the whole of the life of the church and the world beneath the judgment of the gospel. It therefore involves a denial of untruth and a glad and courageous affirmation of truth. A confession that fails to do this—that is not dangerous, that does not venture to contradict—is not a confession worth making, but simply a domestic inventory of Christian attitudes. Real confession is closely linked to martyrdom: both are testimony and attestations of the truth that evokes conflict and suppression. The suppression takes various forms: violence, counterargument, indifference, liturgical routinization. But a church that confesses will demonstrate in its practical attitude a dogged resistance to such pressures. It will simply not conform, because it *cannot* conform. The church that confesses knows that it has been overwhelmed by the gospel and that part of being overwhelmed is publishing the name of Jesus. Once the church allows itself to be arrested in that confession, it has put itself beyond martyrdom and therefore turned away from the lavishness of God. But if—with fear and trembling, with human uncertainty, with anxiety yet with courage—the church refuses to be arrested in making its confession, then it says in public the one word that slays the devil.

Second, a creed or confessional formula is *an indication of the gospel that is set before us in the scriptural witness.* A written confession is a testimony pointing to that which is other than itself. What the confession attests is not, first and foremost, the teaching of the church, nor the commitments and self-understandings of those who make use of the confession to profess their faith.

A confession is most properly an indication of the gospel. The gospel is normatively set forth in Holy Scripture, for Holy Scripture is that collection of writings generated by and annexed to the self-communication of God. Because it is in this way a means of grace, an instrument through which God acts to lay bare the gospel, Holy Scripture is prior to and superior to all acts of confession, and all acts of confession are subordinate to Holy Scripture. A confession always thinks "from below";[6] only by virtue of this subordination does it have any claim on the life of the church. Creeds and confessions have no freestanding existence; they are not a replacement for, supplementation of, or improvement upon Holy Scripture; they are not even a nonnegotiable, normative "reading" of Scripture. Creeds and confessions are wholly a function of the Word of God, which is given in Scripture as, through the power of the Spirit, the risen Jesus testifies to himself. The rule, therefore, is this: "Scripture remains Scripture: unique, incommensurable, outside the series."[7] Hence the authority of the creed is inseparable from its "expository dependance on Holy Writ."[8] Its claim is the claim of an anatomy of divinity, a brief outline of the biblical gospel. Its task is to enable the church's reading of Holy Scripture. We may think of the creed as an aspect of the church's exegetical fellowship, of learning alongside the saints and doctors and martyrs how to give ear to the gospel. But such fellowship is fellowship in a task that is also ours now. The creed is not a substitute for the church's reading of Scripture, a sort of achieved exegetical steady state. It is, rather, the exemplary instance of the church's submission of all aspects of its life to the prophetic and apostolic witness. It may guide and chasten and correct our reading, but it cannot absolve us of responsibility now. The creed does not mean the end of the church's chief occupation, which is hearing the gospel through attention to Holy Scripture. Hearing the Word is not an inheritance but an event: creeds and confessions structure and guide that hearing, but they do not make it dispensable. Nor, in one sense, do they make hearing easier. Truly attending to the creed does not mean finding safe water, but entering into the disruption that is the inevitable accompaniment of encountering the gospel of God.

Third, a creed or confessional formula is *one of the means through which the church affirms its allegiance to God.* Confession, like praise, proclamation, holiness, and service, is a human echo of the electing mercy of God. To confess is to take sides, to pledge involvement with a particular cause, by binding oneself to a particular reading of reality. To confess in the words of a creedal formula is to acknowledge that there are times in the life of the church when indifference, irony, hesitation, or scruple are false spiritual stances and that the church's relation to the truth requires the adoption of a position and the publication of that position in an act of loyalty. Not every moment in the life of the church demands such acts, but some do. Some occasions—not necessarily those that affect our own immediate interests—require an affirmation of allegiance that ties those who make it to certain options, excludes others, and governs the thought and speech of the church's members.

To confess in this way is a countercultural move, and we should not underestimate the extent to which in acting in this way and affirming its allegiance the church goes against the grain of some of the most deeply rooted moral and spiritual conventions of modernity. Those modern conventions are exquisitely set out by Kant in *Religion within the Boundaries of Mere Reason.*[9] Kant fears that public assent to a confessional statement always undermines real integrity and loyalty because profession is mere external conformity, simulated connection, and not the disposition of a free conscience. Kant is quite right, of course, to protest against the deceit that accompanies the enforcement of a confession. But the mistake here is an assumption that Kant shares with modern liberal Christianity—the assumption that confession is always bad faith. And, again like modern liberal Christianity, Kant's remedy for bad faith is conscience, but conscience transformed so that it is a function of will and judgment, not of given truth. If Kant and his modern Christian heirs can make little sense of a confessional formula as an act of allegiance, it is because of a deep commitment to a picture of the human self as free only when undetermined and as fruitful only when engaged in critical inquiry.

An act of allegiance expressed through a confessional formula is not an act of self-determination but of acknowledgment. It is an act whose origins lie not in the will but in the self-presenting, lovingly coercive reality of the gospel. It is an act that involves *trust*—trust in our mothers and fathers in the faith then, and in our sisters and brothers in the faith now. And it is an act of obedient acquiescence rather than of critical appraisal—an act, we might even say, of judgment broken by the truth rather than of enthroned reason. Confessing the creed means leaving behind omnicompetence, conscience, and rationality.

All of that is by way of stressing that the creed is an act of allegiance. Once again, it is very important not to overinvest in the human dynamics of profession. The center of gravity must not become the personal authenticity of the act of allegiance made in assenting to a formula. This is partly to make sure that we do not create a nastily suspicious culture in the church, because if we do so we will oppose the gospel. But it is also because the *fides quae*—those things which are believed—have priority over the *fides qua*—the act of belief by that they are believed. We would be very unwise indeed to defend orthodoxy by attacking the sincerity of those in the church who appear to deny or compromise their profession. What's wrong with false professors is not just that they have broken their oath but that they have denied the truth.

Fourth, through a publically affirmed creed or confessional formula *the church repudiates the falsehood by which it is threatened.* In a creed the church says yes to truth, and in saying yes it thereby also says no to falsehood. It says no only because it first says yes, and it says no with fear and trembling only because it must do so. Nevertheless, in affirming the church, it also denies, turning from its own complicity in falsehood and striding repentantly and hopefully toward the truth.

This means, first, that, as Bonhoeffer put it, "the concept of heresy belongs necessarily and irrevocably with the concept of a credal confession."[10] What is so grievous about the loss of an operative notion of heresy is that it is symptomatic of the loss of an operative notion of truth. Once voluntarism and nominalism grasp hold of the church—once, that is, the Christian faith is no longer considered an onslaught on idolatry but a fertile opportunity for its exercise—then the notion of heresy atrophies and eventually falls away. Very simply, this must not happen, and one of the ways of ensuring that it does not happen is by serious attention to the confessional life of the church.

A confession is a move against falsehood, whether in the form of error or of indifference. A confession worthy of the name will—implicitly or explicitly—include an anathema, an assertion that a teaching or practice is outside the church. We should therefore not be too ready to concede to critics of the confessional attitude that the notion of heresy and the practice of anathematizing are intrinsically flawed, inseparable from the dynamics of scapegoating, exclusion, and diminishment of that which is other than the norm. Certainly it is irrefutable that "orthodoxy" is a political practice as well as a theological concept; certainly an orthodox doctrine is often a successful doctrine; certainly the orthodox have always shown an unwholesome appetite for depicting their opponents in the worst possible light. But to use the notion of heresy in such ways is to abuse it—to deploy it as a means of creating an unpolluted church with a water-tight skin. Truth is not a culture or a political practice or a structure for discipline, however much those things may serve the truth. Truth is a miracle; truth is the creation of the Holy Spirit. The notion of heresy and the practice of anathematizing are ways of following or being caught up in the miracle of truth. They are spiritual practices, aspects of the transformation of human knowledge and government by the coming of the Word of God.

So far, then, I have suggested that a creed is a public and binding indication of the gospel as set out in Holy Scripture through which the church affirms its allegiance to God and repudiates falsehood. In doing these things, a creed is, finally, *a means through which the church assembles around the judgment and consolation of the gospel.* We may ask what happens when the Christian community professes its faith by reciting the creed. If it is to be of any spiritual worth, such an act must be more than a cheerful or even solemn repetition of a safe formula. A creed places the church under judgment. In the paragraph from *Religion within the Boundaries of Mere Reason* to which I have already referred, Kant says, "Let the author of a creed or the teacher of a church, indeed, let every human being, so far as he inwardly stands by the conviction that certain propositions are divinely revealed, ask himself: Do you really dare to avow the truth of these propositions in the sight of him who scrutinizes the heart, and at the risk of relinquishing all that is valuable and holy to you?" And he adds, "I would have to have a very unfavourable conception of human nature . . . not to suppose that even the boldest teacher of the faith must quake at the question."[11] Kant is right—if the creed does not make us quake, if it is not recited with fear and trembling and penitence, then it is not recited with an eye to the one who scrutinizes the heart.

In fear and trembling we place ourselves beneath the truth that we confess. In so doing we come to know that truth as endless consolation. The consolation the gospel brings is its announcement that the world really is a place where God in Christ reigns with the unleashed power of the Holy Spirit; where faith, hope, and love are truthful because they are in accordance with the way the world is. The church's task is to live out the new order that has been made at the resurrection of Jesus from the dead, and so to turn its back on the old order of sin and death. That kind of energetic counterpractice requires that the church be committed to a fierce realism; it needs a deep conviction that the church can refuse the conventions of sin because they are a sham. And not the least of the functions of creedal formulas is to lodge that kind of realism in the church's heart. The world is the place in which it is a truthful and joyful thing to confess that God is the Father Almighty, maker of heaven and earth; that there is one Lord, Jesus Christ, who is one in being with the Father; that for us and for our salvation he came down from heaven; that the Holy Spirit is Lord and life-giver. To confess these things is to confess the gospel's consolation and so to sponsor cheerful and confident practice on the basis of the gospel's announcement that God has once and for all put an end to the pretense of wickedness.

Confessions' Binding Character

Let me now return to the question of the *binding* character of creeds and confessional formulas. What authority do these texts have in the church? In what way do they stand as a norm of teaching and practice?

They have the authority of a norm that is itself normed; they have real yet conditional, limited, and subordinate authority to bind the church; they are a penultimate but not an ultimate word. Creeds and confessional formulas have authority, but only in a twofold subordination. They are subordinate, first and foremost, to the fact that the God of the gospel is free transcendent presence and not merely the immanent soul of the church. God is present as Jesus Christ is present, the one risen from the dead, the one who has been lifted from our sight at the ascension. God is present as the Holy Spirit is present, the one who comes to us but is not a principle of immanence. The creed cannot replace God's presence—it can only reach after it and identify where that presence gives itself to us. Second, creeds and confessional formulas are subordinate, as we have seen, to Holy Scripture, for it is Scripture, not creed, that is appointed by God as the instrument of his self-communication. Whatever else we may say of the creed, therefore, we have to say that it is a *normed* norm. This emphatically does not give us any excuse to fall into soft relativism. To say that the creed is conditional or penultimate is worlds apart from the idea that the creed is merely one not-very-good attempt at pinning down a God whom we cannot really know. The creed is *confident* of its object; it *knows* this God. To talk of the provisionality of the creed is not an expression of skepticism; it is not the antithesis of earnestness; it is not an attempt to undermine genuine confession. It is simply a sober consequence of the fact that sinners—even redeemed sinners—cannot comprehend God's revelation. It simply acknowledges the constantly self-reforming character of the church's thought and speech. Reformation is needed not so we can keep step with the world—why on earth would we want to do that?—but so we can to make sure that we are properly out of step with the world and therefore trying to keep pace with God. Once again, this isn't a matter of promoting instability of having everything open to revision all the time; such an attitude risks denying the reality of the gift of the Spirit to the church. All we are saying is that the creed is not God's Word, but ours; it is made, not begotten.

On this basis we can approach the question of the juridical structures that surround the creed: in what way is it *legally* binding on its subscribers? Church law is an aspect of the church's visibility, that is, of its life as a human historical society. Law is one of the instruments through which the Holy Spirit ensures the orderly shape and regularity of the church's existence in space and time. It is scarcely possible to conceive of any kind of enduring ecclesial reality without legal instruments for the maintenance of its common life, and confessional formulas are clearly part of the statutory life of the community. Creeds need a legal framework of subscription and assent. Creeds without subscription are hardly likely to serve the church's life in the gospel, and they run the risk of becoming what Anglicans call "historic formularies," charming curios that can be safely tucked away at the back of the book.

Creeds need a legal framework. But there is an important qualification here: the juridical and statutory have only instrumental significance. We are sometimes impatient with the transcendence of the object of our confession and are tempted to manage it through law. But church law is not domestication; it safeguards, but it does not codify the free self-presence of the church's Lord and his testimony to himself in Scripture. In short, the authority of the creed, its power to bind, is not primarily positive and juridical, but spiritual.

This means that a confession binds insofar as it is in agreement with Holy Scripture: it binds by saying "Scripture says." As with all instruments of the church's order, the authority of the creed is inseparable from its submission to the Word of God; it has the authority of the herald, not the magistrate.

On the other hand, this means that we should not use the confessions of the church to press the church to take on the wrong sort of visibility—a purely natural visibility in which the church is identified too closely with its visible forms. When this happens and a creedal formula becomes the article by which the church stands or falls, then the transcendent, eschatological reference of the visible church is compromised and confessions come to embody, not testify to, the gospel. When the church becomes visible through its confessions, it does not leave behind Spirit, faith, or the hiddenness and freedom of God; it does not convert the drama of redemption into a set of propositions to be policed. Confessional visibility is spiritual visibility. On the other hand, there is the wrong sort of *in*visibility. We can, for example, so emphasize the incomprehensibility of the object of confession that formulas are simply ruled out from the beginning. Or we can—as many moderns do—treat confessional formulas as merely the external dress of inner conviction and experience, and prefer our church naked. Both rob the church of its proper visibility; both make oversight of the church's public life acutely difficult; both risk undermining the church's relation to the truth of the gospel.

In sum, creeds bind because, and only because, the gospel binds. Hence we have to say (1) that the gospel does bind and that confessions are a place where we encounter the obligatory force of the truth; and (2) that the statutory claim of the creed binds only as it presents the gospel's claim. Figuring out a practice to express these principles is no easy matter. The common options—either libertinism or authoritarianism—are not open to a church with any sense for the gospel. What is required more than anything else is the discernment and prudence that are the gifts of the Spirit and so matters not of policy but of prayer.

Let me sum up these reflections by noting how the creedal life of the church expresses each of the four marks of the church: its unity, holiness, catholicity, and apostolicity. The creed points to the unity of the church, not in mere fellow feeling but in the given realities of one Lord, one Spirit, one God and Father of all. It points to the holiness of the church because it is a confession of election—of the drastic separation between the church and sin that the mercy of God opens up and that the mind of the church must honor. It points to the catholicity of the church because to profess the creed is not to set up a party banner but to read the gospel in the fellowship of the saints. It points to the apostolicity of the church because it is only in confession of the truth that the church can live out the faith and mission of the apostles.

We should be under no illusion that renewed emphasis on the creed will, in and of itself, renew the life of the church: it won't. The church is created and renewed through Word and Spirit. Everything else—love of the brethren, holiness, proclamation, confession—is dependent upon them. Yet I do not believe that we can envisage substantial renewal of the life of the church without renewal of its confessional life. There are many conditions for such renewal. One is real governance of the church's practice and decision making not by half-baked cultural analysis, but by reference to the creedal rendering of the biblical gospel. Another is recovery of the kind of theology that sees itself as an apostolic task and does not believe itself entitled or competent to reinvent or subvert the Christian tradition. A third, rarely noticed, condition is the need for a recovery of symbolics (the study of creeds and confessions) as part of the theological curriculum—so much more edifying than most of what fills the seminary day. But alongside these are required habits of mind and heart: love of the gospel, docility in the face of our forebears, readiness for responsibility and venture, a freedom from concern for reputation, a proper self-distrust. None of these things can be cultivated; they are the Spirit's gifts, and the Spirit alone must do his work. What we may do—and must do—is cry to God, who alone works great marvels.

9

Confessing Christ Coming

Douglas Farrow

"Let us proclaim the mystery of faith: Christ has died, Christ is risen, Christ will come again." This threefold refrain grounds the church's *anaphora* or *eucharistia* in the briefest possible account of Jesus. Theologically it roots the very being of God's people, who offer themselves to God in and through the one acceptable offering that Jesus Christ is, in *his* past, in *his* present, in *his* future. Christ has died—and I with him. Christ has risen—and I with him. Christ will come again—and I, whether then dead or alive, will appear with him and like him in his glory.[1]

The church confesses not only Christ crucified but also Christ risen. It confesses not only the past of Jesus Christ but also his present. Most of us are familiar enough with the desperate attempt of the spirit of Gnosticism to salvage something from its defeat in patristic theology by belatedly embracing the cross while denying the resurrection, by embracing the past of Jesus Christ only to substitute it for his present. It was Hegel who made the best job of this,[2] but it was Albert Schweitzer who wrote the unforgettable epitaph:

> In the knowledge that He is the coming Son of Man He lays hold of the wheel of the world to set it moving on that last revolution which is to bring our ordinary history to a close. It refuses to turn, and He throws himself upon

it. Then it does turn; and crushes Him. Instead of bringing in the eschatological conditions, He has destroyed them. The wheel rolls onward, and the
mangled body of the one immeasurably great Man, who was strong enough
to think of Himself as the spiritual ruler of mankind, and to bend history to
His purpose, is hanging upon it still. That is His victory and His reign.[3]

The church's confession of the bodily resurrection of Jesus Christ is the anti-
dote to Gnosticism in its modern guise, but this confession requires of the
church some elaboration of the present that it claims for Jesus and for itself.
What is more, it requires some elaboration of the future that it claims for
Jesus and for itself, for the church confesses not only Christ risen but also
Christ returning. They tell, says Paul to the Thessalonians, "how you turned
to God from idols, to serve a living and true God, and to wait for his Son
from heaven, whom he raised from the dead—Jesus, who rescues us from
the wrath that is coming" (1 Thess. 1:9–10 NRSV).

Turning, serving, waiting: this is the experience and vocation of the Christian insofar as he or she, with the church militant, acknowledges the past,
present, and future of Jesus as his or her own. It is our task now, in the service of that vocation, to consider more closely, directed by the sixth and sev-
enth articles of the creed,[4] certain aspects of the present and future of Jesus.
The clauses before us in these articles are four:

> He ascended into heaven,
> and sits at the right hand of the Father.
> He shall come again in glory
> to judge the quick and the dead;
> and his kingdom shall have no end.[5]

The documentary history of these clauses can be disposed of easily
enough. All derive directly from the Scriptures and are abundantly attested
there. We have "a great high priest who has gone through the heavens," who
indeed has sat down at the right hand of the Majesty in heaven, says the
author of Hebrews and he "will appear a second time, not to bear sin, but
to bring salvation to those who are waiting for him" (Heb. 4:14; 1:3; 9:28
NIV).[7] Illustrations such as these may be offered from virtually every corner
of the New Testament. The whole construction is entirely primitive to the
Christian faith, as Schweitzer rightly argued. For that reason, it can be no
surprise (to the orthodox) that at least the first and the third of these clauses
are always found in creeds of a narrative character, such as that of Nicea. At
Constantinople the second clause, which can be found earlier in Tertullian

and in Lucian of Antioch, for example, was added in clarification of the first. Likewise, the fourth clause was added in clarification of the third (which itself received minor modification with the addition of the words "again in glory"). Negative in form, however, the fourth clause first appeared only between the councils as a reaction in various local creeds to the teaching of Marcellus of Ancyra; it then made its way into the ecumenical creed in 381 as a safeguard against the Sabellian implications of that teaching.[7]

To dispose our own minds for sustained reflection on "the mystery of faith" as it unfolds in these two articles and four clauses is a more daunting task, and on that has been made all the more difficult by a long history of assault on each of these particulars about the present and future of Christ. Theologians busied by their defense of faith in Christ's resurrection have often become timid, or at least lacked energy and enthusiasm, in defending and expounding faith in his ascension, session, *parousia*, and kingdom. They have been worn down by charges of holding to an outmoded, prescientific cosmology,[8] or to outmoded, exclusivist, and triumphalist views of the Christian religion. It has become all too tempting for them to move more or less directly from faith in the resurrection to faith in the Spirit and in the church, to talk of a Christ who rises into the church or into history or even into the cosmos—that is, to move from Easter to Pentecost without stooping with earlier pilgrims to pass in faith through the low portal of that humble Chapel of the Ascension built by the crusaders on the Mount of Olives.[9] In refusing to do homage to Christ there, of course, one does not eradicate but rather embraces an outmoded, dualistic worldview; one does not eliminate triumphalism, but only gives to it a new and more oppressive form. As a matter of fact, one succumbs—or is in danger of succumbing—to that desperate spirit of which we have spoken. But we are getting ahead of ourselves.

Let us take in turn the article dealing with Christ's present and that dealing with his future, opening them up to further reflection while peeling away a few of the many possible misunderstandings. We begin, then, with a brief discussion of the ascension.

The ascension, we are frequently told—taken as a distinct event in the story of Jesus and therefore as worthy of theological reflection in its own right—is a Lukan invention. The main biblical testimony invites us rather to see the ascension merely an aspect of resurrection, pointing to the divine power and glory that accrue to Christ in that event.[10] It will be asked by some whether the first of the four clauses now before us is not, in fact, the very point in the creed at which we are confronted not with a theological revolution such as that connected to *creatio ex nihilo* or to the *homoousion* or to the doctrine of the resurrection, but rather with a failure of the revolutionary spirit of Christian theology; that is, with a lapse back into a speculative, fanciful cosmology and so into mythological godtalk. We may want to take a lesson on how to avoid this from England's *Church Times,* which once offered the following guidance to Sunday School teachers:[11]

You will need a glass of water and a soluble tablet.

Aim: To begin teaching the meaning of the Ascension.

 . . . Jesus had said he would be ascending to the Father. (Who knows what ascending means? Keep dropping hints if necessary.) Long ago, people believed that God lived up above the sky. Some people still believe that. Some people believe that heaven is a place with pearly gates and golden pavements, but nobody from earth has ever come from there except Jesus, so all we really know about it is what he has told us. The rest is imagination. We do know it is a better life than here because God is there. If we are going there ourselves one day, it will mean being promoted from here—promoted to a higher kind of living. When someone is promoted we sometimes say they are going *up.* That does not mean they are going upstairs. Cub scouts go up into Scouts; Brownie guides go up into Guides; but they don't fly away up into the sky. When we die we hope we shall eventually go up into heaven—not up into the air, but into a better kind of life closer to God.

The time had now come for Jesus to return to heaven. In a way his going would help his disciples. . . .

1. First, it would make clear to them that they would not see him again in the flesh. They could stop waiting around hopefully.

2. Secondly, once Jesus stopped being present in one place at a time, he could start being present everywhere at once. Does that seem strange? Look at this.

Use the glass of water and the tablet. This tablet represents Jesus. All the time he was in the flesh his disciples could see him and touch him, provided they were in the same place as he was. When he went up into heaven they would not see him any more, but he could start being present everywhere at once.

Drop the tablet into the water. You cannot see the tablet now, but it is still present in the water. Jesus was going to heaven; but he would still be in the world. Better still, people could receive him into themselves. Take a sip.

Now this amusing account is commendable for its efforts to nip mythological thinking at the bud without abandoning altogether the historical significance of the ascension as a foundation for the church and its sacramental life. Unfortunately it nips above the bud rather than beneath it, encouraging what it is meant to discourage. Insofar as the doctrine of the ascension was contentious in the early church—let us say, in the second to the sixth century—it was contentious precisely because of a spiritualizing tendency of this sort, first among the Gnostics, then among the followers of Origen. And whence did that tendency arise, if not because a bodily ascension such as Luke describes was *already* incompatible with the cosmology and soteriology of the ancient pagan world? If not because the cosmos was so conceived and union with God so construed as to exclude the presence of gross material forms of existence in the heaven of heavens? But it was obvious enough to the fathers, after some debate, that a deviation on this point for the sake of cosmological orthodoxy would entail a deviation in Christian eschatology as a whole. It was evident to them that the doctrines of the heavenly session, the *parousia,* and the kingdom without end could not be maintained in anything like their original form if a decision were taken in favor of a dissolving Christ—that is, in favor of what Origen had called "ascension of the mind rather than of the body."[12]

We do not have to await the anathemas that would be pronounced against Origenism at the fifth council for a clear statement of this judgment. Consider, for example, the following from Gregory Nazianzen, who notices what the *Church Times* author apparently does not: that the logic of the ascension must correspond to the logic of the *parousia:*

> If any assert that he has now put off his holy flesh, and that his godhead is stripped of the body, and deny that he is now with his body and will come again with it, let him not see the glory of his coming. For where is his body now, if not with him who assumed it? For it is not laid by in the sun, according to the babble of the Manichaeans, that it should be honoured by a dishonour; nor was it poured forth and dissolved, as is the nature of a voice or the flow of an odour, or the course of a lightning flash that never stands. Where in that case were his being handled after the resurrection, or his being seen hereafter by them that pierced him, for godhead is in its nature invisible. Nay; he will come with his body—so I have learnt—such as he was seen by his disciples in the mount, or as he shewed himself for a moment, when his godhead overpowered the carnality.[13]

This is the logic of the angels in Acts 1:11. It is also the logic of the creed, which for good reason (cosmological disputes notwithstanding) treats of Jesus' present in a Lukan fashion, employing two distinct articles and three distinct clauses: resurrection, bodily ascension, and heavenly session.[14]

What exactly is at stake here? Arguments, obviously, about the nature of the *parousia*, to which we will return in due course; about the importance of the body in Christian anthropology; and, yes, about natural and supernatural cosmic order. But also at stake is a right understanding of the relation between Christ and his church, and of the relation of both to the powers and possibilities of this present age. At stake, in other words, is the nature of Christ's heavenly session, together with the sacramental and political theology that are determined by it. It is to these that we must now attend, broadening our discussion of "he ascended into heaven" to include "and sits at the right hand of the Father."

† † †

The church's faith in its resurrected Lord, who has ascended into heaven "until the time comes for God to restore everything," is often presented (as by Peter on the day of Pentecost) in the Melchizedekian terms of Psalm 110. In this paradigm the ascension and heavenly session of Jesus are made intelligible by way of reference to the two institutional roles that he is understood to have taken up. Let us take first his regal or kingly office, adopting the point of view of political theology. Here the ascension of Jesus—as bodily ascension, hence as something historically distinct from the resurrection—is understood as an act of enthronement.[15] The Pentecostal gift, bestowed first upon Jesus' loyal followers in Jerusalem, is similarly interpreted as an act of royal beneficence or patronage marking the occasion of his accession to the throne of his Father. Likewise, the church, as the community of the Spirit, is understood precisely as the community that proclaims publicly, and rejoices at the proclamation, that Jesus and none other is Lord. It is the community that believes, in the words of another popular royal psalm, that YHWH has installed his King on his holy mountain and has begun the process of subduing the Gentiles (Ps. 2; cf. 2 Sam.). The conversion of thousands of Peter's auditors from various parts of the globe, each of whom hears the proclamation of Jesus' inauguration in his or her own tongue, is seen as the harbinger of a new world order—an order that will be revealed fully only when all the king's enemies, not excluding anything that disturbs the well-being of his faithful subjects, have been led to judgment in his triumphal procession.

Such claims as these must have (and did) set the alarm bells ringing in the palaces of Caesar. If the announcement of Jesus' humble birth sent King Herod into a murderous frenzy, how much more dramatic in effect the announcement of his heavenly inauguration? Because a King has been installed by God in heaven over and above every earthly king, their king-doms have become his tributaries. As Oliver O'Donovan observes in his admirable book *The Desire of the Nations*, the subjects of all earthly princes are drawn out from under them by means of the gospel. Christian political theory, argues O'Donovan, interprets the present "secular" age as one in which the rulers of this world have been deprived of any claim to direct authority or to immediate power to rule. What is left to them is merely the vocation of rendering service to a provisional (and for that reason, if no other, a merciful) form of justice, while the reappearance of the one true Ruler and Judge is awaited. Worldly princes embrace lawlessness whenever they shirk or overreach this vocation.[16]

From this point of view, Christ's heavenly session may be likened, *mutatis mutandis*, to a period of transitional government. His session, though heaven-ly indeed, is temporary, not permanent. It is an establishing of the con-ditions under which, and of the officialdom through which, he is to rule in the kingdom without end.[17] These conditions and these officials or vice-regents, while announced and in some sense already in place, are not yet fully accessible, or rather they are accessible only in the form given to them by the church, which is given to the world by Christ as the mystery and sacrament of his coming kingdom (Eph. 1:18–23). This fact may be alter-nately acknowledged and denied by worldly princes, but taken seriously by the church it mandates the church, as need be, to excommunicate princes, to resist the injustices of political and economic powers, and to stand its own ground in the face of persecution, outlasting the murderous rage of jealous gods and potentates. The church knows its King, and knows him to be the King of kings.

Little or none of this can be maintained consistently by those who regard Christ's ascension and heavenly session as a spiritualizing process. In that case, there can be no direct confrontation between his authentic human lordship and its inauthentic imitations. Room is opened up instead for a false compromise in which divine dignity belongs to the invisible, spiritual Christ, while earthly dignity belongs perforce to his visible human repre-sentative. This may be the compromise of an Innocent or a Boniface, which clothes the papacy in the trappings of old-world imperial power, only to see it collapse into its Avignon servitude. Or it may be a Eusebian or an Eras-tian compromise, investing Christ's imperial or national icon with an author-ity that no longer belongs to any worldly prince. Here too the visible church inevitably becomes fractious, vying with itself for a share of this putative earthly dignity, which it derives from the state, rather than vying with unjust and overreaching state officials for the sake of Christ's dignity and that of his subjects. This path has proved treacherous beyond all telling.[18] Perhaps its most dangerous stretch, however, is that which has recently been entered under the banner of secularity, or of separation between church and state. Here vast tracts of human power and authority have now been ceded by the church, as by the general public, to rulers who intend to rule without any reference to the strictly provisional and limited nature of their rule, or to the fact that any authority to rule they might have derives from Jesus Christ, to whom they nonetheless remain accountable.

We will return shortly to this matter. First we must touch also on Christ's priestly office, adopting the perspective of sacramental theology. These two offices are intimately connected, of course, on the Melchizedekian paradigm. But in what does Christ's heavenly priesthood consist? It must be seen first in its Aaronic dimensions, I think, as a continuation of his work of atonement. Thomas Aquinas is only agreeing with the traditional teaching of the Nicene era and with the book of Hebrews when he argues that the ascension rather than the cross is the direct cause of our salvation, for "as the high priest under the Old Testament entered the holy place to stand before God for the people, so also Christ entered heaven 'to make intercession for us,' as is said in Hebrews 7:25." Indeed, "the very showing of himself in the human nature which he took with him to heaven is a pleading for us, so that for the very reason that God so exalted human nature in Christ, he may take pity on them for whom the Son of God took human nature."[19]

In other words, the ascension and heavenly session constitute, after the cross, a further decisive step in Jesus' fulfilling of the mediatorial work typified by the great Hebrew liturgy of Yom Kippur.[20]

Second, however, his heavenly priesthood ought to be seen as it is seen, by John in the Apocalypse, for example, or by the likes of Irenaeus and Maximus; that is, as bound up also with the human stewardship of creation and with realization of the *imago dei*. William Milligan, John Zizioulas, and others have commented fruitfully on this, and I will not try to pursue it here.[21] It should be pointed out, though, that these two aspects or functions of his heavenly priesthood—the soteriological and the ontological, if you like— cohere in the sacraments, and especially in the Eucharist, by which we are authorized and enabled to participate in Christ's priesthood. His disciples too are "Levites and priests," says Irenaeus, sharing with him in "the sacerdotal rank" and making offering to God through him. They are a priestly people in that they present to God the firstfruits of creation in "the new oblation of the new covenant," sanctifying the world through thanksgiving and readying it for the glory that is to come. They are priestly, too, then—here especially—in their suffering and martyrdom for Christ's sake.[22]

When discussing the priestly office of Christ we must once again be diligent to avoid any false spiritualizing tendency. If the work of atonement and intercession conducted secretly in "the sanctuary made without hands" is not performed by a human, it does not benefit humans. If the liturgy of thanksgiving (*eucharistia*) is not led from heaven by a human, it is not a human offering. Likewise, if in the Eucharist there is no actual participation in the body and blood of the man Jesus Christ, then there is no sanctification of this body and blood of mine, nor any eschatological hope for this world of ours. All that remains, then—and in this Hegel was quite right, though he was wrong to think it a triumph over Roman idolatry—is the subjectivity of faith. This faith, it turns out, is a faith that may, or rather must, supply its own objective content through the arbitrary exercise of the will. Welcome to the religion of what is falsely called Spirit, which is also the triumphalist religion of that priestly man who merely imagines that he is divine! Is this not the man of lawlessness, who (to identify but one of his prominent crimes) is happy enough, in the name of progress and even of human rights, to see the warm red blood of the innocents sprinkled on the medical dustbins of Babylon? The man who is secretly against the body rather than for it?[23]

But let us pause a moment and listen to ourselves. If admittedly it is rather awkward (whether for the ancients or for moderns) to try to conceive of the ascension of Christ as a spatiotemporal, bodily event, how much more difficult and awkward is it to interpret his heavenly session by way of reference to the twin offices of Melchizedek? In an age of secular democracy, an age inaugurated by the deliberate debunking of the myths of kingship and priesthood, of what possible relevance is all of this? Is this whole conception, which sprang from a foreign Semitic culture and was maintained by a now equally strange medieval construct known as Christendom, still tenable in any way? Do we not live in the age of the Internet and the ballot box?

Permit me a mundane illustration. In a recent Canadian election, the main challenger for the federal premiership was one Stockwell Day, an evangelical Christian who was ridiculed by the national press for (allegedly) believing that human beings coexisted with the dinosaurs. His opponent, the then and still prime minister Jean Chrétien,[24] took refuge with several of his cabinet members from all probings of their own religious ideas by claiming to be Catholic. The appearance was certainly given that to be

Catholic was to (a) not to believe in a young Earth and (b) not believe, specifically *as* a Catholic, in anything particularly relevant to public life or deserving of public scrutiny.[25] The saddest part of this disingenuous exchange, to my way of thinking, was that the aforesaid challenger, the evangelical Mr. Day, responded that his own Pentecostalist beliefs were no more relevant or deserving of scrutiny than those of his Catholic opponents! Perhaps then we have here a solution to the ecumenical problem, or at least to the division of the Western church. Because neither side believes anything that matters to society at large, no visible division of the church is either necessary or appropriate. Imagine the furor had either Mr. Day or Mr. Chrétien said that he believed that all true public authority was now vested by God in a crucified, resurrected, and ascended Jew, and that, if elected to political service, he would attempt to serve this Jew to the best of his ability by pursuing a sound and merciful exercise of justice for all people within the Canadian dominion! As the election turned out, Mr. Day may as well have said this, but that is not my point. My point is that the public language of Christ's universal kingship and priesthood has been reduced, together with religious ideas generally, to the strictly private language of the church or the prayer closet.[26]

What, then, shall we say in response? Just this: The present situation, if accepted by the church, can only amount to a fundamental reversal of Pentecost and to a denial of Christ's ascension and heavenly session. Of course, it is not accepted and never can be where the church really is the church, or where *Chrétien* really means "Christian". Certainly it is not accepted, and never can be, where the church knows what it means to bear witness to the Christ who is both king and priest. That witness is a stubborn witness, the kind of witness that is willing to be tested by martyrdom—whether political or literal. It is the kind of witness that witnesses not only to Christ's present but also to his future, that is, to the Christ who is coming as judge. It is to that subject, and to the next article (our third and fourth clauses), that we must now turn.

† † †

"He will appear a second time, not to bear sin but to bring salvation to those who are waiting for him" (Heb. 9:28 NIV). Or, as Cyril of Jerusalem puts it, "We preach not one advent only of Christ, but a second also, far more glorious than the first."[27] This faith in the *parousia* is a response to the dominical teaching of Mark 13 and parallels, to the united witness of the apostles, and (behind both) to the pervasive testimony of the prophets regarding a decisive confrontation between YHWH and the nations that will usher in an everlasting kingdom—the kingdom of God and of his Christ.[28] Let us note well that the reappearance of Jesus from heaven in his glory is an integral part of the Melchizedekian paradigm. Whether his heavenly session is regarded in its priestly or its kingly aspect, it demands a *parousia,* a grand public display, a new and further *adventus.*[29] "How glorious he was, surrounded by the people, as he came out of the house of the curtain!" It may be that the author of Hebrews had this wonderful passage from Sirach in mind (referring to Simon son of Onias, who "took thought how to save his people from ruin").[30] No doubt he also had in mind, as did John when he wrote the Apocalypse, the high priest's task upon his emergence from the inner sanctuary where the Shekinah dwells of driving out sin from the camp before pronouncing the blessing that comes from the mercy seat. For he insists that our great high priest will reappear not only to bring salvation, but also to judge the quick and the dead and to set ablaze a "raging fire that will consume the enemies of God" (Heb. 10:27 NIV).[34]

Here too, of course, we confront in Scripture and creed a most awkward claim. I hasten to say that the awkwardness has little to do with the passing of what now seems to some an inordinate amount of time. The so-called crisis over the delay of the *parousia* is essentially a modern invention—though not strictly a modern one, to be sure. We may recall those jumpy Thessalonians whom Paul begged "not to become ... easily alarmed" (2 Thess. 2:2 NIV), to whom he also pointed out that the man of lawlessness must first somehow be brought to maturity (by nature a difficult goal for the lawless to attain!) before divine judgment could fall on him through the return of the man of righteousness. We may recall too those who waited so impatiently for Moses to return from the heights of Sinai and, growing ever more agitated at his absence, built for themselves the golden bull. Of such as these, and especially of the cynical among them—those whom 2 Peter calls the latter-day scoffers (3:3)—we must beware. In writing their premature epitaphs, they deliberately forget the true nature of the "maker of heaven and earth," both his immense patience and his proven decisiveness in judgment. But the real awkwardness is not created by the counterclaims of the scoffers, even when these are sophisticated scholars, influential men of culture, or great philanthropists. It is not generated by those who deny that human history, as well as individual human beings, are moving toward a final appointment with their divine judge. Nor is it generated by the very concept of judgment or of an act of divine wrath as a possible outcome of judgment. It is generated by the creed's own insistence that the Judge is none other than Jesus Christ.[31]

That Jesus is the Judge, and the Judge Jesus, is in the first place wonderful news for the church to share with the world. The one who will judge both the living and the dead is the one who died for those still living and who lives for those already dead. Certainly the judgment he will exercise will be entirely consistent with the judgment he *did* exercise, when out of unfathomable love he became (in a phrase Barth made famous) the Judge judged in our place.[32] And yet *he* is the Judge, and he has a judgment yet to deliver.

> Behold, I am coming soon! My reward is with me, and I will give to everyone according to what he has done. I am the Alpha and the Omega, the First and the Last, the Beginning and the End. Blessed are those who wash their robes, that they may have the right to the tree of life and may go through the gates into the city. Outside are the dogs, those who practice magic arts, the sexually immoral, the murderers, the idolaters and everyone who loves and practices falsehood (Rev. 22:12–15 NIV).

There is no point denying that this is awkward. The gospel's unconditional indicatives of grace do not overturn or undermine its equally unconditional imperatives of faith, loyalty, and obedience (see Matt. 18:21–35). Nor will just any faith, any loyalty, any obedience do for those who wish to pass from death into life, avoiding the wrath to come. To pass from the kingdoms (or even the democracies) of this world into the kingdom of God (which is not a democracy, but "the kingdom of his beloved Son"), faith, loyalty, and obedience to Jesus Christ are required. Jesus is, and on the day of his *parousia* will show himself to be, the Father's one measure of our humanity, for God "has set a day when he will judge the world with justice by the man he has appointed. He has given proof of this to all men by raising him from the dead" (Acts 17:31 NIV).[33]

What the church does not know about the asking and answering of the question of loyalty where those never exposed to the gospel are concerned, it obviously cannot say; but that is no concern of the church. The church's concern is, as far as possible, to put the world on notice of the question, and to show Jew and Gentile alike how a proper answer can be given and a false answer avoided. Let me appeal again to Cyril in order to underline the point about avoiding a false answer. Not for nothing is his catechetical lecture on the present article taken up, in good part, with a discussion of Antichrist and of the signs of Antichrist! Because looking for Jesus is the essential characteristic or distinguishing feature of the church in the present age, it is a point of gravest danger to the church that it should be deceived on this mat-

ter. The devil attacks the church and misleads the world precisely by con-
juring up antichrists of one sort or another.

> Guard thyself then, O man; thou hast the signs of Antichrist; and remem-
> ber them not only thyself, but impart them also freely to all. If thou hast a
> child according to the flesh, admonish him of this now; if thou has begotten
> one through catechizing, put him also on his guard, lest he receive the false
> one as the true. For the mystery of iniquity doth already work.[34]

What is "the mystery of iniquity" but the raising up of more or less plausible alternatives to the righteousness and judgment of God, and so also of
alternatives to the righteous Judge whom he has appointed? "For false Christs
and false prophets will appear and perform great signs and miracles to deceive
even the elect—if that were possible. See, I have told you ahead of time"
(Matt. 24–25 NIV).

Now let me say something controversial. The mystery of iniquity is at work
in the church and at work in this particular way: its theologians and its preachers no longer trouble themselves much to confess Christ coming. The Scripture is read, the creed said, the liturgy prayed; the word of his coming is there
and cannot be avoided, yet it is widely ignored by those who speak to and for
the church, who seem always to have something more pressing to say. Ignored
too is the warning about a great apostasy, a defection to Antichrist. (Such
things are usually left to the depised fundamentalists, whose own lawlessness
stems from the same source: ignoring the mind of Christ as discerned in the
universal church.) "Is it a plausible discourse? all listen to it gladly," remarks
Cyril. "Is it a word of correction? all turn away from it." Yet this very failure
to confess Christ coming is what Cyril would call a sign of his coming, a sign
"proper to the church" because it threatens to controvert the church.[35]

There have been other such signs, to be sure. The Sabellian and Arian
crises, which have reappeared in our time, afford examples. Listen once more
to Cyril:

> If thou hear that bishops advance against bishops, and clergy against clergy,
> and laity against laity even unto blood, be not troubled; for it has been writ-
> ten before. Heed not the things now happening, but the things which are
> written. . . . For men have fallen away from the right faith; and some preach
> the identity of the Son with the Father, and others dare to say that Christ
> was brought into being out of nothing. And formerly the heretics were man-
> ifest; but now the church is filled with heretics in disguise.[36]

Quarrels about the session of Christ (in the form of sacramental and political theology, as well as pneumatology) also qualify. Did they not divide the churches East from West, Roman from Protestant, Lutheran from Reformed, Reformed from Anabaptist? Was blood not spilled along with ink in furious arguments over the spoils of Christ's heavenly beneficence?[37] But this blood and this ink are not redeemed; rather, they are further degraded when the church today, by attrition rather than contrition, imposes on itself the penance of silence concerning either Jesus' present absence or his future coming. For what does this silence do, if not to leave the church, and society with it, prey to Antichrist?

To insist that Jesus is the coming one and himself the judge—that there will be no "coming of God" that is other than the coming of Jesus[38]—still leaves us with a great many unanswered questions, of course. Chief among them is the question as to the form of his coming, and of "our gathering together to Him" (2 Thess. 2:1 NASB; cf. Isa. 27:12–13), so that his future becomes our future. How shall we handle the knotty problems of continuity and discontinuity between the old and the new that here force themselves upon us? What indeed will be the form of Christ's judging, or of the rule and the kingdom he will then establish? "He will reign over the house of Jacob forever, and of his kingdom there will be no end," declares Gabriel (Luke 1:33 NRSV). But how shall this be, and what kind of kingdom is this?[39] Should we not be expected to say *something* plausible about such things, even if we are determined to deliver a word of warning and correction?

Much can be left to a discussion of the creed's final article, and will have to be. We have not the leisure to examine Scripture or the Fathers on these matters, never mind Christian poetry and art.[50] But there are one or two things that may profitably be said here, lest it be thought that having dared to trace the impression of Christ's foot in the rock hallowed by the Chapel of the Ascension we can do little else than take cover ourselves in an obscuring cloud while asserting a highly naive belief in the savior's descent from heaven on some future day. Admittedly, our situation could be considerably worse than that, hermeneutically speaking. Was it Reinhold Niebuhr who advised us to take eschatological "symbols" seriously but not literally? The end of that path can only be Docetism. We must, if we intend to confess the creed in the spirit and sense in which it was written, expect both that the end of history as we know it will come from beyond our history, and that it will come directly *into* it, as did the resurrected one before his ascension. As surely as there will be a last day for you and me as individuals, there will be a last day for humanity collectively when the sign of the Son of Man appears in heaven.[41] We are not thereby committed to the naive notion that Jesus is up there somewhere awaiting his big day, anymore than to the alternative that he is somehow still here, hidden in our midst, struggling from one generation to the next to create the right conditions for his reappearance. Such notions rest on a view of time and history that ignores the fall, is inimical to ecclesiology, and has this in common with the view of the skeptics and scoffers: it too easily equates the present and future of Christ with our own present and future. Oliver O'Donovan, for one, is quite right to insist that the ascension of Jesus entails his elevation beyond any temporal or spatial frame of reference open to us.[42] Not that Jesus has become atemporal or atopic, as if his incarnation had been reversed; but rather that he has been given a time and a place in which and from which to be Lord of every place and time.[43] His enthronement there and then with the Father, and his *parousia* that will one day occur here and now for us, are events integrally bound together, says O'Donovan.[44] They are united and separated not by anything so simple as a stretch of space-time, but by an act of divine power analogous to creation itself. This act is an act of fundamental reordering that impinges upon all creaturely reality, hence equally upon the living and the dead. It is an act centering all things on Christ and committing them to the fiery yet fecund consequences of that centering.

In other words, the *parousia*, like the incarnation from a virgin or the resurrection and ascension, stands in relation to what has gone before it both sequentially and nonsequentially. It effects and entails something that Irenaeus, following St. Paul, called recapitulation. Now this recapitulation, a doctrine that has no true philosophical or theological antecedent, should not be confused with a universalistic *apokatastasis pantōn*.[45] As Irenaeus himself puts it, "the advent of the Son comes indeed alike to all, but is for the purpose of judging, and separating the believing from the unbelieving. . . ."[46] Yet it is also for the purpose of bringing in those "times of refreshing" promised by the Lord, those eternal times in which human beings—led by the Spirit to the Son, and by the Son to the Father—will through communion with the Triune and incarnate God participate in a transformed world wherein all things are ever and again made new.[47] Such is the kingdom that will have no end, the priestly kingdom in which the Melchizedekian reign of Christ and of his saints will know neither boundary nor limit, not because this kingdom is timeless or spaceless, but because in it all things and all people, and the very structures of creation itself, are made free through subjection to God, through being offered up to God with a glad heart, and without reservation.[48]

The coming of the Judge and of a new creation may be still more difficult to conceive or articulate than *creatio ex nihilo* or the appearance in history of he who was born of a virgin. But a church that to many onlookers appears to have given up wrestling with these beliefs, a church whose "Maranatha!" is spoken *sotto voce,* is a church that has lost its nerve together with its christological nerve center. It is a church that cannot hope to understand itself or its vocation between the times. Hegel and Schweitzer are then right after all. What is called for from the church, in imitation of its Lord, is to cast *itself* on the wheel of history in a more or less heroic protest. As a community of protest, however—whether progressive or reactionary matters little—the church is not so much heroic as merely pathetic. On the other hand, the church that knows Christ risen and ascended and takes up the challenge of confessing Christ coming to judge and to reign will not only be renewed in its sense of mission, but will also (of this I am confident) find there open before it new possibilities for an ecumenical undertanding of its own sacraments and order, and for resolving differences related to its privileged participation in the present and future of Jesus. Moreover, it will not falsify or evade its special eucharistic participation in the past of Jesus; it will gladly exchange the heavy yoke of heroism for the lighter yoke of martyrdom.[49] There is no better articulation of its faith in the Coming One than that.

10

The Holy Spirit in the Holy Trinity

Thomas Smail

To turn from the second to the third article of the creed is to move from the eye of the christological storm to the pneumatological periphery, which at the time the creed was written was relatively uncontroversial and so could be disposed of briefly and without too much attention to detail. Indeed, in the version of the creed promulgated at the Council of Nicea in 325, the third article contained the one single and unadorned phrase, "and in the Holy Spirit." When that creed was revised at Constantinople in 381, the third article was expanded into the form that is used in the Christian East to this day.

Even so, if it is true that the church has never known quite what to say about the Holy Spirit, then this creed both shares and sources that reticence. Attention is so concentrated on the binitarian question of the right relationship of the Father to the Son that the properly trinitarian question that deals with the relating of the Spirit to both Father and Son is dealt with in a way that lacks focus and specificity and that, on any reckoning, is quite inadequate to the rich biblical and especially New Testament material that deals with the pre- and post-Pentecostal activity of the Spirit among God's people.

Nevertheless even in the little that the creed does say about the Spirit, we can trace the bare outlines of the classical orthodox approach to the doctrine of the Spirit that has prevailed ever since, and that can still do good service in our own day when questions about the Spirit are very much at the center of theological attention. We can discern here some basic affirmations about the Spirit that can be expanded and expounded to show how vital they are to any contemporary pneumatology.

The Deity of the Spirit

The creed never says in so many words that the Holy Spirit is God, but what it does say clearly implies that conclusion and would make no sense without it. The Spirit is named *kyrios*, the divine name that he shares with the Son, who is God from God, and he is declared to be the "giver of life," which is a divine prerogative. He said to proceed from the Father, and so to be of the same being, the same stuff as the Father, even if the technical term *homoousios*, which has been applied to the Son, is not at this point applied to the Spirit, although it was to be later, in a way that confirmed and consolidated what the creed says. Furthermore, to worship and glorify the Spirit is as legitimate as to worship and glorify the Father and the Son.

In implying rather than declaring the deity of the Spirit in this way, the creed is in harmony with the New Testament, which does the same. In 2 Corinthians 3:17, Paul says that "the Lord is the Spirit" (NRSV), and his analogy in 1 Corinthians 2:11—"For what human being knows what is truly human except the human spirit that is within? So also no one comprehends what is truly God's except the Spirit of God" (NRSV)—clearly implies the identity of the Spirit with the God whom he reveals.

The consequences of this identification are crucial. What the Spirit does is not a human work, or the work of some spiritual energy that is immanent to our humanity or to the created order, but a work of God. If it is through the Spirit that we come to believe the gospel and to appropriate corporately and personally all that the Father has done for us through the Son, none of this is a possibility for or an achievement of our own inherent spirituality; rather, it is a gracious work of God within us. The knowledge of God, the entering into a new relationship with God in Christ, our being renewed into the likeness of Christ, the outcome of our evangelism—all these depend not on human ability or elaborate techniques, but on the promised but uncontrollable activity of the Spirit of God, who, like wind, blows where he wills and is at no one's bidding or command. What matters is not the strength of our spirituality, but the grace of the Spirit of God.

The Spirit is Trinitarian

The Holy Spirit is God in a trinitarian context. The creed affirms that the Spirit is who he is and does what he does in his relationship to the Father and the Son that constitutes his being. The third article of the creed has to be read in the closest relationship to the other two. Precisely how the Spirit is related to Father and Son is not defined here; his relationship to the Son became and has remained a matter of controversy between the East and the West.

Both traditions, however, would be at one in rejecting any unitarianism regarding the Holy Spirit, in which his activity is seen to be self-authenticating and to be discerned in terms of its dramatic nature or its high emotional tone rather than by how it furthers the purposes of the Father as revealed in the gospel of the incarnate Son. To speak in Pentecostal terms for a moment, the initial evidence of the presence and activity of the Holy Spirit in the Christian community is not the manifestation of spiritual gifts but the confession of the Father and the Son. As Paul puts it "No one can say 'Jesus is Lord' except by the Holy Spirit" (1 Cor. 12:3 NRSV) and "God has sent the Spirit of his Son into our hearts crying, '*Abba!* Father'" (Gal. 4 :6 NRSV). By such criteria, anyone who confesses the lordship of Christ and who has been brought into an *Abba* relationship with the Father is a charismatic Christian, regardless of whether or to what degree that person has manifested spiritual gifts. Because the Spirit is who he is in relation to the Trinity, his chief work is to bring us also into relationship with the Father and the Son and to integrate us into their saving work in the world.

The Personhood of the Spirit

The creed does not consider the question of whether and in what sense the Spirit is a distinct trinitarian person or hypostasis within the life of God, although the fact that the Spirit rates a third creedal article of his own, following on the articles dealing with the Father and the Son, may be taken to point in that direction.

The question here is not whether the Spirit acts in a personal way in relation to us; the New Testament witnesses are unanimous that he does. The question is whether what he does can be understood simply as the action of the Father and the Son toward and in us or whether the Spirit, in relation to the Father and the Son, is to be seen as a distinct, though never independent, subject who enters into authentically personal relationships with the Father and the Son.

Wolfhart Pannenberg directs our attention here to the Johannine witness, which we shall look at in more detail later, and specifically to Jesus' understanding of the Spirit as the one who "will glorify me, because he will take what is mine and declare it to you" (John 16:14 NRSV) Through the work of the Spirit, Jesus will receive a glory from outside himself that nevertheless has its ultimate divine source in the Spirit, who shares his divine being and yet is hypostatically distinct from him. Jesus finishes his work and returns to the Father, but the Spirit leads his people in every generation into the unfolding riches and manifold implications of what he has done, and thus brings him new glory. This personal distinctness of the Spirit's work over against the work of the Son is the source of the freedom and spontaneity of our response to Christ. We are not subjected to the external authority of a given revelation, but through the Spirit are enabled to come to an internalized response to that revelation that we bring to Christ—and yet that is the gift of his Spirit to us and the work of his Spirit in us.

All this suggests that the Spirit is a distinct personal subject within the life of God. He is who he is and does what he does within and never apart from his personal relationship to the Father and the Son. But it also suggests that the way in which he is a trinitarian person is different from the way in which the Father and Son are trinitarian persons. They are personal subjects to whom we relate and whom we trust, confess, serve, and approach in prayer and worship. He is the personal subject who enables that relating. He is God on our side of our relationship to God the Father and God the Son who opens us in mind and heart to receive and to answer what the Father has given us through the Son.

As James Packer has memorably put it, the Holy Spirit is like the floodlighting on a great cathedral on a dark night. If the lights are not switched on, you cannot see the cathedral. But if the lights are on, you defeat their purpose if you do not look at the cathedral to which they point, but look instead into the lights and become dazzled and disorientated in the process.

In other words, it can be dishonoring to the Spirit to be too interested in the Spirit in and for himself. As Yves Congar has put it, no face of his own to show us but is concerned only to relate to us the Father and the Son so that through his work they may be glorified. He is the person not to whom we relate directly, but whose presence and activity are evidenced in the multitude of ways he enables us to relate to Father and Son and to the the fulfillment of their renewing purposes for their creation.

The Spirit as Giver of Life

The comprehensive summary of the work of the Spirit offered by the creed is captured in the single Greek word *zōopoioun*, usually rendered in English as "giver of life." It would be in line with the trinitarian understanding that we have been outlining to understand the Spirit's characteristic function in giving life as being its communicator rather than its source. Life has its source in the Father, it becomes incarnate in the Son, and it is imparted to us in the Spirit.

It is also instructive that the word used for life here, *zōē*, is used in the Johannine tradition to describe in a forward-looking way the eschatological new life of the age to come. To describe the created life of the present age, John prefers *bios*. Whether a similar distinction was being drawn by the compilers of the creed we have no way of knowing, but for the New Testament witness as a whole, the Spirit is viewed eschatologically rather than protologically. The involvement of the Trinity in the original creation is viewed chistologically rather than pneumatologically, in terms of the Logos rather than in terms of the Spirit. The brooding of the Spirit over unformed chaos and God's breathing of his life into Adam in Genesis are certainly not denied, but the defining context of the work of the Spirit is the inbreaking of the first fruits and first installment of the life of the age to come that is inaugurated at Pentecost as a result of the finished work of Christ. In the New Testament the Spirit is the Spirit of the future rather than the Spirit of the past, and although the God of the end is also the God of the beginning, in the Spirit we are people whose concentration is directed far less to where we came from than to where are going.

On the uncontroversial periphery of its confession the creed proclaims the Holy Spirit as the divine agent through whom God incorporates us into the life of the age to come, which the Father has opened to us through the incarnation, death, and resurrection of the Son.

The Controversy between East and West

The uncontroversial third article of the creed of 381 became highly controversial some centuries later and indeed led to the Great Schism between East and West. Where the creed had originally affirmed that the Spirit had proceeded from the Father, the West, in an excess of anti-Arian zeal, began to confess that he proceeded from the Father *and the Son* (in Latin, *filioque*). This amendment was first ratified by the Council of Toledo in 589. At first it was resisted in Rome, but soon after 1000 it was adopted by the popes, became the official creed of all the Western churches, and, because it was not a matter of controversy at the Reformation, it has so remained in both Catholic and Reformed churches until the present day.

The addition was, however, violently rejected by the Eastern Orthodox churches, and it became one of the chief causes of the first Great Schism in Christendom in the twelfth century. To understand the violence of that confrontation, it is important to recognize that it had an ecclesiological and political dimension as well as a properly theological one. The ire of the East was aroused by the willingness of the Bishop of Rome to alter in a unilateral way the wording of a creed that had been formulated by an ecumenical council, so that the argument was driven at least as much by disagreements about the powers and claims of the papacy as by disagreements about the procession of the Holy Spirit.

But if we stick to the properly theological question, we may well ask why that ancient controversy over a single phrase in an ancient creed should matter to us in the very different context of the world of the twenty-first century. The answer is that to discuss the *filioque* is to discuss the relationship of the third person of the Trinity to the other two, of the Spirit to the Father and very specifically to the Son. In our time, when questions about the person and work of the Holy Spirit are at the forefront of Christian concern, these questions have both a theological and a practical relevance, as well as a pastoral relevance, which makes them very well worth our pursuit. The way you relate the work of the Spirit to the work of the Son will be a central factor in the way you assess the charismatic renewal and the way you approach interfaith dialogue, to mention but two matters of central contemporary concern.

The Biblical Evidence

To make sure that we keep our feet on firm gospel ground, let us look at what the New Testament has to be say about the part the Father and Son play in the coming of the Spirit. For this purpose the main source is the highly nuanced and sophisticated treatment of the matter in the farewell discourses of John 14–16. We can summarize these chapters by saying that for the Jesus of the discourses, it is the Father who sends the Spirit, but the Spirit's coming is conditioned by and is in the most intimate connection with the person of Jesus and the completion of his work in his death and resurrection.

We can cite John 14:16, "I will ask the Father and he will give you another Advocate" (NRSV), or 14:26, where Jesus speaks of "the Advocate, the Holy Spirit, whom the Father will send in my name" (NRSV). We can also turn to the verse that was to play a key part in the East-West controversy, 15:26, out of which contending theologians often read more than it actually contains, "When the Advocate comes, whom I will send to you from the Father, the Spirit of truth who comes from the Father, he will testify on my behalf" (NRSV). Here it is Jesus himself who sends the Spirit—which is what the West wanted to underline—but it is from the Father that he is sent; it is from the Father as his ultimate source and origin that he proceeds, and that is what the East wanted to underline. The creedal phrase "who proceeds from the Father" is a quotation from this verse.

In John 16:7 we are again told that the coming of the Paraclete is dependent upon the completion of the work of the Son, and for once the part of the Father in his coming is not made explicit: "For if I do not go away the Advocate will not come to you, but if I go, I will send him to you" (NRSV).

In all four Gospels the Spirit comes to Jesus in the context of his baptism by John the Baptist, who says of him, "He will baptize you with the Holy Spirit" (Mark 1:8 [NRSV] and parallels). The gift that he will pass on to us is the gift that has come to him from the Father. The delivery of that gift to his people is ascribed to the ascended Jesus by Peter in his Pentecost sermon: "Exalted to the right hand of God, he has received from the Father the promised Holy Spirit and has poured out what you now see and hear" (Acts 2:33 NIV).

So the New Testament witness, expressed particularly by John but confirmed by the other evangelists, is that the Spirit is sent *by* and *from* the Father but also *through* and *by* the incarnate Son. The manner in which the Father and the Son are involved in that sending is described in a way that enables both the sides in the controversy to make a credible appeal to texts that validate their positions, but we can now go on in the light of the scriptural evidence to assess the strengths and weaknesses of the two positions and perhaps even to see how they can be reconciled.

The Eastern Position—the Father Alone Breathes Out the Spirit

For the Christian East, the Father is the source of both the Eternal Son and the Eternal Spirit. Son and Spirit are as divine as he is, but the divinity of Son and Spirit is a derived divinity that they have from the Father. The Father, within the eternal life of God, begets the Son and spirates the Spirit (see figure one), and when it comes to the incarnation, God's saving self-expression in human history, the relationships of the Father, Son, and Spirit within the life of God are expressed outwardly by the two sendings of the two divine persons. There is in the gospel a coming of the Son and a coming of the Spirit whereby the Trinity that is immanent to God reveals itself in history. As Irenaeus put it, the Son and the Spirit are the two hands of God; the Father is the sender and they are the sent. The Eastern objection to the *filioque* is therefore that it makes the Son into a cosender of the Spirit and thus intrudes upon the personal prerogative of the Father. The Eastern understanding of the trinitarian relationships insists that just as the Son in the second article of the creed is begotten by the Father alone, so the Spirit in the third article proceeds from the Father alone.

When we measure this Eastern Orthodox understanding of the Spirit from the Father against the scriptural evidence that it seeks to interpret, we shall see that it has both a great strength and a great weakness.

Its great strength in that it acknowledges the primacy of the Father in relation to the Son and the Spirit. It is in line with the whole central thrust of New Testament Christianity to insist that the source of everything and the destination of everything is the Father. We shall not come to the Father without Jesus; Jesus is the true and living way not to himself but to the Father. The initial evidence of the Holy Spirit in the life of Christian communities and individuals is that we should cry *"Abba!* Father!" As Paul puts

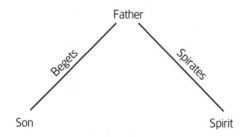

Figure One

it, "Through him[Christ] we both have access in one Spirit to the Father" (Eph. 2:18 RSV).

If the relationships between Father, Son, and Holy Spirit that come to light in human history through the incarnation (economic Trinity) reflect and reveal the eternal relationships between Father, Son, and Holy Spirit within the life of the one God (immanent Trinity), we have every reason to say with our Orthodox fellow believers that the primary and most basic thing about the Holy Spirit is that he proceeds from the Father. The New Testament basis for that statement is clear and sure.

If the Eastern Orthodox position has a great strength, it has also a great weakness; it does not make sufficiently clear how the coming of the Spirit is related to, cradled in, and dependent upon the coming of the Son. If we look again at our diagram, we can see that while it is clear that the Son and the Spirit depend upon the Father, it says nothing about the relationship of Son and Spirit to each other. The Nicene Creed of 381 fails to do justice to what we saw as the rich and complex Johannine teaching about the relation of the Spirit to the work and person of the Son. We have already surveyed that material, and we need only add what Jesus says in John 16:13–15 (NRSV),

When the Spirit of truth comes, he will guide you into all the truth; for he will not speak on his own but will speak whatever he hears and he will declare to you the things that are to come. He will glorify me, because he will take what is mine and will declare it to you. All that the Father has is mine. For this reason I said that he will take what is mine and declare it to you.

This christological orientation of the Spirit goes unmentioned in the creed of 381. Such a silence can have dangerous practical consequences. If we loosen the connection between Christ and the Spirit, we are in danger of severing one of the nerve centers of the New Testament gospel. If Son and Spirit are seen as semi-independent expressions of the divine life of the Father, it might be possible to be in the Spirit without being in the Son, to have a valid relationship to God that is not mediated by Jesus, or to try to reach the Father by some other spiritual path than the one true and living way he has given in Jesus. There is at least the possibility that something like this has happened in Orthodoxy. Karl Barth claimed to have discerned in Russian Orthodoxy a tendency to lapse into a Christless mysticism simply because it did not emphasize clearly enough that the sure sign of being in the Spirit is to confess that Jesus is Lord.

To come nearer home, I have heard an English bishop of a radical cast of mind say that he thought the *filioque* question was totally irrelevant until he realized that if the *filioque* was removed so we could talk about the work of the Spirit without relating it to the work of the Son, that would open the door to an accepting attitude to the other world religions as independent manifestations of the Spirit that can be set alongside God's self-manifestation in Christ.

Those who share the New Testament conviction that God's self-revelation in Christ is the ultimate touchstone of all religious experience will continue to insist that the Holy Spirit is the one who comes through Christ and whose chief work is to bring us to the confession of Christ as uniquely Lord and Savior. An affirmation of the *filioque* is one way in which the normative connection between the Son and the Spirit can be maintained.

Eastern creedal reticence about the relationship of the Spirit to Christ can also leave the door open for a kind of second-blessing Pentecostalism in which Son and Spirit are seen to preside over distinct areas of God's saving activity. I receive salvation from sin from Christ crucified and then, having fulfilled certain conditions, I go to a second stage in which I am baptized in the Holy Spirit into the fullness of God's life and power. Such a bifurcation of salvation is biblically unacceptable and theologically impossible, and it has the potential for all sorts of pastoral disasters; it can very easily run off into a kind of charismania in which speaking in tongues, falling down on the floor, or having tooth fillings turned into gold become the authenticating marks of life in the Spirit, distracting our attention from the priorities of the gospel of Christ.

The same separation between Christ and the Spirit may also underlie the divorce of spirituality from sound doctrine that is such a marked feature of contemporary Christianity. If we construct an understanding of the work of the Spirit that is sparated from an understanding of God's self-revelation in history, the spirit we will find is more likely to be our own spirit than the Spirit of Christ—a spirit that is immanent to our own humanity rather than the Spirit who is given to us by the incarnate, crucified, and risen Lord. To find that spirit we will be tempted to embark on all sorts of introspective inner journeys into ourselves rather than the outward journey beyond ourselves into Christ, who is the authentic locus from which the Spirit of God comes to us. The Holy Spirit does indeed come to dwell in us, but that indwelling is dependent upon and identified by our relationship to the revealed Son by whom the Spirit is given. Any loosening of the trinitarian tie can (and nowadays often does) result in an amorphous spirituality that has little connection with the Christian gospel, with the result that we are, in a profound way, left to ourselves, deprived of access to the recreating energy that is in Christ for us.

In defense of their position, Eastern theologians would be quick to point out that even without the *filioque* clause it does not allow for this kind of separation between what the Son does and what the Spirit does. For them, Son and Spirit have their single source in the Father and are *homoousios* of the same being and nature as the Father, so for that reason alone there can be no question of any division or separation between them.

They would further argue that the fact that the Spirit has his eternal source in the Father alone is not necessarily in conflict with the fact that in the history of salvation he works in closest connection with the Son and is sent into the world in new power and life-giving presence as a result of the Son's cross and resurrection. In gospel history, it is indeed Jesus who sends the Spirit to his disciples, but the Spirit whom he sends is the Spirit of God who proceeds from the Father.

To this last point, the Western theologians would respond that it is difficult to maintain both that the Son is so closely connected with the historical coming of the Spirit at Pentecost and that he has no connection with the origination of the Spirit within the eternal life of God. What knowledge can we have of the trinitarian relationships within the mystery of the life of God except what we can derive from the trinitarian relationships within the history of revelation? If God has acted in history in a way that is consistent with the relationships that constitute his own being, and if the Son as well as the Father is involved in the historical coming of the Spirit at Pentecost, is that not a pointer to the fact that in the eternal life of God the Spirit is who he is by virtue of his relationship to both the Father and the Son?

The Eastern theologians would reply that although they have not affirmed the eternal relationship of the Spirit to the Son in their creed, they have by no means denied or ignored it in their theological teaching. Gregory of Nyssa says that although the Spirit proceeds from the Father, he is also "of the Son," and indeed we may say that he proceeds "from the Father *through* the Son." The Spirit, says Gregory, is like a third candle lighted from a first candle through a second candle. The light has its source in the first candle (the Father) but it is transmitted to the third candle (the Spirit) through the second candle (the Son).[1] We can see here how such a theology fills the gap we have identified in Eastern pneumatology and, in its own way, asserts the dependence of the Spirit on the Son that was so important to the West. Gregory's formula, "The Spirit proceeds *from* the

Father *through* the Son," has great possibilities for a future reconciliation of East and West, affirming as it does both the primacy of the Father, emphasized by the East, and the dependence of the Spirit on the Son, emphasized by the West.

The Western Position—Both Father and Son Spirate the Spirit

The Western church, whose theology was massively shaped by Augustine (who himself affirmed the *filioque*) was less concerned about the primacy of the Father and, in reaction to Arianism, much more concerned to affirm the equal deity of the Son. Augustine argues that because the Son is as much God as the Father, and because it belongs to the divine nature to originate other divine persons or hypostases, the Son and the Father, who share equally in the divine nature, must also share equally in the origination of the Spirit. Therefore, to fully affirm the full deity of the Son alongside the Father, we have to affirm that the Spirit proceeds both from the Father and the Son. We may sum up this position in another diagram.

In figure two we can see the characteristic features of the Western position that constitute both its strengths and its weaknesses.

The Father alone begets the Son, but the Father and the Son together breathe out the Spirit—as Augustine puts it, acting "as one principle in a single act."[2] The Spirit, in other words, proceeds from the divine being and nature that Father and Son share, rather than, as in the East, from the single person of the Father.

To this Augustine adds that the Father is the *principle* source of the Spirit because ultimately it is from him alone that both Son and Spirit come. The Spirit comes from the Father directly and also indirectly through the Son, who himself is begotten by the Father. This is the way in which Augustine acknowledges the primacy of the Father that is so important to the East.

The Western position is strong precisely where the Eastern position is weak—it acknowledges that the Holy Spirit is the Spirit of the Son whom the Son sends upon his people from the Father, and thus provides a theological defense against the mystical, relativistic, and charismatic excesses to which a pneumatology that is not firmly anchored in Christology can easily give rise.

One of the chief weaknesses of the Western position is that it involves a downgrading of the Holy Spirit in comparison with the Son. For Augustine, it belongs to the divine being and nature to generate divine persons,

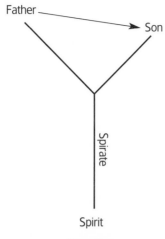

Figure Two

so for the Son to be fully divine he must, with the Father, have a part in bringing forth the Spirit. But in the Western scheme the Spirit has no part in the bringing forth of any divine person, so we must ask whether then the Spirit is divine at all. The Son exercises his divine prerogative in relation to the Spirit, but the Spirit has no such prerogative in regard to the Son. Within the divine life the Son is creative in a way that the Spirit is not. The Son shares in bringing forth the Spirit, but the Spirit has no share in bringing forth the Son.

The East has always protested that that the trinitarianism of the West, which comes to expression in the *filioque* clause, involves a subordination and depression of the Holy Spirit in relation to the Son, so that the West has never been able to do justice to the distinctive contribution that the Holy Spirit makes to our salvation. Attention is so concentrated on Christ that the Spirit and his work can be neglected and sometimes almost forgotten. It is possible to be Christ-centered in a way that stops believers from being open to the Spirit and causes them to see the Spirit not as a distinct divine person who, with the Father and the Son, is to be worshipped and glorified, but simply as the postascension mode of action of the exalted Christ. Hendrikus Berkhof has proposed to reduce the three divine persons to two, thus carrying to its formal conclusion the Western tendency to depreciate the Spirit in favor of the Son. From this point of view, we can understand the Pentecostal movement as a protest against the exclusive christocentricity of Western Christianity in both its Catholic and Protestant manifestations. The Pentecostals, on the positive side, have reminded us that as well as the fixed point of what Christ has revealed to us and done for us once and for all, there is the spontaneous and creative action of the Spirit with all the expectation, enthusiasm, and openness that it brings. The ordered "givenness" of the Word has to be set in the context of the "living-ness" of the unpredictable Spirit. The saving deed done on Good Friday and Easter long ago has its contemporary effect in the present inbreaking of the Spirit in Pentecostal power.

Alasdair Heron summarizes these accusations by saying that Western trinitarianism "involves a subordination of the person of the Holy Spirit to the person of Jesus Christ which tends towards a 'depersonalisation' of the Spirit, his reduction to a mere 'power' flowing from Christ and so loses sight of his sovereign freedom and initiative as the Spirit who, like the Word, is one of what Irenaeus called 'the two hands of God.'"[3]

Because the Western church downplays the living and immediate pres-ence of the Spirit in this way, it is easy to see how the pope has come to be seen as the earthly vicar of an absent Christ and the church has been under-stood predominantly in terms of earthly power and jurisdiction, not in terms of a free and direct encounter with God the Holy Spirit.

In other words, where the Spirit does not have his rightful place, author-itarianism easily creeps in: all the emphasis is on the given word of an infal-lible pope on the Catholic side and an infallible Bible on the Protestant side. When that happens, the gospel can be regarded as something imposed from outside rather than something seen and freely accepted through the work of the Spirit inside. In worship, this can lead to the rigidity of a fixed liturgy and the even greater rigidity of a minister-dominated free church service where the freedom of the Spirit to act spontaneously among and through the congregation is inhibited rather than encouraged, feared rather than expected.

It was precisely such defects in the Western churches that led to the protest of liberalism on behalf of the freedom of the Spirit of man and to the protests of pietism and Pentecostalism on behalf of the freedom the Spirit of God, but in ways that, once again, for the sake of the freedom of the Spirit, downgraded the normative authority of the work and person of Christ.

Furthermore, if we turn back for a moment to the biblical evidence, we will see that what the New Testament presents is not a one-way depen-dence of the Spirit on the Son which the *filioque* model implies, but a mutual interdependence of Spirit and Son, on each other. It is true that the Spirit is dependent on the Son for the normative content of what he conveys to us, but it is equally true that the Son is dependent on the Spirit for his powerful words and action in human history.

The Son owes his incarnate life to his conception by the Spirit in the womb of Mary. The Spirit is the gift of the Father to the Son in his Jordan baptism, and he acknowledges his dependence on the anointing of the Spirit by quoting Isaiah in his sermon at Nazareth: "The Spirit of the Lord is upon me because he has anointed me to bring good news to the poor" (Luke 4:18 NRSV). The Son is who he is because he has received the Spirit from the Father and does what he does in the power of the Spirit. It is the Spirit who has been at work perfecting Jesus' humanity that Jesus then breathes on us to perfect ours. The incarnate Son first receives the Spirit and then bestows him. John's Gospel says both these things in the same sentence and through the mouth of John the Baptist, "I saw the Spirit descending from heaven like a dove, and it remained on him. I myself did not know him, but the one who sent me to baptize with water said to me, 'He on whom you see the Spirit descend and remain is the one who baptizes with the Holy Spirit.' And I myself have seen and have testified that this is the Son of God" (John 1:32–34 NRSV).

The incarnate Son is both the eternal Word made flesh and the model of the man who is filled with the Holy Spirit. His person is constituted by both his relationship to the Father and his relationship to the Spirit. An incarnational Christology and a pnematological Christology have often been seen as exclusive alternatives, but John has both. What we need is a trinitarian Christology that sees Jesus as the eternal Son of the Father who, precisely because of his unique relationship to the Father, is uniquely indwelled by the Spirit of the Father, which he then conveys from his humanity to ours. One of the chief defects of the Chalcedonian Christology is that it seeks to define the constitution of Christ's person without any reference to the Holy Spirit. It falls far short of the gospel, in which the very highest incarnational Christology is taught and professed.

All this has practical import when we realize that it is the pnematological element in the incarnate Christ that makes his humanity not only normative for but creatively empowering of ours. That is what Paul is indicating in when he says of him, "The last Adam became a life-giving spirit" (1 Cor. 15:45 NRSV). The incarnate Son of the Father is, in the power of the Spirit, the ultimate human being, who gives the Spirit who has dwelt transforminaly in his humanity to work in the same way incurs. The mighty works of Jesus are not unique to him as the divine Son of God, but they are works that are accomplished in the humanity he shares with us in the power of the

Spirit that he has received from the Father. Because that Spirit is conveyed to us, the mighty works of that Spirit are made accessible to us. It is precisely when he is promising the Holy Spirit to his disciples that Jesus says to them, "The one who believes in me will also do the works that I do and . . . greater works than these, because I am going to the Father" (John 14:12 NRSV).

The Christ who receives the Spirit and depends upon him is the Christ who provides the theological basis for an effective and life-giving reception of the same Spirit by us.

A Possible Solution

A final diagram (figure three) shows the Father-Son-Spirit relationships that we have discerned as we have looked at the strengths and weaknesses of the Eastern and Western formulations.

If we are to be true to the total New Testament witness, we have to say that if the trinitarian relationships revealed in history reveal the eternal relationships within the life of God, then the Spirit comes *from* the Father *through* the Son. This, as against the *filioque,* clearly expresses the primacy of the Father over the Son in the giving of the Spirit; but also, as against the christological inadequacy of the Eastern formulation, shows that the Son has his own distinct part in the sending of the Spirit.

By the same token, we also have to say that if the historical relationships point to the eternal relationships, then the Son comes from the Father through the Spirit. There is not just a one-sided dependence of the Spirit on the Son, as the *filioque* suggests with all the resultant downplaying and subordination of the Spirit that it implies, but rather a mutual interdependence of Spirit and Son on each other. Both have their ultimate source in the Father, but each does what he does and is what he is in dependence upon the other. Their relationship is better described in terms of coordination than of subordination.

On this basis there may well be a good case for proposing not one, but two alterations to the Nicene Creed as we have received it. If in the third article we are in faithfulness to the biblical data, we are to say that "the Spirit proceeds from the Father *through the Son.*" Might not the same faithfulness to the same data lead us to say in the second article that the Son "is eternally begotten of the Father *through the Spirit*"?

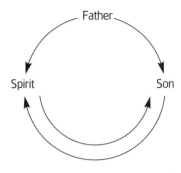

Figure Three

To remove the present ecclesiological barriers to the discussion of these theologically important questions, the Western churches will need to repent of their unilateral insertion of the *filioque* that has so offended the East and return to the original form of the creed of 381 as a basis for ecumenical study and possible agreed ecumenical advance, perhaps in the direction that we have just been outlining.

To sum up, from the Father there originate two converging movements of divine self-giving. On the one hand, the Son comes from the Father through the Spirit; on the other, the Spirit comes from the Father through the Son. The Son and the Spirit, the two hands of God, are clasped in the closest embrace of mutual support and cooperation before they are stretched out to gather in the world. To have faith in the Son of God who has come from the Father is to be made ready to receive the Spirit of God; to be in the power of the Spirit of God who has come from the Father is to be made ready to confess the Son of God and, through him, to come to the Father. We can have no valid relationship with the Son without receiving the Spirit; we can have no valid relationship to the Spirit that does not propel us toward the Son. Paul expresses the one side of it, "Anyone who does not have the Spirit of Christ does not belong to him" (Rom. 8:9 NRSV). John expresses the other, "By this you know the Spirit of God: every spirit that confesses that Jesus Christ has come in the flesh is from God, and every spirit that does not confess Jesus is not from God" (1 John 4:2–3 NRSV). In the life and work of God, Son and Spirit are joined together; neither in our theology nor in our practice are we to pull them apart.

11

He Spoke through the Prophets
The Prophetic Word Made More Sure

Kathryn Greene-McCreight

"How sweet are thy words unto my taste! yea, sweeter than honey to my mouth! Through thy precepts I get understanding: therefore I hate every false way. Thy word is a lamp unto my feet, and a light unto my path" (Ps. 119:103–105 KJV).

The phrase "He spoke through the prophets" of the third article of the creed raises some of the most important of theological problems of all of Christian confession. In a sense, everything hangs on this one little phrase. Almost everything. By it we refer to the inspiration of Holy Scripture, to the theological unity of the two testaments, to the conviction that Scripture, one Scripture in two testaments, has a content or goal toward which it draws us, indeed the goal of history toward which the Lord of history draws us. Of course, all of this then raises the pressing question for our time: Does the Holy Spirit still speak today in Holy Scripture?

By the phrase "He spoke through the prophets," we assert that the Holy Spirit, whom the creed links with the Creator and with Jesus, is not merely a principle of the supernatural but is quite concrete. This is one of the only two references in the creed to what we call the Old Testament. The first is to God the Creator in the first article, and the second to the Holy Spirit speaking through the prophets. This sets the Holy Spirit in time, the Spirit who spoke originally through and within a specific community, a community with the demands and blessings of the covenant of God's righteous law, and it begs the question that has at many points in the history of Christian theology become a *bête noire:* What do we do with the Old Testament? From the statement in the creed, it is apparent that we are to understand the Old Testament to bear the Holy Spirit and to attest to the Triune God. The creed's affirmation that the Holy Spirit spoke through the prophets sharpens the matter implied in the earliest statement of Christian confession, "Jesus is Lord." This pithy phrase equates Jesus with the one God of Israel, and that one God now present as the Holy Spirit in the Christian community is the same God who spoke through the prophets.

We must note that the phrase "who spoke through the prophets" is not in the Apostles' Creed. The assumption that the Old Testament witnesses to Jesus was, of course, present in Christian confession very early on. After all, Jesus gives a Bible lesson about himself to the travelers on the Emmaus road: "Beginning with Moses and all the prophets, he interpreted to them in all the scriptures the things concerning himself" (Luke 24:27 RSV). Jesus also points out that the Scriptures testify to him, even though the Jews do not see this: "You search the scriptures, because you think that in them you have eternal life; and it is they that bear witness to me; yet you refuse to come to me that you may have life" (John 5:39–40 RSV). Paul writes to the Romans that scripture of former days is not a dead letter from the past, but is for the present and for the future: "For whatever was written in former days was written for our instruction, so that by steadfastness and by the encouragement of the scriptures we might have hope" (Rom. 15:4 RSV).

This phrase "He spoke through the prophets" also raises the matter of the inspiration of Scripture. It recalls the verses 2 Peter 1:20–21, "First of all you must understand this, that no prophecy of scripture is a matter of one's own interpretation, because no prophecy ever came by the impulse of man, but men moved by the Holy Spirit spoke from God" (RSV). It is worth looking closer at this passage at this point. In 2 Peter 1, the role of memory is important: "Therefore I intend always to remind you of these things," these things being the call and election of the brethren. Peter continues "I think it right . . . to arouse you by way of reminder," and links the role of memory to the future, "since I know that the putting off of my body will be soon. . . . And I will see to it that after my departure you may be able at any time to recall these things" (vv. 14–15 RSV). What Peter reminds them of is a very concrete kind of memory, that is, his own experience of witnessing the "power and coming of our Lord Jesus Christ" and his "majesty" (v. 16 RSV). He recollects hearing the voice at the transfiguration that attested that Jesus is the beloved Son of God. The typological linking between the transfiguration on the "holy mountain" (1:18 RSV) and the giving of the law at Sinai, so popular in the early and medieval church, is difficult to rule out as a possible intended meaning here in first Peter, especially when he says that, in addition to these eye- and ear-witness memories, "we have the prophetic word made more sure" (v. 19 RSV). In witnessing the manifesting of Jesus as the Son of God, the disciples were given the lamp that is the light to our path (Ps. 119:105) even more surely. It would light the dark places until the future day when the morning star would rise in their hearts (v. 19). Here we come to the clincher: "No prophecy of scripture is a matter of one's own interpretation" (v. 20 RSV). Even the witness of the transfiguration does not allow Peter to concoct his own interpretations because prophecies have never come by the impulse of people moved by their own individual interpretations; instead, "men moved by the Holy Spirit spoke from God" (v. 21 RSV). These prophetic writings are not the fancy of a brilliant religious leader, but are from the very Spirit of God.

Second Peter can be read to include Christian prophecy along with the prophecies of the Old Testament. The letter goes on to speak of "false prophets who arose among the people—Peter meant the people of Israel—and these false prophets find their parallel in the false teachers among the Christian communities (2:1 NRSV). It can be argued that Peter is claiming that the apostles' Christian words about Jesus, for example, the retelling of the eyewitness experience of the transfiguration, are from the Holy Spirit just as are the prophecies of Holy Scripture. So in 2 Peter 3:16, the assumption is that Paul's writings are held to have authority equal to that of the "other scriptures." We remember the scene of Pentecost, how the community of different nationalities and ethnicities and languages gathered, how the apostles were filled with the Holy Spirit, who allowed them to speak in languages not their own (Acts 2:4, 11). Peter then stood up and preached, interpreting the prophet Joel and various Psalms insofar as they speak of Jesus. This story and this speech themselves become Scripture for us; they are early Christian prophecy, inspired by the Holy Spirit. It is the Holy Spirit who safeguards the truth of Christian teaching and who is not contradicted. We see this to be the whole basis of early Christian preaching. For example, in Acts 8 Philip preaches Christ to the Ethiopian eunuch on the basis of Isaiah, and in Acts 28 Paul testifies to the kingdom of God on the basis of the law of Moses and the prophets. Early Christian preaching is not a matter of individual interpretation because it is based on Scripture and is of the Holy Spirit.

The other passage like 2 Peter 1:21 is, of course, 2 Timothy 3:14–17. Here Paul urges Timothy to continue in the things that he has learned and received in faith since his childhood. That "sincere faith" first dwelled in his grandmother Lois and his mother, Eunice, and now in him (2 Tim. 1:5). By the way, this is no small detail, especially coming from a writer who speaks of "weak women" who "never arrive at a knowledge of the truth" (2 Tim. 3:6–7 RSV) and who rejects the teaching office of these women (1 Tim. 2:11–12). That Timothy learned his faith from women is signifi- cant, but the important thing to point out here is the role of remembrance: "Continue in what you have learned and firmly believed" (2 Tim. 3:14 RSV). Timothy has been instructed from childhood in the sacred writings (*hiera grammata*) that have the power (*ta dynamena*) to make wise for salvation through faith in Jesus Christ. The writer goes on to say that Scripture is "of the spirit of God" (*theopneustos,* often translated "inspired"), profitable "for teaching, for reproof, for correction, and for everyone who believes in train- ing in righteousness, that God may be proficient, equipped for every good work" (2 Tim. 3:16–17 NRSV). Not only does Scripture pertain to recollec- tion; it is also the object of expectation, and the content of the recollection and of the expectation is the same. The clauses before and after the phrase about Scripture being inspired of God are parallel: the Scriptures are able (*dynamena*) to instruct us for salvation through faith in Jesus Christ (v. 15) and are profitable (*ōphelimos*) for correction and training in righteousness. The first clause refers to Scripture's past use in Timothy's life, and the sec- ond to its present and future use. The clauses are bridged by the phrase "All scripture is inspired by God" (*pasa graphē theopneustos,* 2 Tim. 3:16 RSV). The inspiration of Scripture thus has to do with this backward and forward effect, receiving faith and passing it on.

This backward and forward effect of Scripture is thus dependent upon the work of the Holy Spirit. In addition, to affirm with the creed that "the Holy Spirit spoke through the prophets" is to accept the assumption that Scripture as Old and New Testaments has an overall unity and therefore a unified content or goal. Scripture is not a series of random statements and signs collected by the winners of history; it is a coherent whole bearing a single Truth, namely the Triune God. We see this in Athanasius's discus- sion of the scope (*skopos*) of Scripture.[1]

According to T. F. Torrance, the term *skopos* was used to refer to the goal and turning-post in the race course and also to the bounds of the course.[2] When Athanasius uses the term *skopos*, he therefore means both the goal or intent of Scripture as well as its bounds or content.

> *Skopos* thus can be used in a wide sense to describe the general perspective or frame of reference within which the Scriptures are rightly to be interpreted *(kata skopon),* and in a deeper sense to denote the basic pattern of meaning that is perceived when the interpreter not only looks at the written words but looks through them at the objective centre of reference beyond *pros skopos*.[3]

With either meaning, we can see that speaking of the *skopos* of Scripture assumes an objective reality not entirely identifiable with the text itself but related to it and borne by it. So Athanasius says,

> Now this scope and character of Holy Scripture, as we have often said, is twofold in its announcement about the Savior namely, that he was eternally God and is the Son, as the Word and Radiance and Wisdom of the Father, and afterwards for our sake took flesh of the Virgin Mary, the bearer of God, and became man. And this is what is signified throughout all inspired Scripture, as the Lord himself has said, "Search the Scriptures, for they are they which testify of me."[4]

Frances Young has argued that more central than *skopos* to Athanasius's biblical interpretation is his use of the concept *dianoia*, the "mind" of Scripture.[5] In defending the use of theological but nonbiblical terms such as *homoousios*, Athanasius argues that even if the term does not appear in Scripture, it still expresses the mind (*dianoia*), or meaning, of Scripture.[6]

> Wherefore, if a person is ready to learn, let him know that even if the terms are not found as such in the Scriptures, nevertheless, as has been said already, they derive their meaning (*dianoian*) from the Scriptures, and by expressing it communicate it to those who have their hearing unimpaired for divine experience. This is what you are to consider (*skopein*) and what the uninstructed are to give ear to.[7]

This may mean that appropriate divine meaning may not be identical with literal or lexical human meaning. According to Young, Athanasius's exegesis is neither literal, nor typological, nor allegorical. Rather it is deductive. The deductive process involves attention to the meaning of words, their particular biblical sense, the syntax and the context of the text in question, . . . but the overriding principle concerns the discovery of a proper way of reading . . . which accords with both the unitive mind of scripture and the appropriate conception of the one God. The irony is that that concern demands innovative exegesis.[8]

One can see that under the concepts both of the *skopos* and of the mind of Scripture lies the hermeneutical use of what is alternately called the rule of faith or the rule of truth. The rule of faith was the pre-creedal, creedlike material outlining the basic points or narrative moments of the Christian faith. One example of the rule of faith can be found in Justin Martyr's *Apology*, in which he links the Holy Spirit with the prophets:

> Over him who has elected to be reborn and has repented of his sins the name of the Father and the Lord God of the universe is named, the officiant who leads the candidate to the water using this, and only this, description of God . . . Moreover, it is in the name of Jesus Christ, Who was crucified under Pontius Pilate, and in the name of the Holy Spirit, Who through the prophets announced beforehand the things relating to Jesus, that the man who is enlightened is washed.[9]

Irenaeus also includes this linking of the Holy Spirit with the prophets, interestingly enough at one point inserting this material under both the second and the third articles. In the material under the second article he even includes the linking of the prophets with the Father, thus including the first article:

> This then is the order of the rule of our faith, and the foundation of the building, and the stability of our conversation: God the Father, not material, invisible; one God, the creator of all things: this is the first point of our faith. The second point is this: the Word of God, Son of God, Christ Jesus our Lord, Who was manifested to the prophets according to the form of their prophesying and according to the method of the dispensation of the Father: through Whom (i.e., the Word) all things were made; Who also at the end of the times, to complete and gather up all things, was made man among men, visible and tangible, in order to abolish death and show forth life and produce a community of union between God and man. And the third point is this: the Holy Spirit, through Whom the prophets prophesied, and the Fathers learned the things of God, and the righteous were led into the way of righ-

teousness; and Who in the end of the times was poured out in a new way upon mankind in all the earth, renewing man unto God.[10]

This version of the third article makes especially clear the uniting of the witnesses of the Old and New Testaments, so important even from the earliest times, as is evident throughout the New Testament (see Romans 9–11) and in post–New Testament writings such as those of Polycarp, who summons the Philadelphians to accept as their standard Christ with "the apostles who preached the gospel to us and the prophets who announced our Lord's coming in advance."[11]

We see here how one of the theological functions of the rule of faith is to hold together theologically the confession of God the Creator and Jesus Christ, and analogously in hermeneutical terms, the old and new covenants.[12] Understood to be derived from Scripture, the rule of faith is reapplied to Scripture in interpretation, much as the *skopos* or *dianoia* was understood to be a hermeneutical guide. The rule of faith functions as an outer limit that places constraints on what can be argued as a legitimate reading, whether such a reading is literal in the human or lexical sense or not. The rule of faith is the "real content of revelation, the fundamental tenor of the one message of scripture,"[13] such that to interpret Scripture according to this rule is to let it interpret itself (*scriptura sui interpres est*).

Even while the rule of faith, the hermeneutical application of which is indicated by the phrase "he spoke through the prophets," acts to unite Creator God and Jesus Christ, old and new covenants, it does not determine the interpretation of Scripture. Likewise, asserting the inspiration of Scripture does not define either the method or the content of the interpretation given. "The framework of interpretation, then, does not so much solve the problem of what Scripture means as supply the *context* in which the quest for that meaning may take place."[14] The context in which meaning is to be sought is specifically the community that confesses the Triune God, the community that unites in worship around the old, old story told in the rule of faith. But this does not mean that we should set up the church as that arbiter of Scripture, merely as the context of its interpretation. Barth had a striking image for this: "Christians have to see themselves standing as it were between two choirs singing antiphonally—the apostles on one side and the prophets on the other."[15] This is a profound understanding of our place. We are not to understand ourselves as though after the apostles, even though obviously they preceded us chronologically. They who testified to Jesus in the law and and prophets and writings are on one side, and they who experienced the Lord Jesus in the flesh are on the other. We are all one choir, all singing antiphonally, but we sing as led by them, neither leading them nor drowning them out, not changing their song.

This brings us to the future element implied by the phrase "he spoke through the prophets." Not only does it unite the Old and New Testaments and unite us with those who came before us, but it also binds us to the hope of the final redemption. Our faith is not a narrative per se, but it does have narrative elements. It presupposes a setting (the created order and its fallen state), a theme (redemption through Christ), a plot (Israel's wanderings, Christ's deeds) and a resolution (the eschatological hope).[16] The claim that the Holy Spirit spoke through the prophets is followed in the creed by material on the church, that is, the present, and is then followed by the promise of the resurrection of the dead and the life of the world to come. This puts our faith into a very real dimension. This is no cleverly devised myth (2 Peter 1:16) but a remembrance of God's deeds in the past that promise us a very concrete future of life with God.

Now as we move into the future, we need ask the thorny question of where and through whom the Holy Spirit might be speaking today. After all, "we have the prophetic word made more sure" (2 Peter 1:19 RSV). Yes, but Jesus said, "You search the scriptures, because you think that in them you have eternal life; and it is they that bear witness to me; yet you refuse to come to me that you may have life" (John 5:39–40 RSV). In other words, there may easily be an interpretation of Scripture that neglects the very thing Scripture bears: the truth of Christ. The old hymn is profound here:

> How firm a foundation, ye saints of the Lord,
> Is laid for your faith in God's excellent word!
> What more can he say than to you he hath said
> To you who for refuge to Jesus have fled?

What more indeed? The Holy Spirit speaks today, yes, but never in contradiction with or dissonance to Scripture. An example of a contrary claim in the present time is that of the Mormons. My Mormon students tried to tell me that I just did not want to believe that Jesus came and spoke to ancient Native Americans. I firmly said I had no trouble believing that could be possible, because Jesus can do whatever he pleases, but that he never would have taught the Native Americans that they would all be gods of their own planets. Unlike the White Man, God does not speak with forked tongue.

How do we then discern where the Holy Spirit is speaking today? The rule of faith is to be our guide here. As I have pointed out elsewhere,[17] the rule demands an adequate theological relating of the two covenants such that the old covenant is made clear in the new and the new lies hidden in the old (to use the traditional Augustinian formulation). This is why we can't run around claiming that we will become gods of our own planets: not just because it sounds nutty, but because it doesn't lie hidden in the old covenant any way you turn it around. Again, according to the rule, we need to have a proper understanding of law. As Christians, do we obey the law? Remember, Jesus made all foods clean, ate with Gentiles, and broke the Sabbath, yet there are specific commandments we are to keep, such as refraining from idolatry and magic and adultery, to name just a few, and we are to "fulfill the law of Christ" (Gal. 6:2). The Holy Spirit will not speak against the law of Christ. The rule of faith requires that whatever we claim to be "of the Spirit" must account for the unity and faithfulness of God with Israel and with those of the New Covenant. Are we talking about the same God? This is the problem Paul wrestles with in Romans 9–11. We will have our own Romans 9–11s. We may feel that we have already had more than our share of theological controversy in which we are called on to give account for the unity of God. We must not be discouraged. By following the rule of faith, we can be sure that God's Word will be a lamp unto our feet and a light unto our path. God's Word will be sweeter than honey, and through its precepts will we grow in understanding. It will be the very stability of our conversation and the prophetic Word made more sure.

12

I Believe in One Holy, Catholic, and Apostolic Church

William J. Abraham

Contemporary Christians have come to look upon the church in a wide variety of ways. Four images come to mind as competing snapshots of what the church is.

Some see the church as a country club. It is a nice place to visit regularly. It has a loyal band of officers, on occasion it does laudable charitable work, it provides a network for meeting important people in the community, it has beautiful facilities in which to meet, and sometimes the music is excellent.

Others see the church as a kind of Noah's ark. The world outside is stormy and difficult, and the church is a place to which we can escape for shelter. It provides a protected space to shield us from the harsh realities of the world. When the church itself becomes harsh and corrupt, we remind ourselves of the aphorism: "We can endure the smells inside the church because we know the floods outside are always worse." So we grin and bear it.

Yet others see the church as a waterbed, a warm, fuzzy, therapeutic community that provides rest and acts as a support group. It is not a place of service or challenge; it is a place to relax, unwind, and lie down and receive psychic and spiritual massage.

Still others see the church as a loose confederation of states. In the political arena each state has its laws, principles, customs, ethos, ethnic makeup,

and so on. The task of leadership is to foster tolerance, hold the ring in disputes, and work for as pluralistic and inclusive a community as possible. The
church holds to as much of past tradition as is apt and feasible, and its goal
is to accommodate as much diversity as is manageable within a minimalist
vision of unity.

Now, to be sure, these images are overdrawn, and they need not be taken
in a wholly negative manner. Moreover, even in recent centuries, much more
positive images have surfaced, as we can see in the naming of new Christian communities or denominations. Consider, for example, the church as
the Society of Friends. This is a very positive spin on the church as country club. Or consider the church as the Salvation Army. This is a sharp contrast to the church as Noah's ark or even the church as the ark of salvation.
Or consider the church as the Vineyard of the Lord. In this case we envisage the church as an orchard bearing grapes to be made into wine to enliven
our spirits. This is close to the therapeutic image of a waterbed, but one in
which the image is bent in a positive direction.

I began this way for two reasons. First, it illustrates a useful and long-
established way to focus our thinking about the church. It is very fitting and
relatively easy to think in terms of images of the church. This is extremely
popular in the biblical traditions, and we will return to these later. A crucial
issue here is where we locate the images of the church in the bigger picture.
To what do these images apply? What is the subject of which they are the
predicate? It is at this juncture that the creedal phrase "I believe in One
Holy, Catholic, and Apostolic Church" becomes pivotal.

Second, the images employed here are intended to correct what is endemic
in much thinking about the church, namely a tendency to idealize. Ecclesiology is one area in theology where there is enormous temptation to think
in abstract and utterly unrealistic terms. We find it difficult to think historically, concretely, and realistically.

This is unfortunate because many people, both laity and clergy, are deeply
alienated from and frustrated by the church. Therefore, realism is imperative if a deep theology of the church is to be believed and practiced. In the
case of the creed's article on the church, we are dealing with our everyday
life and work over a long span of years. If we have only a textbook theology
of the church, we are setting ourselves up for disillusionment.

Our difficulty in thinking concretely is unfortunate, also because if we
do not have a relatively firm theological conception of the church, we will
inevitably fall into sub-Christian conceptions of the church that adversely
affect our ministry and the ministry of the whole people of God. Many sim-

ply think of the church as a collection of political caucuses to be manipulated and mastered; or a vast, unfriendly bureaucracy organized by bishops and superintendents; or a business with its own CEO, trade unions, perks, and pension funds. If we do not have a proper theological vision of the church, then other visions, expressed informally in images borrowed from hither and yon, will rush in to fill the vacuum and rule the day.

We need a theological vision of the church that does three things. It allows us to acknowledge reality as we find it empirically in the church as it is and as we can predict it will be in the future. It provides a narrative of the divisions and chaos in the history of the church. And it acts as a norm that can deepen our experience, call us to accountability, and evoke a straining toward renewal and revitalization at a crucial junction in our history.

Finding and articulating such a vision is a very tall order. My attempt in this regard will be sketchy and tentative. I will develop my remarks first by insisting that the arrival of the church is the outcome of the presence of the kingdom of God in history. To put this in different terms, the church is a gift of the Holy Spirit in time and space. With that in place, I will briefly unpack what is at stake in confessing that the church is one, holy, catholic, and apostolic. I will end by returning very briefly to the various images of the church, tying my conception of these to my reading of the church depicted in the creed.

The Church and the Kingdom of God

Alfred Loisy provides a useful point of entry to our topic. He says, "Jesus foretold the kingdom and it was the church that came."[1] The great merit of this aphorism is that it insists on a clear distinction between the kingdom and the church. Its negative side is that it is an expression at best of disappointment, at worst of cynicism.

The church is not the rule or reign of God, but it is surely intimately connected to the rule of God. Just how this is to be worked out is a delicate theological issue. My own approach to it requires a radical historical orientation that attempts imaginatively to enter and relive the history of the church in the first millennium.

The church was a tangible and formidable historical reality before there was any formal reflection on ecclesiology. No formal definition had yet been agreed ecumenically. There was no canonical definition. The creed provided not a description per se, but a promise veiled as a description.

What we had initially was a very specific community rooted in Jerusalem, which soon spread across the ancient Mediterranean world. It was not just a collection of voluntary societies, nor was it a network of religious communities loosely banded together for support. It was a mysterious, diverse, historical reality held together in extraordinary unity. The reality was so self-evident that it did not need to be defined. Christians did not need to theorize formally and grandly about the Christian community because they already knew the church from firsthand experience: in catechesis, baptism, and Eucharist they had came to participate in this rocklike, diverse, mysterious reality.

The church held together over time, and it gradually ordered its life over the centuries. That it held together for so long is absolutely amazing. This comes home to us when we contrast it with the history of Methodism over two hundred years. It spread in an extraordinary way until it became the largest Protestant denomination in North America in the nineteenth century. Yet consider how it has splintered and broken into dozens of pieces, divided now into caucuses and interest groups galore; as Albert Outler used to quip: "United Methodists are as united as Free Methodists are free."

The angle of vision here is important. There was a church before there was a canon of Scripture, before there were creeds, before there were agreed ecclesiastical structures. There was from the beginning a discernible people with a recognizable historical narrative. This was an earthy, noisy, imperfect community; the last thing I want to do is idealize it. The warts show through in the traditions for all to see. Yet it has recognizable boundaries, and it can be seen to have grown and spread, proving as it expanded to be an enormous threat to the religious and political establishment of the day. If I had been a provincial Roman governor in the first or second century, I would not have been able to make heads or tails of these people.

What then brought the church into existence? It was not Jesus and the twelve apostles, although the nucleus was already there with them. Nor was it even the death and resurrection of Jesus per se. These, to be sure, were pivotal, but even after these events the earliest form of the church was simply that of a minor, insignificant society within Judaism.

What brought the church into existence was the action of the Holy Spirit. The church was first and foremost a charismatic community, a community created, founded, and guided by the Holy Spirit. Pentecost was the constitutive and originating womb of the church. I am presupposing here that the Holy Spirit is a dynamic personal agent, as real as Jesus, who acted decisively and specifically at the feast of Pentecost in Jerusalem. Pentecost was not just an ecclesiastical seminar where the penny dropped about Jesus and his relation to God. It was not just a special representation of grace in the early community that emanates from Jesus. It was a datable, memorable event in history. It was a decisive new encounter with God in the action of the Holy Spirit that was a milestone in the history of the cosmos.

To be sure, Pentecost is presented relatively casually in the literature. Yet Pentecost is more than a moment in the history of religious archeology. It is the unfolding of a new, dynamic, personal reality, so much so that the disciples and others had to wait for the appearance of this reality. Once the Holy Spirit had come decisively, there was now a new actuality that is always existentially available. This helps explain the extraordinary confidence of the early Christians as a distinct group.

These people did not even have a name for themselves. *Christian* came as a nickname. Some of them called themselves "The People of the Way." They got along without a canon of Scripture as we know it today, without a creed, and without a formal identity because they could and did trust the Holy Spirit to lead them. The Holy Spirit gave them a security, a freedom, a confidence, even a sure-footedness that nothing else can give. This is as true today as it was on and after the day of Pentecost. The Holy Spirit is the primary and fundamental horizon within which the church comes into existence. This good and life-giving Holy Spirit cannot be collapsed or reduced into a prosaic structure or a network of religious experiences.

The presence and action of the Holy Spirit provides the clue to solving the riddle of the relation between the church and the kingdom of God. Where the Holy Spirit reigns or rules, there God rules, there is the kingdom of God. Where the kingdom comes, there is the creation of a new community, the community of the Holy Spirit. Constitutive of the activity of the Holy Spirit is the creation of the church. So constitutive of the coming of the kingdom is the creation of new people; within the kingdom of God the Holy Spirit creates a people. The rule of God subsists in but is not reducible to the life and work of the church. The church is a glorious treasure contained in the rule of God in history.

There is another corollary to be noted and explicated. The Holy Spirit does not work in a historical vacuum; nor is the activity of the Holy Spirit generic, abstract, and unspecified. These two points are intimately connected. Consider the intimate connection between the life and work of Jesus and the activity of the Holy Spirit. It was the action of the Holy Spirit that enabled Jesus to do what he did in his mighty acts of redemption and salvation. When this was achieved once and for all, part of the ongoing work of the Holy Spirit is to bear witness to Jesus. Hence a community created by the Holy Spirit is one that will see who Jesus is and give him his rightful place as Lord and Head of the church. A truly charismatic community will acknowledge, welcome, and celebrate the Lordship of Jesus Christ, risen and coming again. This is a trademark of the activity of the Holy Spirit.

In creating, the Holy Spirit bypasses neither Jesus nor the apostles whom he has trained and taught. The Holy Spirit acts at Pentecost in fulfillment of the promise to the disciples. The continuity between the work of Jesus and the activity of the early church is to be located in the ongoing action of the Holy Spirit. So the Holy Spirit gathers up what has already been done in Jesus Christ and carries it over into a new day in the history of the people of God. The Holy Spirit works in and through the apostles and other disciples already gathered around Jesus.

This is why I need now to qualify my earlier remarks about the emergence of the church, when I spoke of how surprising it is to see it begin without a canon of Scripture as we know it today, and without a creed or formally defined structure. I do not want to give the impression that the church came as a bolt from the blue, or that it was a body without leadership, without oversight, and without tradition. From the outset the church gathered as a group around the apostles and other disciples of Jesus, including his brothers and his mother. These were real live people who had customs, memories, insight, prejudices, and everything else a creature of history possesses. These, that is, Jesus and those first disciples, are necessary conditions for the emergence of the church. If there had been no Jesus and no apostles, there would not have been a church. However, these were not sufficient conditions. The Holy Spirit works in and through them to create the church. This is the crux of the issue theologically.

Let me summarize the matter thus far: Jesus actualized the kingdom in his life and ministry; the kingdom continues in the mighty acts of the Holy Spirit since Pentecost; one of the mighty acts is the arrival of the church; the mighty act of forming the church was carried out not apart from but through the apostles in the earthy, contingent realities of the first century.

One Holy, Catholic, and Apostolic Church

We are now ready to tackle directly the creed's article on the church: "I believe in one holy, catholic, and apostolic church."

This is not a definition but a verbal confession or witness. It is an attempt to describe four crucial aspects of a living historical reality, that concrete network of communities that emanated from Jesus and the apostles in history. Both the noun and the adjectives are crucial. The church is the *ekklēsia*, meaning an assembly of the sovereign people in a city, a general congregation of all regular citizens. Hence *church* in secular language denotes both the people and the city. But it carries Hebrew overtones, for it translates also the Hebrew term (*qahal*) for the chosen people, the people of God construed as a whole. The church is the true Israel, the people of God, a new people grafted together by God into "a chosen race, a royal priesthood, a holy nation, God's own people" (1 Peter 2:9 NRSV).

This community is not perfect; there is not a hint of ecclesial utopianism here. There is no claim to infallibility, although I would argue that we can and should expect the Holy Spirit to provide reliable access in the canonical heritage of the church to all that God intended for his people, including those truths essential for their spiritual and moral welfare. Rather, it is *holy:* it is set apart, called out to be different to serve the purposes of God. It is *catholic:* it operates according to the sense and judgment of the whole and is not parochial or partial in its commitments. It is *apostolic:* it stems from the apostles. It is not a departure from the apostles even though it grows, develops, and changes. Moreover, it shares the faith of the apostles and carries out their missionary work. Then, finally, there is *one* church. There are not many churches or denominations or chosen peoples; there is one people that has descended in succession from the apostles. Once a group puts itself outside that, it becomes a sect. Either it then finds an ecclesiology that will legitimize it as a sect—perhaps this is the route of denominationalism in the modern period—or it has to face up to historical ecumenical reality and accept that it may have been unknowingly and unintentionally cut off from the historic succession of the apostles.

What I am reaching for here is the idea of a historical people with definite institutional continuity and history from one generation to the next. I am convinced this is how the clause in the creed is to be construed. It cannot be construed in the ethereal, abstract, idealistic sense in which it is construed in much modern Protestantism. It is not the company of all true believers, whether known only to God as the elect or partially known to human subjects; it is a mixed bag of wheat and tares, of good, bad, and indifferent. Nor is it the invisible church; it is a visible body that can trace its lineage more or less in a succession of bishops across the centuries. Nor am I happy with the claim that the visible church of Christ is a congregation of faithful people in which the pure word of God is preached and the sacraments duly administered according to Christ's ordinance. The one holy, catholic, and apostolic church is that community that has existed as one people since the days of the apostles, that hammered out a shared canonical heritage, that designated bishops sworn to uphold its treasures across the generations, and that gathered week in and week out to celebrate the resurrection in its Eucharist. It is not simply a network of congregations functioning according to some preferred ideal.

What is unresolved here is where and how to relate the historical continuity of this body to the Christian communities of the medieval and modern world. The gaping difficulties that meet anyone who takes my preceding point seriously are obvious: Where is this church now? What do we make of those communities created by the Holy Spirit outside its boundaries? I can only speak telegraphically at this point. Two points need to be made immediately.

First, whatever the merits of the notion of the invisible church, or of the elect, or of the body of true believers, or of visible congregations rightly ordered with word, sacrament, and discipline, none of these can stand as the referent for the body identified as one, holy, catholic, and apostolic. The referent, in my view, is a concrete historical body, not some platonic ideal or some pious or theological will-o'-the-wisp substitute. What, then, is this referent? We must acknowledge, of course, the contested claims of Rome, the churches of the East, and the Anglican Church to be the true bearers of continuity with the relatively undivided church of the first millennium. If we must resolve this dispute, the contest, in my judgment, goes to the East. Aleksei, despite the polemical edge to his writings, got it exactly right.[2] The West broke the collegiality of the church by going its own way, especially in the disastrous addition of the *filioque* clause to the creed.[3] In time, to justify itself, the West sold its soul to a vast and extraordinary epistemological captivity that remains intact in the current shift from modernism to postmodernism. Nowhere is this captivity more visible than in the reduction of the canonical heritage of the church to Scripture and in the transformation of the Scriptures away from a magnificent means of grace into a criterion of truth, warrant, justification, and knowledge.[4] Whatever we make of this claim, the fountainhead of unity stands with Constantinople and the East.

Second, we cannot dechristianize those communities that have been created by the Holy Spirit either in the wake of the division between East and West or in the wake of the Protestant Reformation or more recently in the wake of the extraordinary growth of Pentecostalism. The old claim that all we have here is heresy or mere enthusiasm will not stand the light of historical or theological scrutiny. Nor will it do to claim that we know where the church is but that we do not know where it is not, as if we can be agnostic about the work of the Holy Spirit in the rest of the Protestant underworld. We must reckon with the genuine working of the Holy Spirit wherever we find it, and such working involves not just individual conversions but also the creation of radically diverse communities.

The challenge now is this: How might we hold these two convictions in place while we search for the visible unity of all Christians? Again, I can write only telegraphically. This time I have three points.

First, every effort needs to be made on all sides to recover and reappropriate the full canonical heritage of the church of the first millennium before the split between East and West. Paradoxically, in this process the East may be provoked to make full use of its own canonical traditions; it may rediscover the significance of its treasures by observing the plundering of its resources by friendly aliens in the West.

Second, we must find a way to relativize our varied epistemological commitments. The biggest challenge here will be our handling of *sola scriptura* and papal infallibility. Neither of these claims should be canonical for the whole church, no more so than empiricism, rationalism, fideism, postmodernism, or the host of other proposals that crop up in epistemology. These, unlike the content of the creed, are not canonical. They are efforts to secure an epistemology for Christian truth claims that are radically secondary in the economy of the church. This is in no way a call to be diffident about such matters; in their time and place they are interesting and even important. They should not, however, be canonical; making them canonical has been one of the chief sources of division among Christians.[5]

Third, we must reckon with the real possibility of divine judgment on all of us for our sins. Maybe our situation is analogous to Israel after the monarchy when God handed his people over to the full consequences of their rebellion.[6] God maintained his faithfulness to the covenant despite the lust for monarchy; indeed, God continued to work in and through the flawed institutions of his people. He continued his ministry of mercy and healing to the world despite rebellion and sin. There is here an analogy for understanding God's relation to the divisions among Christians. While maintaining continuity in history and preserving the canonical treasures of the church, God has scattered his people and driven them into exile so they may come to terms with their sin. While remaining faithful to his covenant and continuing to pour out his Holy Spirit, God has withdrawn the fullness of his blessing, waiting patiently until we repent of our manifold sins and disorders.

If there is any merit in this last possibility, then we can surely see our way forward, for the future lies in a fresh Pentecost in the life of the children of God. If the one holy, catholic, and apostolic church is the fruit of the working of the Holy Spirit, then it is here in the working of the Holy Spirit that we must relocate ourselves afresh today. Applying this insight to the references in the creed (one, holy, catholic, apostolic), these descriptions are more normative descriptions than they are simply straight historical descriptions. They pick out features of the church as seen by insiders who captured crucial features of their life that they were determined to maintain. They are promises of what the church can be in the power of the Holy Spirit. Consequently, we may not really know the fullness of the marks of the church anew until we all repent and seek the fullness of the presence of the Holy Spirit. In our current Christian communities, scattered near or far from the original fountain, we only partially know the full treasures the Holy Spirit has in store for us. These lie in the future. The Holy Spirit may yet gather up her scattered treasures and join them all in one visible community that stands in historical continuity with the church of the apostles.

Construing the church as a community brought into being by the Holy Spirit undercuts all forms of triumphalism and arrogance. We possess nothing we have not received, and the preservation of what we have received must ever be an act of gratitude rather than a weapon to discredit the work of the Holy Spirit in others or a mechanism to exalt ourselves. This is pivotal in securing the genuine freedom of the Holy Spirit and in fostering a minimum of ecclesial civility.

Back to the Future and the Many of the Images of the Church

As we make this journey into the fullness of the life of the church, we can once again employ the rich imagery the New Testament applies to the church. Think of five of the many images available in the New Testament. There is the image of the church as the body of Christ. The image of the church as the branches of the Vine. The image of the church as the holy city. The image of the church as a royal priesthood. The image of the church as the light of the world. How shall we read these metaphorical descriptions of the church? Like the normative adjectives given in the creed, they should be read as veiled promises. What is at issue is not that we might take them literally. The greater danger is that we will take them flat-footedly and apply them to ourselves as we are and thus reduce them to what we find in our communities. What these images do is evoke a picture of what we can be when we allow the Holy Spirit to act fully among us. They display features of the church as it is meant to be in the power of the Holy Spirit. Hence they are an amazing treasury of hope and a charter of new creation. That we fall short of such descriptions is to be expected, but this is no warrant for despair, depression, or pessimism about the church. These images should summon us to a deeper repentance and to a firmer reliance on the work of the Holy Spirit.

So we do not give up if our church is now a country club, a Noah's ark, or a giant waterbed. These were not what it is meant to be or what it is called to be. We are called and empowered to be the salt of the earth, a letter from Christ, the vineyard of the Lord, the bride of Christ, exiles in a foreign land, the Israel of God, the holy temple in which the living God dwells, a remnant, chosen by grace, the slaves of Christ, a light to the world, a royal priesthood, the holy city, the branches of the true vine, and the very body of Christ. Each of these metaphors provides a glimpse of the true greatness God has in store for the church today.

13

I Acknowledge One Baptism
for the Forgiveness of Sins

Susan K. Wood

Reflection on the line, "I acknowledge one baptism for the for-giveness of sins" in an ecumenical context invites reflection on three questions. First, how can we adjudicate between those Christians who practice believer baptism and require a conscious, explicit, adult profession of faith for the mutual recognition of baptism and those other Christians who practice infant baptism? Second, how can we profess belief in one baptism in an environment of a divided Christianity? Third, how can we articulate the relationship between baptism and the forgiveness of sins?

"I Believe"

The acknowledgment of one baptism for the forgiveness of sins occurs within a creedal statement of belief. Who does the "I" refer to in the creedal confession "I believe"? What kind of faith is required for baptism? An area for exploration in an ecumenical context is not the necessity of faith for the reception of baptism, but the relative emphasis on individual faith versus the faith of the church in our respective traditions. The Nicene-Constantinopolitan Creed is a doxological prayer recited in the liturgy. The baptism it acknowledges is also liturgical prayer. Liturgical prayer is the public, official prayer of the church, not the prayer of a private individual. In the profession of faith within liturgical prayer, the "I" of "I believe" refers not only to the individual but to the whole church professing its belief.[1]

In the opposite way of viewing this, an individual comes to personal faith, confessing Jesus Christ as Lord and Savior, and then unites with other Christians for support in that personal affirmation of faith. The first reality, communal faith, is the paradigm for infant baptism. The second, individual adult faith, is the paradigm for adult believer baptism. Both practices reveal important aspects of baptism and baptismal faith in the life of the church.

Since the restoration of the catechumenate, the baptism of adult believers at the Easter vigil service is normative for our understanding of the theology of baptism. Here *normative* does not mean the statistically most frequent practice, but the practice that best expresses the theology of baptism. This understanding of baptism presupposes a sequence and pattern within Christian initiation, including formation in the faith or conversion, baptism in water in the name of the Triune God, postbaptismal chrismation in the sacrament of confirmation, participation in the public prayer of the church (especially through admission to the Eucharist), and finally, life in the Christian community.[2] This sequence, simplified as formation in faith, baptism in water, and participation in the life of the community, common to many Christian communities, essentially follows the pattern of Acts 2:41–42: "So those who welcomed his [Peter's] message were baptized, and that day about three thousand persons were added. They devoted themselves to the apostles' teaching and fellowship, the breaking of bread and the prayers" (NRSV).

The emphasis on conversion and mature faith as the norm of our theology of baptism brings Roman Catholicism closer to those communions that practice believer baptism even while the majority of Roman Catholics continue to be baptized as infants. Adult baptism is normative because of the faith engaged and also because the rite involves a conversion of life not experienced by an infant.

However, the long tradition of infant baptism in many Christian communions also gives us insight into baptismal faith. From earliest times, the Roman Catholic Church has baptized infants as well as adults. In the case of infant baptism, there is faith by proxy—the faith of parents, godparents, and the Christian community. Children "are baptized in the faith of the Church, a faith proclaimed for them by their parents and godparents, who represent both the local Church and the whole society of saints and believers."[3]

The primary difference between those communities that baptize infants and those that practice believer baptism is not whether faith is present or not—faith is required for the reception of all the sacraments—but rather where faith is located. Baptists and other groups issuing from the Anabaptist arm of the Reformation require a personal profession of faith on the part of the person who is baptized. In the Roman Catholic tradition, as in many other Christian traditions, faith is expressed by proxy by the godparents and the parents. In other words, the faith is located first in the Christian community, which then initiates the child into the community of faith. The child is thus welcomed into the faith of the community.

In the rite of baptism, after the profession of faith by the adult being baptized or the proxy profession of faith by the godparents, the celebrant and the congregation then given their assent to the profession of faith in these words or in some other way in which the community can express its faith:

> This is our faith. This is the faith of the Church. We are proud to profess it, in Christ Jesus our Lord. Amen.

Here there is a mutual recognition of faith between the faith community and the individual being received into that community.

The community of faith is where the gospel is proclaimed and where a person is drawn to belief through hearing. Henri de Lubac, in his study of the Apostles' Creed, states that the "I" of the "I believe" is the Christian community before it is the individual.[4] There is a complex dynamic between the faith brought to the sacrament by an individual and the faith of the community that invites, supports, and sustains that faith. Faith is first of all communal faith, and an individual participates in that larger communal reality. In this way of thinking, the community of faith precedes the individual believer.

Nevertheless, this faith must be appropriated and personally confessed by that individual at some point. Infant baptism requires a postbaptismal catechesis in the faith. In this process, individual faith matures and grows more deeply in conformity with the faith of the community at the same time that it becomes part of the identity of the believer who professes it. Just as the Rite of Christian Initiation for Adults (RCIA) is not merely instruction in the faith but also Christian formation in the patterns and practices of becoming a Christian, so too postbaptismal catechesis is not simply catechetical instruction but also ongoing formation. Becoming a Christian is a lifelong process and presupposes a vital local community of faith capable of this task.

Roman Catholicism emphasizes the need for a community of believers, for "it is only within the faith of the Church that each of the faithful can believe." The church does not require a perfect and mature faith for baptism, but "a beginning that is called to develop." The rite asks of a catechumen or godparent: "What do you ask of God's Church?" The response is "Faith!"[5] The presupposition is that the church's faith precedes that of the catechumen, who is invited to adhere to it.[6] The sacraments in the Roman Catholic Church presuppose faith and also nourish, strengthen, and express it.[7]

Martin Luther conceded a measure of causal efficacy of the sacraments, and considered them to have salutary value insofar as they aroused or strengthened faith.[8] He also supported infant baptism as illustrative of the gratuity of grace. However, there exists in Reformation thought a suspicion of, if not a rejection of, mediating authority in favor of the direct, existential, intensely personal experience of faith. This raises a number of questions. Does this represent a certain tension in the Reformation worldview between the ecclesial practice of baptism inherited from its Catholic origins and Luther's view of faith acquired in his adult experience of reading Romans 4:4–6? This tension may reflect the fact that the Roman Catholic theology of justification originates in the experience of baptism while the forensic model of the Reformation finds its origin in the sacrament of penance, hence the forensic and declaratory nature of justification. This difference represents one of the major asymmetries in the approaches to justification on the part of Roman Catholics and those of groups issuing from the Reformation. Finally, is the Anabaptist focus on believer baptism what results when an exclusively forensic model is taken to its logical conclusion?

This reflection on baptismal faith reveals its ecclesial foundations. Baptismal faith is not individualistic, but oriented to the Christian community. The faith of the Christian community in some sense precedes the faith of an individual and invites that person's participation.

"One Baptism"

Confession in one baptism has a biblical basis in Ephesians 4:4–6: "There is one body and one Spirit, just as you were called to the one hope of your calling, one Lord, one faith, one baptism, one God and Father of all, who is above all and through all and in all" (NRSV). The unity of baptism is grounded not in the unity of churches, but in the one Lord in whom all are baptized. Through the one baptism all Christians are initiated into the death and resurrection of Jesus Christ, the saving event that occurred once and for all. They are anointed in the one Spirit. The forgiveness of sin, which will be discussed in more detail in the third section of this chapter, occurs through the self-gift of Jesus and reception of the Holy Spirit. Through baptism we are incorporated into that saving event. This association is also alluded to in Ephesians, which says that Christ gave himself up for the church "in order to make her holy by cleansing her with the washing of water by the word" (5:25–26 NRSV).

One baptism, then, is not the result of ecumenical efforts for Christian unity. We will not achieve one baptism when we will have achieved mutual recognition of one another's baptisms. Rather, there is now only one baptism because there is but one Lord and one saving event of his death and resurrection. Our burden is to account for our disunity rather than to account for our unity. Or to turn this in another way, unity is not something to be achieved by the churches, but a gift to be received.

The historical context for the confession of "one baptism" in the Creed of Constantinople was probably a reaffirmation of the church's ban on rebaptizing heretics.[9] The Donatists were in the practice of rebaptizing everyone who was not baptized by one of their own ministers. In recent times many Christian communities have been more mindful of this ancient practice. For instance, the 1982 Faith and Order document *Baptism, Eucharist and Ministry* states that "Baptism is an unrepeatable act. Any practice which might be interpreted as 're-baptism' must be avoided." It comments,

> As the churches come to fuller mutual understanding and acceptance of one another and enter into closer relationship in witness and service, they will want to refrain from any practice which might call into question the sacramental integrity of other churches or which might diminish the unrepeatability of the sacrament of baptism.[10]

Within the Roman Catholic communion, the rite of the Reception of Baptized Christians into Full Communion[11] of the Catholic Church stipulates:

> The sacrament of baptism cannot be repeated and therefore it is not permitted to confer it again conditionally, unless there is a reasonable doubt about the fact or the validity of the baptism already conferred.[12]

Nevertheless, practical problems persist in the implementation of the rite. Baptized Christians being received into the Roman Catholic Church from other churches are sometimes treated as if they were unbaptized when candidates (those already baptized) are indiscriminately joined with catechumens (those never baptized) in the same rites, catechesis, and formation programs. Small groups of uncatechized candidates are combined with even smaller groups of catechumens for practical reasons. However, I do not believe that we as Roman Catholics have adequately reflected on the RCIA's instruction that

> even though uncatechized adults have not yet heard the message of the mystery of Christ, their status differs from that of catechumens, since by baptism they have already become members of the Church and children of God. Hence their conversion is based on the baptism they have already received, the effects of which they must develop.[13]

All validly baptized Christians are members of the priestly people of God and as such are deputed to public liturgical worship. Yet in many parish communities we dismiss them along with the catechumens after the Liturgy of the Word and do not permit them to be present for the Liturgy of the Eucharist. Were we to permit them to remain for the remainder of the eucharistic liturgy, they would not be admitted to the table. Here we find ourselves at the heart of the most profound ecumenical dilemma: How can we profess one baptism and yet be divided at the eucharistic table? How can we acknowledge a common baptismal priesthood and yet not allow its complete exercise by full eucharistic participation?

Baptism effects both a union with Christ and an ecclesiological unity. In the theology of Romans 6, we are baptized into Christ Jesus and his death so that we may walk in newness of life just as Christ was raised from the dead (Rom. 6:3–4; Col. 2:12). Baptism in the name of the Father, Son, and Holy Spirit (Matt. 28:19) leads us into communion with the Triune God. It also knits believers together into a communion with each other because "in the one Spirit we were all baptized into one body—Jews or Greeks, slaves or free—and we were all made to drink of one Spirit" (1 Cor. 12:13 NRSV). Christians who recognize one another's baptism affirm a common unity in Christ and a unity in the Spirit. We affirm a unity in the christological body of Christ, but we balk at affirming an ecclesial unity effected by baptism. Why?

A key to this conundrum can be found in the primary baptismal text in Vatican II's Decree on Ecumenism, which takes up the baptismal theology of Romans 6:4 and Colossians 2:12 and speaks of baptism as incorporation into Christ and as constituting the sacramental bond of unity existing among all who through it are reborn. The text says, however, that it is only a beginning, an inauguration: "Baptism, therefore, is oriented towards the complete profession of faith, complete incorporation into the institution of salvation such as Christ wills it to be, and finally the completeness of unity which eucharistic communion gives."[14]

According to this text, unity is not found absolutely in baptism because the unity achieved there is only an "imperfect" one and baptism is only a "point of departure" for full unity.[15] Completeness of unity is associated with eucharistic communion. This is consistent with the Decree on Ecumenism as a whole. Chapter one of the decree, which gives the Catholic principles of ecumenism, begins with the Eucharist rather than baptism as the sacrament by which "the unity of the Church is both signified and brought about."[16] The third article of that chapter, where baptism is finally mentioned, affirms that "all who have been justified by faith in baptism are members of Christ's body, and have a right to be called Christians, and so are deservedly recognized as sisters and brothers in the Lord by the children of the catholic church." This same paragraph states that "those who believe in Christ and have been truly baptized are in some kind of communion with the catholic church, even though this communion is imperfect." The theological questions are the following: What is the difference between perfect and imperfect communion? And what, if anything, is missing in baptism with regard to unity?

What baptism is ordered toward but cannot contain within itself belongs to the visible elements of unity identified primarily as participation in eucharistic communion. Baptism initiates us into a soteriological unity in Christ and makes us members of his body, invisible elements of *koinōnia*. Baptism is incomplete at a certain level of visibility and particularity. Visible communion involves the concrete particularity of ecclesial communities in space and time. *Lumen gentium* 14 stresses this visibility where it states that "they are fully incorporated into the society of the church who, possessing the Spirit of Christ, accept its whole structure and all the means of salvation that have been established within it, and within its visible framework are united with Christ, who governs it through the supreme pontiff and the bishops, by the bonds of profession of faith, the sacraments, ecclesiastical government and communion." The church is not just a communion of the baptized, but a visible society with a visible framework and offices of governance. The emphasis is not just on faith but also its profession.

As far as I am aware, the rites for baptism in Christian churches do not include mention of the particular faith tradition into which a person is baptized or, at a more concrete level, the name of the local congregation. The unity of our baptism is signified by baptism by water in the name of the Trinity accompanied by a profession of faith in this Triune God. We are not explicitly baptized Roman Catholics, Lutherans, Methodists, or Anglicans in the words of the rite of baptism. Yet in conversation we say that we were baptized as Roman Catholics, Lutherans, and so on. Best pastoral practice would preclude the minister of one faith tradition baptizing a niece or nephew who will be raised in another faith tradition not in full communion with that of the minister.[17] Wherein lies this particularity? It resides not in the rite of baptism, but in the place of baptism and in the particular community that receives the baptized into their faith.

We are baptized into both the universal one church of Christ and into a local church. Even within Roman Catholicism emphases on the two vary. Avery Dulles, for example, emphasizes membership in the universal church and notes that "baptism can be validly administered where no community is present" and that "some baptized Christians, while lacking any stable relationship to a particular parish or diocese, are entitled to receive the sacraments wherever they go."[18] In his theology of the universal church, Dulles identifies this church within the particularity of Roman Catholicism in the spirit of *Lumen gentium*'s famous statement that the church of Christ "subsists in the catholic church, governed by the successor of Peter and the bishops in communion with him, although outside its structure many elements of sanctification and of truth are to be found which, as proper gifts to the church of Christ, impel towards catholic unity."[19] Jean-Marie R. Tillard, on the other hand, identifies the local church eucharistically and baptismally as "the community of those who are 'in communion' (*communio*) through that which is 'communicated' (*communicatum*)."[20] From this theology of the local church, the universal church is conceptualized as a communion of particular churches.[21]

Most concretely, we are baptized into a local church as a worshiping assembly. Both the place, ordinarily the parish church, and the minister of baptism, the bishop, presbyter, or deacon of that place, are determined by that assembly.[22] This place gives us the particularity of our confessional identity. Furthermore, this place is identified by the Eucharist, and in a very real sense we are baptized into the Eucharist. The local church is defined eucharistically in Roman Catholicism as "an altar community under the ministry of a bishop" and in Reformation communities as "where the gospel is purely preached and the sacraments rightly administered." Through baptism we enter into the priestly community (1 Peter 2:4–10) that is deputed for eucharistic worship. Within these local communities the faith is professed, the community receives the baptized, and the Eucharist celebrates and proclaims the sacramental presence of Christ within the community. The new rites of initiation are simply unthinkable outside of a local community because they presuppose a local church where the catechumens are evangelized and formed and where the neophytes are nurtured.

Both baptism and Eucharist celebrate the same mystery, namely the death and resurrection of Christ in the power of the Spirit. We are baptized only once, but our regular celebration of the Eucharist recalls the once and for all sacrifice of Christ represented on the altar and enables us join ourselves to Christ and to one another as the body of Christ (1 Cor. 10:16–17). Kathleen Hughes says as much when she describes the Eucharist as "our daily dip in the font." In the Eucharist, our communion in the body of the Lord, both in Christ dead and risen and in his ecclesial body, achieves a repeatable visibility. Our participation in the Eucharist is as profoundly baptismal as our baptism is profoundly oriented to the Eucharist. In baptism we become the priestly people of God, and in the Eucharist we exercise that priesthood. The incomplete unity achieved in baptism finds completion in the Eucharist because it is there that ecclesial and christological communion achieves repeatable sacramental visibility.

Unfortunately, this perceived connection between baptism and the Eucharist has largely been lost in the West due to the separation of the sacraments of initiation. The West, wishing to keep the bishop as the ordinary minister of confirmation, delayed that sacrament until such time as the bishop visited a local church. The reception of the Eucharist was also delayed until an age of maturity with the result that the order in which most Roman Catholics receive the sacraments is baptism, first penance, Eucharist, and confirmation. Since our theological thinking is formed by our practice of prayer, the principle of *lex orandi, lex credendi*, it is no wonder that our theology of baptism has become separated from our theology of the Eucharist. A reunified rite of initiation would ensure that our baptismal spirituality is a eucharistic one and that a eucharistic spirituality is baptismal.

The particularity of our place of baptism and its relationship to the Eucharist explains why we sadly and paradoxically experience division among Christian communities at the same time that we affirm a unity in

Christ bestowed upon us in baptism. We are baptized simultaneously into the universal church of Christ and into a particular church. These particular communities where we are baptized and where we celebrate the Eucharist are not in communion with one another. Full baptismal unity will only be achieved ecumenically when we heal the divisions between particular communions and achieve eucharistic unity. Sacramental unity, the full mutual recognition of baptism and admission to a common eucharistic table, follows upon ecclesial unity. Only when we will have achieved this unity will we no longer experience the paradox of unity forged by the one baptism in Christ in the name of the Trinity and the disunity of divided eucharistic tables.

Yet the reverse also seems to be true. There are times when ecclesial unity seems to be dependent upon sacramental recognition. *Dominus Jesus,* the recent document from the Congregation for the Doctrine and the Faith, links ecclesial recognition to recognition of the sacrament of order and the Eucharist.[23] Those groups are called churches that have episcopal ministry in apostolic succession and a valid Eucharist. This is determined to a great extent by recognition of the minister of the Eucharist. We have not adequately clarified whether recognition of sacraments leads to recognition of churches, or whether recognition of churches leads to mutual recognition of one another's sacraments. Clearly the two are mutually conditioning, an indication that ecumenical dialogue needs to address sacraments in their ecclesial signification and issues of ecclesiology in terms of their sacramental expression. This points to the profound interrelationship between sacramental reality and ecclesial reality. Moreover, ecclesial recognition does not guarantee full communion, as Roman Catholic relations with the Orthodox demonstrate.

We are accustomed to thinking that ecclesial unity will result when we will have achieved mutual recognition of each other's baptism and Eucharist. We have failed to recognize that, for the most part, our historical divisions did not result from a lack of mutual recognition of sacraments, but from what were perceived as discrepancies from the apostolic faith. We will not mend these divisions with mutual sacramental recognition or common sacramental practice.

This leads us to the conclusion that we may have to complete our assertion that sacraments signify and create unity with a corresponding claim that ecclesial unity leads to the mutual recognition of sacraments. The two assertions stand in a relationship of mutual polarity. They cannot be separated. We are baptized into Christ and into the church, inseparable from him and identified as his body. The church is not simply the place of our baptism. We are baptized not simply *in* the church, but *into* the church. In John Zizioulas's meaning of the term, we are ecclesial beings.[24] This is much more than church membership or a matter of confessional identity; it is an ecclesial way of being in the world. Baptismal unity forges ecclesial unity, and ecclesiastical being witnesses to the one baptism in Christ.

"For the Forgiveness of Sins"

Scholarship has provided evidence that the creed we know today as the Nicene-Constantinopolitan Creed actually predated the Council of Constantinople in 381. J. N. D. Kelly places it as the official baptismal creed in Constantinople and the surrounding region before 451. It later became the sole baptismal creed of all the Eastern churches. Within a few decades, it was incorporated in the Eucharist in the East. The same incorporation took place in the West more gradually over several centuries, and the document became the creed *par excellence* of Christian worship.[25] The phrase "confession of one baptism for the forgiveness of sins" receives its interpretation from its baptismal setting.

Certainly in the West, the specific historical polemic of the confession of one baptism for the forgiveness of sins concerned, by the first part of the fifth century, the baptism of infants. The issue was the presence of sin in infants. Both sides of the Pelagian controversy affirmed the necessity of the baptism of infants even though they disagreed concerning the purpose of the practice. Julian of Eclanum supported the baptism of infants even though they were created good, arguing that this would make them better through renewal and adoption as children of God.[26] Pelagius evidently argued the necessity of the practice in order that infants could be reborn in Christ and be with him in the kingdom of God. The Synod of Carthage in 418 confirmed the Augustinian interpretation and decreed that "anyone who denies that newborn infants are to be baptized or who says that they are baptized for the remission of sins but do not bear anything of original sin from Adam which is expiated by the washing of regeneration, so that as a consequence the form of baptism 'for the remission of sins' is understood to be not true but false in their case—let him be anathema."[27]

One historical interpretation of the creed in the fifth century involved the baptism of infants, but consciousness of sin, belief in the salvific character of Jesus' death, and the practice of baptism for forgiveness of sin date from the first century. Baptism is associated with the forgiveness of sin from the earliest days of Christianity. In Acts 2:38, Peter tells the Israelites to "repent, and be baptized every one of you in the name of Jesus Christ so that your sins may be forgiven; and you will receive the gift of the Holy Spirit" (NRSV). The confession of baptism "for the forgiveness of sins" follows from baptism's relationship to the death of Jesus Christ. In Acts we find a series of short pericopes that summarize and interpret Christ's death and resurrection (Acts 4:10–12; 5:30–31; 10:36–43; 13:23–39; 17:2–3). Jesus Christ died and rose that those who would believe in him would find salvation and the forgiveness of sins.[28] Romans 6 interprets baptism as a baptism into the death of Christ Jesus so that we will walk in newness of life, be united in a resurrection like his, and be freed from sin. Paul links washing with sanctification in 1 Corinthians 6:11.

Forgiveness of sins in baptism entails more than the once-for-all forgiveness of sins present in the person being baptized. It also signifies that the person is committed to a life of repentance and conversion. As the Rite of Christian Initiation of Adults states, "The rite of Christian initiation presented here is designed for adults who, after hearing the mystery of Christ proclaimed, consciously and freely seek the living God and enter the way of faith and conversion as the Holy Spirit opens their hearts."[29] Repentance and conversion are lifelong, for although one becomes a Christian at baptism, in another sense one becomes a Christian over a lifetime. Forgiveness of sin is not only an event in the life of a Christian; it entails entrance also into a lifestyle characterized by the gratitude of one who has been forgiven. This thanksgiving is sacramentalized in the Eucharist—the word *Eucharist* meaning "thanksgiving"—where the ethical implications of baptism come to visibility through the proclamation of the Scriptures and the anamnesis of Jesus' life poured out for others.

Finally, baptism for the forgiveness of sins identifies the community into which a person is baptized, namely a community of salvation. Certainly the church offers the sacraments of Christ's forgiveness, among which baptism is primary. The church is also a community of those for whom Jesus Christ died, whose sins are forgiven. However, to be identified as a community of salvation also expresses the demands of Christian living. By taking the name *Christian* in baptism and being incorporated into Christ's body, the baptized assume the responsibility to offer forgiveness to one another in imitation of the one into whom they are baptized.

Conclusion

The creed's confession of one baptism for the forgiveness of sins occurs in a specific fourth-century historical context. It reflects the ecclesiological and liturgical issues of that time. The creed does not summarize the whole of Christian life. In the ancient church baptism was the most important sacrament, but given the place of the Eucharist in the life of the church, we may be surprised at its absence in the creed. The theology and practice of the Eucharist was simply not a disputed issue at that moment in the church, as was the relationship between the Father, the Son, and the Spirit; the recognition of baptism by schismatics; and the question of infants being baptized for the forgiveness of sins. If we interpret the creed within its liturgical setting—either within a comprehensive rite of initiation or in its eucharistic setting in the Sunday liturgy—the confession of baptism is inseparable from the particularity of its eucharistic setting, and its theology must be articulated in the light of eucharistic theology. Baptism and the Eucharist are linked as early as 1 Corinthians 10:2–4 and perhaps even John 19:34 and 1 John 5:6.

Both baptism and the Eucharist are ecclesial sacraments in the sense that they are constitutive of the church. The confession of one baptism is also essentially the confession of one Lord, one faith, and one church. There is only one baptism because there is only one Christ, dead and risen, into whom we are baptized. Baptism proclaims the Christian interpretation of Jesus' death; that it was "for us and for our salvation." Baptism effects something, namely life in Christ and life in a community of salvation, the church.

14

And I Look for the Resurrection . . .

Vigen Guroian

My mother suffered a stroke on the Monday before Christmas that weakened her right side and paralyzed her arm. She will need to undergo lengthy therapy in order to regain her strength. The following day, I lamented on the phone to a young friend: "Last year at this time my mother had a heart attack, and now it is a stroke. Christmas is bittersweet. Gladness has gotten mixed with sorrow, and hope with trepidation." My friend consoled me and then he said: "Vigen, maybe there is a reminder in this that even as we welcome our Savior joyfully into this world, we should not forget that here is not our true home."

Wisdom in a young man's speech and the unsettling last stanza of T. S. Eliot's "Journey of the Magi" leapt to mind.

> . . . I had seen birth and death,
> But had thought they were different; this Birth was
> Hard and bitter agony for us, like Death, our death.
> We returned to our places, these Kingdoms,
> But no longer at ease here, in the old dispensation,
> With an alien people clutching their gods.
> I should be glad of another death.

I have begun to understand the wisdom of the Armenian Church's stubborn persistence in celebrating Jesus' birth and baptism *together* on the sixth of January, as was ancient practice. His birth shines light into this darkling world and commences the death of death itself. His baptism reveals this world's true Maker and Ruler and the path of repentance, self-renunciation, and sacrificial love that each of us must travel to inherit eternal life. In the same manner, by our personal baptism we not only receive the gift of the Holy Spirit and adoption as sons and daughters of God, we also recapitulate Jesus' crucifixion, death, burial, and resurrection. This is the death Eliot commends because it is also birth into eternal life. The ninth century Armenian patriarch Zechariah proclaims in a sermon for January 6 (Eastern Epiphany):

> To-day being illuminated in the font together with Christ, we have been made radiant and gleaming with light, and having had the divine and royal image delineated in us, having been invited to the mansions above, [we join] our voices with those of the heavenly hosts . . .

> To-day we were buried with Christ in the waters of baptism, being born along with him unto his death. And together with him shall we also be made alive, and with him reign in life eternal.

The following is addressed to my mother, Grace Guroian

Mother, I have been reminded these past two Christmases that I was brought into this world by a woman who is mere mortal flesh and who is the source neither of her immortality nor of my own. In the night Jesus responded to Nicodemus, "Truly, truly, I say to you, unless one is born anew, he cannot see the kingdom of God" (John 3:5 RSV). The bright wonder of my own birth by a woman is marked darkly by the mystery of her mortality and mine. In perplexity and with irony, Nicodemus had asked Jesus: "How can a man be born when he is old? Can he enter a second time into his mother's womb and be born?" (John 3:4 RSV). By giving birth to me, Mother, you have ensured my death and in some real sense hastened your own. Even if you could give birth to me a second or third time, death would still lay claim to me. Now, as I watch you diminish with years, I tremble as I am made to confront not just your mortality but mine, because they are deeply and mysteriously tied other. Still, I am grateful that you gave birth to me and so also this life to live. And I am happy that if you must die, so must I. Love moves me to say this. Love also makes me want immortality for you and a share for me in it as well.

I do not think that this is a vain hope, Mother, because Love, Love Divine, came into this world for your sake and mine. The Son of God condescended to be born of a woman in order that motherhood might be made a means once more to immortality, as it was in the beginning when Eve came to be. Her name was Mother of the Living, but tragically she forfeited that grace when she sinned, and henceforth she became Mother of the Dying. Mother, I do not blame you for my mortality. Instead, I wish to honor you, as God honored womanhood by making Eve the Mother of the Living and chose blessed Mary to conceive and give birth to the source of our salvation so that she would be the New Mother of Life. Mother, by baptism you became one of Mary's daughters. That is why I draw hope in your birth-giving as a promise of eternal life for me and you. And perhaps now, as you heal to live on this earth yet a little while longer, God is inviting you also to take hope in me, whom you call your son. I mean, Mother, that as surely as the Son of God loves his Father, he also loves his mother. Thus Jesus' compassion for his own mother embraces all mothers and their children and will permit love not to be confounded by death, but rather to be consummated in a communion of eternal life.

Mother, the other evening as the sun set on an icy blue sky, I laced up my new Christmas boots and visited the vegetable garden. It lay barren, half buried in the snow that fell a week ago. I abandoned it for travel in the fall. And now in winter at dusk, it is haunted by skeleton vines and wisps of asparagus plumes stripped of their filigree leaf. This couldn't be paradise. How easy it is in winter to forget what we have been waiting for, or to lose hope that it will ever come. St. Gregory of Nyssa reminds us in the *Commentary on the Canticle,* however, that "the *Sun of Justice* rose in this cruel winter, the spring came, the south wind dispelled that chill, and together with the rising of the sun's rays warmed everything that lay in our path. Thus mankind, that was . . . chilled into stone, might become warm again through the Spirit, and receiving heat from the rays of the Word, might again become as *water leaping up into eternal life.*"

On the third morning the blessed women arrived with oil and spices at the dark cave, three of them, like the Magi at the manger, but this time the Master had been wrapped in a shroud and not in swaddling clothes. They came to anoint his fractured body one last time, he who as a babe wiggled with new life in his mother's arms. Mary Magdalene tremulously entered the cave. "It was dark, but love lighted her way," says St. Romanos the

Melodist in his *Hymn on the Resurrection*. The Master was gone, the tomb lay empty, and the burial linens were folded neatly in a corner. Someone was standing behind her. She turned, thinking it it was the gardener. Then he spoke her name. "Mary," he called, and she knew at once it was *He,* though his body was more beautiful than Adam in paradise. The garden tomb was bursting with life. The tree in blossom as it was on the first day. The fragrance of the flowers more sweet than any perfume for the dead. That is the true story, Mother. No matter that this day is the darkest of the year and that the winter garden is desolate. From this day forward the Sun increases and chases off death's shadows with his uncreated light. He renews the whole earth and will warm your frozen limbs so that they are all like "water leaping up into eternal life."

Sometimes when our body hurts or is numb and does not answer our commands, when it will not let us savor life, we want to leave it behind. But this is a trick of the devil. A wise man, Bishop Kallistos Ware, reminds us in *The Orthodox Way:* "Man is not saved *from* his body but *in* it; not saved *from* the material world but *with* it." What is the sweet fragrance of the rose without the petals? What is perfume if not worn by womanly flesh? Modern people need to be reminded that our humanity is an indivisible oneness of body and soul and that our salvation is no less of the body than of the soul. So many have got it in their heads that the body is disposable and that the soul alone is who we are. That is a very old and mistaken notion that the church rejected long ago, but modern people think it's up-to-date. It's what they call spirituality.

The author of the Book of Genesis has a different vision of life. He says God molded Adam from earth and water, like clay in the potter's hands, and "breathed into his nostrils the breath of life" (Gen. 2:7 RSV). Then God "took the man and put him in the Garden of Eden" (Gen. 2:15 RSV). According to that ancient writer, human beings are of the earth and belong to the earth. What makes modern folk think that their flesh is not worthy of eternal life? What silly stories have they got lodged in their heads?

Mother, when our bodies are afflicted by disease, as the stroke has afflicted you, that is an intimation of our mortality, but no reason to despise one's body. Death wants to undo us, and death has called God back into this world in his Son so that he might make us whole again. By him and in him all of the broken images of God littered outside of Eden's gates shall be restored and returned to paradise, body and soul together and forever. That, too, is the true story.

Mother, Jesus' enemies set a crown of thorns on his head that tore his brow and covered his eyes with blood so that he stumbled on the stairs. Then they led him up a craggy rock on which spectral trees sprouted not leaves but lacerated flesh. Yet he did not detest his body. Instead, he raised it glorified, a rose without thorns. He took his flesh and ours to the Father, like incense at the altar. St. John tells us that "in the place where he was crucified there was a garden" (John 19:41 RSV), and in it a newly hewn tomb. Might we not assume that Jesus saw that garden from the cross and that it stirred in him great sorrow and great joy. Says Jesus in George Herbert's poem "The Sacrifice," "Man stole the fruit, but I must climb the tree;/The tree of life to all, but only me." Through his death the Son of God revealed the cursed cross to be the tree of life for you and me, and by his resurrection he transformed every lifeless winter garden back into green paradise.

St. Cyril of Jerusalem proclaims in his Catechetical Lecture 14:11,

> A garden was the place of His Burial and a vine that which was planted there; and He hath said, *I am the vine!* (John 15:1). He was planted therefore in the earth in order that the curse, which came because of Adam, might be rooted out. The earth was condemned to *thorns and thistles:* the true Vine sprang up out of the earth, that the saying might be fulfilled, *Truth sprang up out of the earth, and righteousness looked down from heaven* (Psalm 85:11).

While on that cross Jesus promised the repentant thief who hung next to him like a withered vine that they would see each other in paradise that day; not in some penumbral realm where the dead exist in a disembodied state, but in a luxuriant garden filled with perpetual light. On Holy Saturday Jesus descended into dark Hades and took Adam and Eve back with him to paradise. And on Sunday, the first day of the new creation, Jesus sprang up from the tomb, a vine laden with the fruit of resurrection. Yes, and Mary found Jesus in the garden tomb and thought he was the gardener. And she was right, although she mistook him for another. St. Ephrem the Syrian says in Armenian Hymn no. 490, "Whereas Eden's other trees were provided/for that former Adam to eat, /for us the very Planter of that Garden/has become the food for our souls." What a strange thought that the Planter is the food for our souls. Weren't we taught in grade school not to mix metaphors? But God is not a metaphor. God *became* the planter. God *became* the gardener. God *became* the vine and its fruit. And he *is* the drink and food of eternal life. He is all of them because he has clothed himself with these symbols in the same way that he has worn our flesh, to make us new, as in spring when the dead seeds sprout shiny new leaves and the unclothed vine bursts with bright buds.

What is it with modern people that if they believe in God, God is pure spirit, and if they believe in immortality, immortality is disincarnate existence? Do they detest this world that much? Is it that they despair that love abides? Or perhaps they don't spend time enough in a garden? Why won't they believe that God is himself the vine and the grape, and also the wine pressed for our sake? The Son wore our flesh and watered a garden with drops of blood that we drink at the table that he has set. Mother, the daisies and violets that grew in your garden held more truth and hope in them than all this human knowing put together. The Christian faith has got it right. If eternal life is God's life shared with us, then it is truly a garden of delight, and we are the flowers that grow within it.

> And now in age I bud again,
>   After so many deaths I live and write;
>   I once more smell the dew and rain,
>   And relish versing: O my only light,
>   It cannot be
>   That I am he
>   On whom thy tempests fell all night.
>   These are thy wonders, Lord of love,
> To make us see we are but flowers that glide:
>   Which when *we* once can find and prove,
> Thou hast a garden for us, where to bide.
>
>   George Herbert, *The Flower*

Mother, I have passed fifty, and the years that separate us seem to have shrunk. My children are still too young to really know what George Herbert means about budding in age again. They do not see naturally that their lives are like "flowers that glide," that want to root in a garden "where to bide." Rafi works the Internet and finds power there. Victoria thrills in political wills. You and I, however, are drawn back to the garden, where "after so many deaths," we live to "smell the dew and rain." Each day is an epiphany of love divine, or it is not a day at all. And each day draws us nearer to eternity, or it has no meaning at all.

I do not know of a better place to count the days or the seasons or to take measure of my life than in a garden. Mother, try to remember the gardens you grew in my youth.

And you will not despair in this cold December,
Though the trees have lost their crowns
And shiver naked in the north wind.
For the *Sun* with a radiant diadem,
Has illuminated the dark cave
And is thawing the frozen ground
For the advent of Eternal Spring,
When he will heal your weakened body
And make it whole,
As it was in my youth,
When you lingered in the flower garden,
Kneeling among the poppy and the primrose.

It is hard for any gardener to accept that no matter how hard she tries, the garden she grows cannot be paradise. Yet among some ancient Armenian stories concerning what happened after Adam and Eve were expelled from the Garden of Eden, there is this one tale that I want to tell. It is a source of comfort and hope to all of us who garden; not easy hope or fast comfort, mind you, because it reminds us that since the time when that first couple ate the fruit of the tree and tasted death our mortality is the condition under which we hope for eternal life. Here is the story, Mother. It begins with an admonition, not unlike my young friend's about where our true home lies.

One day Adam said to Seth, "Son, this is not our home. Rather, our home was Eden towards the east, in the garden. For God created your mother and I and put us in the garden, and he commanded us from which fruit to eat and from which not to eat. But we did not keep the commandment, and deprived ourselves of the garden." Seth was moved by his father's lamentation and fasted for forty days and forty nights, and asked God if more could not be made right for his father Adam. God sent an angel with a branch in his hand, which was a branch of joy from the Tree in the garden of delight. And the angel gave him the branch and said to Seth "This is your father's consolation."

Seth took this branch to his father and said, "Father, this is from your home." Adam took the branch and saw that it was from the tree of the forbidden fruit, which produced death. And Adam said to his son, "Seth, my son, this is of the tree from which the Lord commanded us not to eat." Seth, the son of consolation, said to his father, "Father, know that just as it causes death, so also it gives life and light."

It is that way with every garden, isn't it Mother? In winter a garden is a place of darkness and death and desolation, but in spring of light and bountiful life.

The story ends this way:

Time passed and one day Seth's son Enoch asked his father why his grandfather Adam was so sad. And Seth told Enoch "He is sad because he tasted of the fruit, for which he went out of the garden." This troubled Enoch whose heart was pure and sensitive. To his father Enoch exclaimed, "The son must pay the debts of his father." So Enoch fasted for forty days and forty nights, after which he planted a comely garden filled with every kind of flower and fruit-bearing tree. And Enoch lived in that garden a very long time until one day an angel came to the garden and picked Enoch from it, like a ripe pomegranate, and placed him in the midst of Paradise, and he is there until today.

The Armenian Apocryphal Adam Literature

I was a young man when June and I dug our first garden. It was strictly for economy and provision that we made it: less spent at the grocery store and plenty of plastic containers stored for winter in the freezer. Mother, do you remember that vegetable garden in Richmond, Virginia? Just behind it, on the other side of a chain link fence, a man with a withered arm grew his vision of paradise, and what he raised with his other, good arm he gave away. Mother, who would question that in paradise Christ will make that man's shriveled arm whole, as he did for another in the Gospels, or that in paradise God will cause his garden to grow more beautiful than any that he had on earth? And, Mother, God will make your arm whole too, because you, like Enoch, have grown a garden in your life, not just of flowers and trees but of family also. And you have taught me that a garden and a family are about more than food to eat or provisions to keep, but about love and joy given and shared, which must, if God is good—which God is—continue into eternal life.

Friday before Christmas, Mother, I took Scarlett out on her leash through the porch door. The flowerbeds that ring the backyard lay before us monochrome and naked. The peony plants that bore big fragrant blossoms in May were shrunken to frail twigs. The hosta hedge beside the screened porch that in June grew lush green leaves lay shriveled and matted on the frozen ground. The tall aster stems that were lit in September with wild bouquets of pink and purple stars were turned to straw. I thought to myself: "Was all that growing, all that greening, all that flowering just for this, to become a withered winter waste?" I was thinking of you, Mother, in your weakened

state, and I was tempted to despair. I returned to my study and I read the
Epistle of St. Clement of Rome, which was written at the dawn of our faith
in the first century of our Lord. In it St. Clement writes:

> Let us consider, beloved, how the Lord continually proves to us that there
> shall be a future resurrection, of which He has rendered the Lord Jesus Christ
> the first fruits by raising him from the dead. Let us contemplate, beloved, the
> resurrection which is at all times taking place. Day and night declare to us
> resurrection. The night sinks to sleep, and the day arises; the day again departs,
> and the night comes on. Let us behold the fruits of the earth, how the sow-
> ing of grain takes place. The sower goes forth, and casts it in the ground, and
> the seed being thus scattered, though dry and naked when it fell upon the
> earth, is gradually dissolved. Then out of its dissolution the mighty power of
> the providence of the Lord raises it up again, and from one seed many arise
> and bring forth fruit.

First Epistle, 24

Anyone who has grown a garden has stood amidst sacramental signs of
eternal life. On one level the lesson nature teaches is fairly simple: what
looks like death is merely preparation for the regeneration of living things.
One needn't be a supernaturalist to take comfort from this natural procession of life, death, and new life. Yet St. Clement sees nature with the new
vision of Jesus' resurrection. He is not claiming that nature's cycles are evidence of eternal life. Rather, he is saying that nature is an epiphany of the
resurrecting power of God. What the naturalist sees in nature as proof of
its regenerative strength, the Christian embraces as revelation of the power
of God to raise us all to life everlasting. We are not interested merely in
nature's regenerative cycles. Our wonder, yours and mine, Mother, is in the
garden that reveals the resurrection of each one of us, indeed of each of our
bodies buried in the ground and raised up on the last day. "Unless a grain
of wheat falls into the earth and dies, it remains alone; but if it dies, it bears
much fruit," says our Lord (John 12:24 RSV). And he affirms this, not only
with his words, but by his very death, burial, and resurrection.

That is why, even in this darkest moment of the year, when the earth is
cold and life has gone out of it, still we may rejoice, Mother, in the light that
Christ's birth brings into our lives. And we may draw hope from having
been refreshed in baptismal waters and renewed by the breath of God. In
nature no flower loses its form from year to year. The lily that in winter falls
to the ground rises up again that same flower the next spring. Likewise,
Mother, in the great spring we will be nourished by the divine dew and

warmed by the heavenly Sun, and each of us will blossom into a flower of its own distinct kind. Our likeness will be as it was during the seasons of our earthly lives, only more real and more radiant under the light that God shines upon us. The psalmist says, "May people blossom in the cities like the grass of the field" (Ps. 72:16 NRSV), and "Their children become a blessing" (Ps. 37:26 NRSV). Amen.

15

To Desire Rightly
The Force of the Creed
in Its Canonical Context

Ephraim Radner

The Canonical Context of the Creed's Articulation

What is the context, or the means even, by which this creed we have been celebrating reflectively "makes sense" for the church, and indeed for the world? It seems to make sense to *us*, of course. Yet we would not be here if we did not somehow also feel that we are guardians of something that may be slipping from our grasp, and has already slipped for many. What does it take that this "canon of the truth," as it has been early called, should be and remain alive in our day? Is it a new hermeneutic, or some retrieved way of relating Scripture to doctrine? Is it a readjusted model of truth itself and its formulation within historical consciousness or time? Is it some refashioned mode of catechesis? Shall we pound our fists?

I want us to dwell a bit now with the way that these words of the creed and their meaning *themselves* dwell within a practice of order, of ordering. That is, I want us to reflect on the way that the Christian truth is spoken in a well-ordered church. In doing so, I wish to carry through with insights lifted up by postliberal traditionalists like George Lindbeck and emphasize the way in which the creed's words only go so far in acting as theological explicators of the truth. They limit, they guard, they point. But the demand for wisdom to fill in the sinful gaps of human (and Christian) existence, so pointed in our churches and so desired, cannot be fulfilled apart from the creed's articulation within a certain *kind* of church, that is, in an ordered church. The creed, in other words, is not the gospel; it speaks the gospel, but then only from the posture of an evangelical practice.

Now in much of what I am going to say about order and the creed, Episcopalians may assume that I am simply responding, perhaps parochially, to certain realities now challenging our own denomination. They would not be wrong in thinking this, of course. But at the same time, I must emphasize that exactly the same challenges now face many other denominations. They do so in part because these challenges are endemic to dynamics of church life as it has been bequeathed to the world by earlier forms of catholicism still evident in Catholic and Eastern Orthodox traditions. The question of order and the creed is all of ours.

I should add, furthermore, that it is a question that cannot be overleapt through some sense that "conservative" (or "orthodox" or "traditionalist") forces within denominations can somehow coalesce in faith so as to make the question irrelevant to the doctrinally adept. Not at all; just the opposite! The question of order and creed is at the center of what it means to be the Christian church, especially because this church has become all of these churches that we call ours. It has always been *the* question of the *oikoumenē*, the ecumenical question par excellence. We must be forthright about this.

So let me say something brief about the the order of Nicea, to use the prime example of the First Council, whose name attaches to our creed, as all subsequent councils were clear to admit. We all remember the problem of the Arians. Isn't that what Nicea was all about? Much of what we have heard about the creed properly speaks to the profound and variegated realities of divine life that are bound up with overcoming Arian claims and implications. The theological and doctrinal issues at stake in speaking about the creed are immense.

But we must also remember that there was a second motivating occasion for the gathering of the "the three hundred," or however many bishops were actually at Nicea. This was the problem of when to celebrate Easter. That might seem like a minor matter, but Athanasius tells us this at one point, when trying to summarize the purpose of the council: "As to the Nicene Council, it was not a common meeting, but convened upon a pressing necessity, and for a reasonable object." What was that object? Well, he goes on to say, "the Syrians, Cilicians, and Mesopotamians were out of order in cele-brating the Feast and kept Easter with the Jews."

That, according to Athanasius, is the first matter for this "uncommon" gathering—the order of festal celebration and uniform calendars. Oh yes, he continues, "in addition, the Arian heresy had risen up against the Catholic Church."[1] Now whether the council was ultimately any more successful at getting us all to celebrate Easter together than at having us speak of Christ faithfully is a question we shall not broach now. But it is crucial to see these *two* questions—Easter and Arius—as being both worthy of extraordinary conciliar authority.[2]

To be sure, Athanasius himself seems to distinguish the character of these two concerns. The matter of the Arians touches upon the apostolical faith. The matter of Easter's date, on the other hand, touches only upon common submission to a common worship. Who would not wish to keep such a hier-archy of importance intact? Still, we must note that Athanasius *does* lump the resolution of both topics together as common marks of the council's sin-gular authority, over and against other, false councils. In fact, the Synodal Letter of Nicea—the message of the bishops sent out to all the church's faith-ful—describes both matters as having to do with the singular "peace and har-mony" of the church. It is this "peace" that is the mark of the Catholic church's authority to speak in the first place.

Finally, the actual letter of the emperor regarding the fixing of Easter's celebration as quoted to us by Eusebius[3] makes it clear that matters of inter-est beyond tidiness were at issue in the date of the great feast. If one can get behind the dripping and repulsive antisemitism that colors the decree, it is still possible to see that, at base, the ordering of Easter's celebration had to do, in the mind of the council, with God's honor, with the integrity of the church's common speech and worship, and with the unity of the church of God under one divine will.

What we could call "the principle of Easter and Order" was therefore embedded in the Nicene Council's very being, and it is congruent with this principle that a third item is noted in the synodal letter as being at the cen-ter of the council's business. This third item is the problem of solving a schism in Egypt—involving the breakaway church of the rigorist Melitius. (This, too, was a problem whose actual resolution proved debatable.) So it is not surprising that linguistically, along with whatever distinctions one might wish to make about matters of more or less importance—Arianism vs. Easter, say—the question of "order" given in the council's many other decrees gave creative coherence to the character of the council as a whole.

Thus, we find early commentators on the creed[4] using the term *canon* to refer to the creed itself and its significance, as well as to the various portions of the decrees the council made, that is, the *canons*. The *canon* of the creed and the *canons* of the many decrees are therefore terms that often ambiguously overlap in the writings of the early church. Pope Julius, contemporary and supporter of Athanasius, for instance, speaks of the "the Canon" of Nicea, in the singular, as well as the "canons" in the plural. It appears in some places as if by the singular he refers to the whole body of the conciliar canons (and those from the past), and in other places as if he is speaking of the *general* ordering of the council, including the creed, by which the church has been formed in a living and structured opposition to Arianism and heresy at large. Arians, Julius writes, act "contrary to the Canon," and they do not organize their church's life "according to the Canon." What is the referent to the word *canon* here is not precisely clear.[5]

What becomes clear, however, is that this general "ordering" or "canonizing" of the church, enacted by the council, included not only the creed but also the creed's relation to and its articulation within the particular and practical framings of common life that we assign usually to "canon law." The "canons" of the council were understood as church law, in other words, as reflecting the same authoritative and divine power, however peculiarly, that lies behind the creed's enunciation of the "truth" of the gospel. Thus, Julius can speak of the canons, in the plural, as being "apostolical," and can describe their contradiction in terms of an "offence" against the integrity of the word preached to Christ's "little ones."[6] Not abiding by the canons is literally a "scandal," he says, worthy of hell. Athanasius, in an even more explicit paragraph, speaks of the canons as things not constructed for or from the moment, but "wisely and safely transmitted to us from our forefathers," just like the "faith" itself, which has "come down to us from the Lord through His disciples." "Ordinances" "from of old," Athanasius says, quoting 1 Corinthians 4:1, ought literally to be equated with "the mysteries of God."[7]

The Contemporary Setting of Our Day for the Creed's Relation to Canon

We must try, therefore, to reorient our attitudes to the creed away from purely abstract, however devotionally tethered, theological reflections. We must seek the connections between creed and the ordering of ecclesial life that hold the "canon of truth" and the "canons of the church" together.[8] This requires effort. It is not uncommon to read the creed in exclusively doctrinal or even scriptural terms, devoid of the ecclesially ethical or (as I shall say in a moment) the "ascetical" character that gives it mass. It was Andre de Halleux who wrote that the Nicene Creed, in a sense, served to "consecrate a dogmatic communion already existing,"[9] and the conjoining of "dogma" with "existing communion" is what is crucial to note in this phraseology.

Another way of expressing this was put by the Faith and Order Commission itself when it described the ancient councils, like Nicea and Constantinople, as "taking place on the basis of the existing fellowship,"[10] and not as gatherings whose aim was to discover a unity not yet in existence.

Shall we not say that the creed is expressive of community? Is reflective or formative, or even *re*formative of it? However we wish, in the end, to formulate the exact historical and sociological relationship of the Nicene Creed to the community of faith that articulated, adopted, and promoted it, there can be no doubt that the notion of an existing or evolving community fundamentally tied to that creed is accurate.

There is an irony, then, that we contributors to this volume have gathered, in a sense, as explicators of a creed that today goes *in search of* its community. Or, again in the words of the Faith and Order Commission, today any "conciliar process" has as its "point of departure" "plural ecclesiastical communities in confrontation with one another." Who are we, after all? We are representatives of a diversity of communions, of denominations, even of parties within diversified denominations. To speak more truthfully, we are representatives of *divided* churches that in no way could be described, as a whole or even in part, in terms of "dogmatic communion," even within our own denominated Christian bodies. Who are we? Among ourselves we do not, for the most part, share the Eucharist; we do not share our pastoral and missionary resources and energies; we do not share our money; we do not share our mutual subjection; we do not share the scripturally directed shape of our vocations in Christ. Yet we say that we have the same creed; we gather to lift it up, to celebrate it, to draw from the wealth of its embedded treasure and truth.

Let us go further. Many, if not most, of us do not represent, in our relationship to this creed, the very Christian institutions that count us as their members. We are unrepresentative exactly insofar as we gather for the purpose of reflecting on a creed that has lost its central purchase on our churches' common life! Ecumenically, therefore, it is an interesting phenomenon that we gather at all. What does this gathering evidence? Ever since Robert Wuthnow's popular books of the late 1980s,[11] among others, we have been instructed that American Christianity has been realigning itself according to conservative and liberal poles across denominations. Perhaps, then, we are the conservatives of this social dynamic, throwing off the ecumenical strategies of seventy years of denominational rapprochement as we forge a new "Nicene Christianity" that rises from outside the boundaries of our now overcome traditions.

Or perhaps—to follow another sociological theory of class and religion—we are simply erudite misfits, unable to dwell within the educated liberalism of John Spong's successfully marketed attempts to reach the inquiring professional on one side, yet at the same time far too knowledgeable to remain within the class of the socially striving evangelical bourgeoisie. As an advertising friend of mine said to me, "No one wants you in a focus group, because you represent a niche too small to make money off of."

Who are we, after all? To press this question about this community gathered here is to press the question not only of whose creed it is but also of the nature of creed itself. De Halleux's point deserves our most careful scrutiny: If the creed is organically tied to a discursive community—a community, that is, that communicates effectively within itself—what therefore defines the character of that effective communal life that in its work embodies the creedal act? We have a creed, but it does not seem to belong to us. So the question gets more specific: not only "Who are we?" but also "Who are we to become, if the creed is our creed?

My purpose, then, is to suggest that an answer to this lies within the context of the creed's formal adoption—both at Nicea and Constantinople—by *self-ordering* bodies. That is, the creed is the speech of a church that acts to order itself, presumably according to the perceived will of God, but to order itself nonetheless, within the shape of formal and mutual accountability. This is the simple fact upon which I want us to reflect: with the Nicene Creed came twenty canons, and with Constantinople even more. These canons were from the first understood as informing not just the church that put the creed together, but the *kind* of church that is creed-speaking. In short, the "canon" or "order" that is the creed (and it was early so designated, as I said) is at one with the "canons" that proceed from the councils' coincident work of ordering its constituent members. There is no effective creed without order. And we must become self-orderers *with one another* if we are in fact to be creedal Christians.

Now this may seem on its face to be based on a standard description of the character of theology in general as we have learned it in our linguistically sensitive postliberal and postmodern age. Our era, after all, has an intellectual maxim. It states clearly that "discourse" is both necessarily shaped by and necessarily coherent within integral communities. In other words, so this piece of popular intellectual wisdom goes, there is no coherent language apart from a coherent community that does the talking. Because this maxim is so current, I need quickly to qualify its pertinence to our discussion in two ways.

First, however current it may be, the maxim is only partly believed in ecclesial circles, and then only in ways that undercut its ecumenical significance. Take, for instance, the 1982 Faith and Order document entitled "Towards the Common Expression of the Apostolic Faith Today." The document is a good example of how the creed today hovers paralytically within our ecclesial character. The "Ecumenical Creed" of Nicea and Constantinople, we are told, should be "recognized" by all member churches of the World Council of Churches as the only "common expression" of faith that can adequately "connect" churches to the "one, holy, catholic, apostolic church." Only this creed, that is, can "express the integral unity of the Christian faith."[12]

But having said this, the commission then immediately goes on to tell us that the nature of our "divided" Christian communities compromises this fact. If the creed is useful at all, given our divisions, it cannot be to form us into a *new* unity; rather, it can only serve as a fuel for diverse "reexpressions" of the faith we already share. The creed can play a singular role as "ground" to our multiplied realms or orders of communication. You could say that the creed's job, in this light, is to act as a kind of national boundary for multicultural identities. Of course, such a boundary could be like that of either the United States or the Yugoslav Federation, depending on the forces that order those identities from within.

So despite the common acceptance of the necessity of theological-communal coherence, in the face of the intractability of Christian fragmentation the challenge of coherent creedal discourse is not easily grasped by the horns. This, then, is the first note of qualification I need to give to the claim that the connection between creed and its communal ordering is self-evident: it is clearly *not* self-evident to those who accept division and yet still call themselves Christians. It is not self-evident, in any practical sense, to many readers of this volume and to me.

The second qualification I would make is this: the ordering of creedal meaning according to the self-ordering of its articulating church is not a theoretical problem to be addressed by theological constructs. It is a matter, as Nicea and subsequent councils demonstrated, of canonical discipline. And this is a way of describing the self-discipline of the body of Christ. As theologians speak of the "grammar of faith" and the "rules" of theological or doc-

trinal discourse, or indeed of how doctrines themselves act as "grammar" to
the expression of the Christian faith—and these are all properly accepted
ways of construing Christian speech in our day—we must realize from the
start that the communal ordering of the *creed's* speech was given in the context of *canon law*. What Nicea and Constantinople did was to formulate and
promulgate a creed among churches that at the same time were ordered by
canons of mutual and internal discipline.

This is not merely a historical coincidence. It grew out of the fundamental and lived conviction of the early church that to speak truly was the gift
of those who followed Christ most truly, that is, the saints, and that the truthful church was the holy church. To order truthful theological speech, therefore, is to order the church *ascetically*, in the sense of those practices by which
the Holy Spirit trains ecclesial structures in the forms of his pneumatic powers—of hope, of humility, of charity, of patience, and so on.

To say, then, that the communally ordered character of the creed is one of
ecclesial asceticism is a qualification to the current notion of communally
coherent discourse. That is because the discipline of communal life is dis-
cordant with the magically self-evolving character that people of our day
attribute to communal identity, not to say communal unity. When the Faith
and Order Commission has addressed the issue of canon law, for instance,
it has not done so in the context of its discussion of the creeds; these last seem
to be free-floating documents of the tradition, available to all Christians
through some kind of abstracted familial genealogy. Canon law has, instead,
been addressed as a problem for the ecumenical movement that needs somehow to be overcome.[13] All these "laws" that govern our divided churches, we
are told, get in the way of coming together.

However, many of the "laws" in question derive, often quite literally, from
the presupposition that the church is one, much like the Nicene Creed itself
speaks from such a canonical perspective. Unity and discipline presuppose
each other. The issue thrust to the fore, then, is how these "laws" are not so
much obstacles to be overleapt as signs of deeper realities to which we must
more deeply submit.

So let's bear these two qualifications in mind, those of us who are wise
and knowledgeable about the character of theological life. First, we are not
as forthright as we claim to be when we affirm the intimate connection that
exists between theological speech and community. We are wedded to the
freedoms of autonomous Christian life far more than we care to admit (perhaps more than many we scholars whose community is so judiciously chosen for the sake of our work). Second, and just because of our ingrained habits

of autonomy, any reassertion we may seek for that connection between speech and community, as it touches upon the creed especially, will have a bite, a sharp bite indeed, that jumps out at us from the fact that order in word and deed comes from a vigorous ecclesial discipline.

With these qualifications in mind, I can state again the main point I wish to make about the creed as a coherent statement of conviction by the Christian church: if the creed makes any sense or points to any sense within the faith of the Christian community, it does so only within the context of the ascetically ordered life of the church. To the degree that the creed does not, to the degree that we gather pressed by a looming sense of the theological disorder of our churches, it is because this theological disorder is inseparable from the ascetic disorder of our ecclesial life. It is not, on the one hand, simply for lack of truthful speaking that our churches are in disarray—although we need so much of this, and so need the creed's words now more than ever. Nor is it only for want of the civic virtues of courtesy and tolerance that we struggle so in our divided churches—although a little more of each could hardly hurt. Rather, the spiritual fruits that mark particularly *Christian* virtue will be the gifts of self-giving that, clothed in the political garb of ecclesial practice, will push the ordering capacity of our faithful language to its purposed end.

The Particular Meanings of the Creed's Canonical Context

Now let us return to the canons of Nicea (and later councils for that matter), so we can see how the creed takes its shape quite explicitly within the context of such self-ordering. In doing so, we can see the nature of this self-ordering in a light that must surely judge our own common lives.

I have said that there is a kind of semantic overlap between the "canon" of the creed itself and the "canons" that make up the various decrees of the council. Let us be more explicit about the theological significance of this overlap. We tend to think of the creed as both the product and the instrumental expression of "unity in faith." If we cannot join in the faith expressed by the creed, it is said by many ecumenical confessions, like the Chicago-Lambeth Quadrilateral, we cannot be one in the church. I need to emphasize, then, that patristic explicators of Nicea understood the canonical decrees of the council much as we do the creed itself in this respect. For instance, Athanasius was insistent that the political orderings given in the "canons" of the council—those canons, say, that dealt with the jurisdictional constraints on bishops—were precisely what upheld and often coincided with the integrity of the apostolic faith. To dilute the practice of these canons and to accept such dilution, he asserted, was to engage, quite literally, in the "corruption" of the faith. These two elements, "ecclesiastical canons" and "faith of the Church,"[14] in Athanasius's mind, are conjoined, and to dislodge one was to subvert the other "by degrees."

Thus we find that much of the material someone like Athanasius marshals and cites from others in his apologies and histories of the Arian conflict—episcopal letters, letters from popes, decrees from local synods, and so on—speaks to the general conviction that the "unity" constructed by an adherence to political and jurisdictional canons given at Nicea and before is integral to the integrity of the faith given in the creed.[15] The examples are too numerous to cite, but a simple look at Nicea's synodal letter demonstrates the loose way in which references that touch on "matters of the faith" are mixed up, on the one hand, and those that by "canon and decree" "establish peace and harmony" do so from the midst of contention and "fatigue," on the other hand. So it must be stated firmly that, in the context of the creed, the bald distinctions between "faith" on the one side and the political processes of "ecclesial unity" on the other cannot be played off against each other. Such distinctions, as we use them today, are the product of sixteenth-century separative logic that simply fall outside the theological world of the creed. The canons that order the church's practical life in unity are themselves expressions of the creedal faith of the church.

To look at the specific referents of the canons, then, is to reveal the concrete meanings of the creedal life of the church. Of the twenty accepted canons of Nicea, fourteen can be self-evidently "thematized" into categories. They are the following: three canons (2, 9, and 17) deal with the moral purity of the clergy; four canons (8, 10, 14, and 19) deal explicitly with the reception of repentant heretics; 7 canons (4, 5, 6, 15, 16, 18, and 20)—the most by far that fall into a single category—deal with the ordering and political jurisdiction of the church's leadership. If one were to state briefly how these three categories relate, one might say that the canons as a whole speak to a concern over turmoil and division within the church that is marked not only by doctrinal conflict with heretics, but even more deeply by the moral pride of individuals.

Let me explain this a bit further. Moral pride forms the ground of the ecclesial elements the canons address. From a negative perspective, the Nicene canons show that doctrinal division is mirrored in institutional and jurisdictional confusion. This, in turn, is influenced by the interior moral corruption of Christian leaders. Hence, questions of ethical purity with money and sexual behavior and Christian immaturity go hand in hand with the extensive concern over priests and bishops who violate diocesan boundaries, who have no desire to stay put, who make decisions autonomously and independently from other dioceses and metropolitan provinces, who accuse colleagues capriciously and without due process, and who refuse discipline and repentance. From a positive perspective, the common shape of the canons demonstrates how divine "truth" itself is mirrored in common discipline, mutually accepted orderings of institutional life, the stability and self-discipline of church leaders, and the maintenance of the geographical integrity of jurisdictional boundaries and structures.

These particular meanings and their mutual interaction seem to articulate a common orientation, which is properly brought under the heading of "canon." That is, there is a theological reason why the "canon" of the creed and the "canons" of institutional decrees semantically overlap. This theological reason lies in the undergirding evangelical significance of ordering itself, understood as self-ordering. In the case of both creed and canons, the governing force in their expression is the obedience os submission to the will of God within the context of the concrete life of both the church and the world. What does such submission represent? It represents the very character, indeed the historical reality, of God's own life given to the world, to which the church is the gifted response. To order one's life as a believing church and to submit to that ordering canonically (which is what the canons constitute) is to embody the shape of God's own self-giving in the world.

It would be tendentious, of course, to read the creed's dual affirmation of the Son's substantial divinity and his historical incarnation as somehow explicating this divine shape of self-ordering in a way that directly informs particular canons. The early church, in general, did not have a robust theology or devotion of *imitatio Christi*, let alone one that explicated the order of the institution in particular.[16] Athanasius, for instance, was inclined to speak of the "imitation of the saints," rather than of Christ. Their courage and love, furthermore, leading even to martyrdom, was based less on the model of Jesus than on the gift of freedom from mortal fear that his redemption of human flesh gave them.[17] The incarnation was not a principle of self-ordering in this sense.

It is still significant that the ordering of the church's life, shaped by its canons, was something clearly tied to the holiness of the apostolic life in union with Christ. It is interesting to find the suffering of and submission to canonical confusion within the church literally called a form of "martyrdom,"[18] according to Athanasius. But even further, the very acts of ordering the church, in the form of episcopal organization in canonical integrity, are called "saintly" acts of "apostolic" character tied to the life of Christ. The episcopal order of ministry, with all of its most practical and burdensome functions of governance, is a "trust" from Christ, the acceptance of which, with all of its dirty administrative work, places us in the order of St. Paul himself (as Athanasius writes in the wonderful letter to Dracontius [Letter 49]). Paul's own sufferings as a leader of ecclesial order, in turn, draw on the truth of Christ's incarnation (see also Athanasius's second paschal letter, of 330). "We ought to imitate the saints and fathers," Athanasius then asks, "And whom do *they* wish you to imitate?" The ultimate and implied model is clear: they imitate the first apostles, whose lives were directly touched by Jesus' own.

Church canons, then, do not directly mirror the incarnation, but it is not surprising to see a logical evolution of the vision of canon and apostolic imitation taking place in the direction that did, in the end, make "ecclesial order" and "historical incarnation" mutually reflective realities. Gregory of Nazianzen's famous apology for his refusal to accept his ordination founds explicitly the deep-seated tradition, later picked up by Gregory the Great, by which the ordering of the church describes, in a sense, the truth of God's own self-giving in the flesh of Christ.[19] Athanasius had tried to elevate the sanctifying dignity of ecclesial ordering by tying it to St. Paul's ministry. Gregory of Nazianzen, just for this reason, is frightened of its holy burden and of his own incapacity to fulfill it. What is interesting is the way he describes his own and the larger church's failures in terms of their inability to order themselves and finally resolves his fears in terms of a literal "submission" to order, whose painful progress—and frequent failure—is nothing less than an image of the accepted cross of the Incarnate One. Ultimately, Gregory perceives only one solution to the "anarchy and disorder," the "confusion" and "war against love" among the members of the church[20] from which he shies away; that is, his own "submission" to the "order" and "rule" of the apostle's outline of the institutional roles of the church, given especially through his own ordained father who calls him back to work as a priest.[21] It was a vocation, as we all know, that he found almost unbearable; but in submission to it, he understood himself to be "taking up the cross" of the Lord's disciple.

It is *not* tendentious, therefore, to see the growth of and existence of the canons, the orderings of the church's life, as distinctly reflective of the life of Christ, as the apostolic character of that incarnation in the eyes of the Nicene fathers. It was Gregory who quoted from Galatians 6:14 (or perhaps Phil. 3:3) in the context of a discussion of the orders of ministry, "Far be it from me to glory except in the cross of our Lord Jesus Christ, by which the world has been crucified to me, and I to the world."[22] It was St. Paul himself who called this, literally, the "canon" or "rule" by which the "Israel of God" should walk (Gal. 6:16). It is also, according to a later gloss on Philippians 3:16, the "canon" by which our imitation of Christ's own incarnated self-humiliation was to be "held in mind."

Nor was the direct connection between cross and organizational canon foreign to this scriptural root. For St. Paul himself, there was a particular place wherein such a canonical adherence to the form of Christ's service was given bite in his own life. This lay precisely in his submission to what was later to become jurisdictional discipline (2 Cor. 10:13–16; cf. Rom. 15:20): he would not work in, and would therefore not boast of, the field—or "canon," literally—of labor that other missionaries had planted, not wishing to build on someone else's foundation, already laid. To imitate the apostolic model, therefore, did indeed include subjection to geographical limits upon one's authority—a self-limitation that not only helped to maintain unity, but tied one to the lineage of the true disciple of Christ Jesus.

It is hardly a coincidence, therefore, that the jurisdictional question loomed large at Nicea as well. Among the many canonical issues articulated by the council was that which concerned the self-limiting of the teaching authority by which both heresy and orthodoxy were confusedly advanced. In this case, that ordering limitation, which in several canons prevented the movement of priests and bishops outside their immediate jurisdictional residencies, was deemed a necessary buttress to a church bound to the form of Christ's own disciplined self-revelation. It is interesting to note how many centuries later the founder of one of the church's most famous itinerant orders and a self-conscious disciple of the Lord's cross, that is, Saint Francis, listed the self-limitation of preachers within foreign jurisdictions as a primary characteristic of the faithful follower of Christ (see the opening of his *Testament*). The line of connection between cross and organizational self-dicipline was obvious for centuries.

The fundamental element of self-ordering, and thus of self-limitation, that informs the canons of the creedal church, is therefore properly understood as a practical and critical explication of the doctrine of Christ that the creed articulated. Indeed, the canonical context of the creed must be seen as essential to a grasp of its very meaning, in a way analogous to the Christian tradition's understanding of mortification as essential to the flourishing of charity within the Christian soul.[23] We should, in fact, see the canons as structures of ecclesial mortification in that their purpose in ordering the church is to leave space, through the limiting of human pride's self-assertion in the corporate life, for the divine assertion of Christ's own gracious form upon his body. This, finally, is the underlying thread that holds together the thematic categories of Nicea's twenty canons as they emerge from the resolution of the Arian turmoil: no longer will heresy cripple the church if the church can order the pride from which heresy springs through a limiting of the power of its members that rightly reflects the Lord's own willingness to give himself over to humankind.

The Canonical Challenge of Creedal Christianity

On its face none of this perhaps seems very notable: the church orders itself so it can teach effectively. Who would disagree? Every denominational body has its institutional origins in such a functionalist motive. Further, the fact that I am making a simple point should not lead to the conclusion that it is a simplistic one. The claim I am making is much broader than such a functionalist observation about ecclesial organization for the sake of the gospel's propagation. The principle of "Easter and Order" with respect to the creed is fundamentally tied to the living reality in this world of God's truth in Christ Jesus.

In the first place, I am claiming that the self-ordering of the church is evangelically essential, not only functionally supportive.

In the second place, I am explaining the character of this evangelical essence as ascetically self-mortifying. The kind of order that comes from organized and disciplined self-limitation on the part of the institution's players is an essential instance of the declarative grace by which God, through the church, sets forth the form of her proclaimed Lord.

Third, by corollary, I want to emphasize how the absence or confusion of such ecclesial self-mortification—that is, the church's disorder—is destructive of the reality of the gospel.

Finally, we must conclude that the standard of order ought rightly to evaluate, coherently with other normative elements, the whole character of our gathered ecclesial vocations.

This last conclusion, of course, touches upon the ecumenical reality that informs the present gathering of scholars. It is not simply that we gather in contradiction to about every explicit canon of Nicea (and Constantinople). We do. But even more to the point, we gather in disinterest of them altogether. We gather, that is, as positive exponents of overlapping jurisdictions upon jurisdictions, for that is what a modern denomination is; as exponents of free-ranging ministerial entrepreneurialism of the mind; of atomized Christianity incapable of even beginning the process of preparatory discipline and mutual accountability and subjection. All of these work against basic elements of the creed's canonical articulation.

If there is something new about the ecumenical placement of our discussion, then, it surely touches upon this reality as it informs our condition. You see, we are gathered here because we are all touched by the angelic wording of the creed (and I do not hesitate so to locate the sanctity of the creed's speech). These phrases and their referents have become properly enticing of our yearning spirits that, after a long hunger for the divine sounds of scripture's elucidation, now seek a rest amid this ecclesial and cultural desert in the deep treasures of Christ's truth. We are driven people, seduced by God's truth. Yet here and now, in a time when such truth is so belittled, so misunderstood, and unheeded, and alien in its very character as truth for an enveloping world culture of materialist autonomy, just now in our awakened desire we discover ouselves incompetent, disordered into incompetence—to know fully and uphold firmly in our flesh this very truth for the sake of both church and world.

A yearning disordered into incompetence. Of course, who would deny that Christian churches have been expanding at a remarkable rate across the globe, seemingly belying the worries of our ecumenical forebears? Who needs Christian unity to grow? And yet more than ever our churches are tossed about, transformed by, and reflective of a God-forgetting global materialism that is frightening in its ability to remake ecclesial life into its own image. The church's disorder is now celebrated as the freedom and creativity of a new paradigm of unhindered self-assertion whose very progress is a blasphemy against the character of the incarnate and self-giving God who is the crucified and risen Christ.

So if anything is new ecumenically, it is in part the awareness of the astonishing extent of that insight original to the ecumenical movement one hundred years ago: no longer is our disunity an obstacle only to the effectiveness of our evangelism of the world, as was once thought. It is even more pertinently now shown to be a fundamental obstacle to our grasp of the truth that is the basis for our evangelically fired speech in the first place. The yearning for God itself is what has been disordered into incompetence. What is wholly new is the revealed conjunction of this yearning and incompetence: creedal Christianity is unable to hold the object of its desire. As St. James writes, "You desire and do not have. . . . You do not have, because you do not ask.

You ask and do not receive, because you ask wrongly, to spend it on your passions" (James 4:2–3). James's comment to his church is an assessment of today's deepest evangelical longing shorn of its self-ordering.

The revelation of this conjunction of yearning and incompetence does not, however, in itself provide a view of some practical future; but it does unveil a motive by which those who find life in the Christian faith must seek to live it. None of us now controls our interdenominational condition, but the order of our personal and immediate institutional lives is both ours to mold and, at present, our self-evident failure to maintain. The assertion of human pride in both personal and institutional settings has never been so in need of the mortifying restraints of mutual subjection and humiliated self-denial. That is why the struggles over marriage and sexual behavior in our midst are hardly irrelevant to our ecumenical being. But it is also why the virtues of our financial spending are equally essential, along with the character of our local jurisdictional self-limitations and the discipline of our common interactions.

Particular canons are not at issue. What *is* at issue is the recognition by theological adepts, such as those gathered here and all ecclesial leaders, that our desire for God's true life in Christ must find its focus today in the press for this kind of order. It is an order that embodies the canonical demand for the institutional "form of Christ" that alone can speak the truth after which we so ardently thirst. We must, as James says, desire rightly, for such right desire—the desire of personal and institutional mortifying order—is the opening of grace by which the way forward in unity can be discovered. After all, only such grace as this will clarify the further paths of self-ordering that can draw long-separated churches together. They are paths that today still remain wholly obscure and about which we are still unable to say much of anything. We should not be discouraged, however. For the creed, in its true articulation, drives us to the place where our asking, our bare asking through the submission of our wills and passions and pride to the orderings of our fellow believers, must find its proper form.

Let us take our minds, let us take our money, let us take our wills and our plans, our strategies for reform, our manifestos and demands, and let us give them over to one another. That is order. And at that point, *"credo in unum deum et in Iesum Christum, et unam ecclesiam"* will be a sound with a startling swell.

Notes

Introduction

1. For a more thorough discussion of Luther's views see Reinhard Hütter, *Suffering Divine Things: Theology as Church Practice* (Grand Rapids: Eerdmans, 1997), 128–45.

2. Quoted in J. N. D. Kelly, *Early Christian Creeds*, 3rd ed. (New York: Longman, 1985), 1.

3. Stephen W. Sykes, *The Integrity of Anglicanism,* (London: A. R. Mowbray & Co., 1978), 20–24.

4. Michael Ramsey, *An Era in Anglican Theology, From Gore to Temple* (London: Longmans, 1960), p. 14.

5. For a nice expression of this point see Christopher Brown, "More than Affirmation: The Incarnation as Judgment and Grace," in *The Rue of Faith: Scripture, Canon and Creed in a Critical Age*, ed. E. Radner and G. Sumner (Harrisburg, Pa.: Morehouse, 1998), 77–91.

6. Douglas Farrow, *Ascension and Ecclesia: On the Significance of the Doctrine of the Ascension for Ecclesiology and Christian Cosmology* (Grand Rapids: Eerdmans, 1999).

7. Thomas F. Torrance, *The Trinitarian Faith: The Evangelical Theology of the Ancient Catholic Church* (Edinburgh: T & T Clark, 1988), 1–13.

8. *Nicene and Post-Nicene Fathers of the Christian Church* (second series), vol. 14, *The Seven Ecumenical Councils* (Grand Rapids: Eerdmans), 8.

9. Ibid., 11.

10. Ibid.

11. Ibid., 190.

Chapter 1: Our Help Is in the Name of the LORD, the Maker of Heaven and Earth

1. David Yeago, "The New Testament and Nicene Dogma: A Contribution to the Recovery of Theological Exegesis," *Pro Ecclesia* 3 (1994): 152–64.

2. John Pearson, *An Exposition of the Creed* (London: George Bell & Sons, 1902).

3. Frances Young, *Biblical Exegesis and the Formation of Christian Culture* (Cambridge: Cambridge University Press, 1998); Richard Bauckham, *God Crucified: Monotheism and Christology in the New Testament* (Carlisle: Paternoster, 1998).

4. Mark Tooley, "Apostasy at 2000: Episcopal Institute Promotes Pantheism, Syncretism," *Touchstone* (January 2001).

5. Augustine, *The Confessions of St Augustine,* trans., Hal M. Helms (Brewster, Mass.: Paraclete, 1986), 3.

6. C. FitzSimons Allison, *The Cruelty of Heresy: An Affirmation of Christian Orthodoxy* (Harrisburg, Pa.: Morehouse, 1994).

7. John Betjeman, *Collected Poems* (London: John Murray, 1997). The final two lines have been added for this context.

8. Robert Jenson, *Systematic Theology,* vol. 1, *The Triune God* (Oxford: Oxford University Press, 1997), 42–60.

9. See Pearson's own dicussion (*Exposition*, 75ff.).

10. Ibid., 38, n. 4.

11. Barth, *Church Domatics* 1/1, 400.

12. Pearson, *Exposition*, 40–41.

13. B. S. Childs, *Biblical Theology in Crisis* (Philadelphia: Westminster, 1970), 217.

14. James Barr, *Old and New in Interpretation* (Harper and Row, 1966), 149.

15. Lee Keck, *A Future for the Historical Jesus* (Philadelphia: Fortress, 1980), 213.

16. P. Zahl, *A Short Systematic Theology* (Grand Rapids: Eerdmans, 2000).

17. Kendall Soulen, *The God of Israel and Christian Theology* (Minneapolis: Fortress, 1996), 50–1.

18. Childs, *Biblical Theology*, 226.

19. Ibid

20. "Walter Brueggemann's *Theology of the Old Testament: Testimony, Dispute, Advocacy,*" *SJT* 53 (2000): 228–33. Brueggemann's book was published in 1997 by Fortress Press.

21. Jenson, *Systematic Theology*, 50–51.

22. Martin Luther.

23. P. T. Forsyth, *Positive Preaching and the Modern Mind* (London: Independent Press, 1907), 240.

Chapter 2: And in One Lord, Jesus Christ . . . Begotten, Not Made

1. Maurice Wiles, "In Defence of Arius," in *Working Papers on Doctrine* (London: SCM, 1976), 28–37. See also R. C. Gregg and D. Groh, *Early Arianism* (London: SCM, 1981); and Rowan Williams, *Arius: Heresy and Tradition* (London: Darton, Longman and Todd, 1987).

2. Wiles fails to note one crucial piece of evidence. He offers evidence that the Cappadocians, like Augustine after them, failed to attribute any functional distinctions between the economic work of the three persons of the Trinity, but he does not give attention—to cite one example—to Basil, *On the Holy Spirit*, XV: 36 and 38. While affirming the unity of the one God, he says that we must also distinguish "the original cause of all things that are made, the Father, . . . the creative cause, the Son, . . . the perfecting cause, the Spirit."

3. Maurice Wiles, "Eternal Generation," in *Working Papers on Doctrine* (London: SCM, 1976), 19.

4. The problems of this are immediately apparent. Origen continues: "I so not think that our mind must stray beyond this to the suspicion that this hypostasis or substance could possibly possesses bodily characteristics . . ."

5. Origen, *On First Principles* 1. 2. 2.

6. Wiles, "Eternal Generation," 24–25.

7. G. L. Prestige, *God in Patristic Thought* (London: SPCK, 1952), 51

8. G. R. Beasley-Murray, *John*, 2d ed., Word Biblical Commentary (Nashville: Nelson, 1999), 14.

9. Here, as in other places, Origen sails far to close to the wind of Gnosticism. "This abstraction [the Gnostics'] from Jesus to the Christ, and then back again to ourselves, is a movement which has been repeated over and over again in subsequent theological speculation and sermonizing. It is the second and more important reason why gnosticism is to be identified as the archetypal heresy." Douglas Farrow, "St Irenaeus of Lyons: The Church and the World." *Pro Ecclesia* 4 (1995): 333–55 (337).

10. Robert Jenson, *Systematic Theology*, vol. 1, *The Triune God* (Oxford: Oxford University Press, 1997), 76–77. The langauge may be rare, but it comes in significant places, for example in Exodus 4:22 NIV: "say to Pharaoh: . . . "Israel is my firstborn son"; and compare Hosea 11:1.

11. As Jenson also sees, describing Israel as the people created by God's Word. Jenson, *Systematic Theology*, 1:68.

12. In Origen's terms, as god rather than *the* God.

13. Indeed, such a concession goes some way to obviating those tendencies, especially strong in Western theology, that render the three persons of the Trinity functionally identical.

14. For recent unsatisfactory attempts, Catholic and Protestant respectively, to mimimize or abolish the doctrine of the immanent Trinity, see Catherine Mowry LaCugna, *God for Us: The Trinity and Christian Life* (New York: HarperCollins, 1991), and Ted Peters, *God as Trinity: Relationality and Temporality in Divine Life* (Louisville: Westminster/John Knox, 1993).

15. Athanasius, *On the Incarnation of the Word* 4, in *Christology of the Later Fathers,* ed. E. R. Hardy, Library of Christian Classics, vol. 3 (London: SCM, 1954), 59.

16. Athanasius, *On the Incarnation* 7, 61–62.

17. Athanasius, *Against the Arians*, 1:28.

18. Irenaeus, *Against the Heresies* 3.16.6. This ought surely to dispel all the nonsense that Irenaeus's is only an economic trinitarianism and that the "evil" of ontology came in only with Nicene theology.

19. This discussion assumes an essentially Eastern approach, in contrast to the Western tendency to conceive the persons in terms of relations of opposition.

20. Wolfhart Pannenberg, *Systematic Theology*, vol. 1, trans. G. W. Bromiley (Edinburgh: T & T Clark, 1991), 320.

21. Pannenberg, *Systematic Theology*, 1:319 n. 183, recording his disagreement with Robert Jenson.

22. Pannenberg, *Systematic Theology*, 1:315.

23. I owe the latter point to Shirley Martin, to whom I am grateful for a number of comments on this paper that have assisted in its preparation for publication.

24. "A Trinity which is absolutely locked within itself—one which is not, in its reality open to anything distinct from it." (Karl Rahner, *The Trinity*, E. T. by Joseph Donceel, [London: Burns and Oates, 1970], 18.)

25. Athanasius, *Against the Arians*, 1:29.

26. Heinrich Heppe, *Reformed Dogmatics, Set Out and Illustrated from the Sources*, translated by G. T. Thomson (Grand Rapids: Baker, 1950), 122.

Chapter 3: Being of One Substance with the Father

1. An extended version of this paper, replicating much of the material, appears in *The Cambridge Companion to Jesus*, ed. Markus Bockmuehl (Cambridge: Cambridge University Press, 2001).

2. The "Programme for Theology and Cultures in Asia" exemplifies the view that "indigenous theology" is best carried out by considering the spirituality immanent in the symbols of a particular culture. If the symbols of Scottish culture are taken to be its indigenous, national drink (whisky), its national recipe (the haggis) and its famously indigenous musical instrument (the bagpipes), this would seem to suggest that indigenous, Scottish theology should be characterised by spirit, guts . . . and large quantities of wind!

3. John Hick, *The Myth of God Incarnate* (London: SCM, 1977).

4. Such was the plethora of terms appearing in the titles of books on the topic, that the cynic would have been excused assuming that theologians had been hunting through their thesauri with the aim of claiming relevance and originality by finding another word for myth!

5. For this discussion I am particularly indebted to Alasdair Heron's outstanding article, "Homoousios with the Father," in *The Incarnation*, ed T. F. Torrance (Boot of Garten: Handsel Press, 1981), 58–87.

6. Integral to Arius's thinking here was the supposition that if the Father and the Son were conceived to be coeternal, they must be identical with each other, thereby destroying the foundational doctrine of divine simplicity.

7. To deny this and to conceive of the Son as consubstantial (*homoousios*) with the Father was, in Arius's view, to destroy the divine simplicity such that the Father becomes "compound and divisible and alterable and a body." This is taken from a fragment of Arius's *Thalia*, cited by Athanasius, *De Synodis*, 15. Cf. Heron, "Homoousios," 62 and n. 5a.

8. Cf. Heron, "Homoousios," 78 n. 15.

9. Here I am indebted to articles by T. F. Torrance on Athanasius and the patristic understanding of revelation found in his two books, *Theology in Reconciliation* (Eugene, Ore.: Wipf & Stock, 1996) and *Theology in Reconstruction* (Eugene, Ore.: Wipf & Stock, 1996).

10. Heron, "Homoousios, " 70.

11. Frances Young translates *dianoia* "sense" (*Biblical Exegesis and the Formation of Christian Culture* [Cambridge: Cambridge University Press, 1997], 34). As Frege showed, the sense of an expression is the mode of designation of its reference.

12. *Dianoia* refers to the penetration of our theological conceptualities (*noein*) "through to" (*dia*) their reference.

13. Heron, "Homoousios, " 70–71.

14. Josef Jungmann, *The Place of Christ in Liturgical Prayer* (Collegeville, Minn.: Liturgical Press, 1989).

15. Like Arianism before it, Apollinarianism was condemned by the church in the "Tome of Damasus" (382), which emerged out of the Council of Rome.

16. For a fuller discussion of these issues and their practical ramifications, see James B. Torrance, *Worship, Community and the Triune God of Grace* (Downers Grove, Ill.: InterVarsity Press, 1996).

Chapter 4: By Whom All Things Were Made

1. George Coyne, S.J., "The Universe: Scientific Understanding and Theological Implications," *Origins* 26 (1997): 480.

2. In his recent book *The Fifth Miracle: The Search for the Origin and Meaning of Life* (New York: Simon & Schuster, 1999), Paul Davies states: "What remains to be explained—what stands as the central unsolved puzzle—is how the first microbe came to exist" (29).

3. In "Biological Evolution and Christian Theology—Yesterday and Today," in *Darwinism and Divinity*, ed. John Durant (New York: Blackwell, 1985), A. R. Peacocke summarizes the evidence for evolutionary relations among living organisms: "Twentieth-century biochemistry, notably in its phase of molecular biology, has now demonstrated fundamental similarities at the molecular level between all living organisms from bacteria to man. Not only is nucleic acid (DNA or RNA) the prime carrier of hereditary information in all living organisms but the code that translates this information from base sequences in DNA, via messenger RNA, to amino acid sequences in proteins (and thence to their structure and function), is the *same* code in *all* living organisms. This code is arbitrary with respect to the relations of the molecular structures involved and its universality is comprehensible only as the result of evolution: the code now universally operative is the one which happened to be present in the living matter that first successfully reproduced itself fast enough to outnumber other rivals. Molecular biology has provided another independent and powerful confirmation of evolutionary relations through its ability to compare amino acid sequences in proteins with the same chemical function (e.g. cytochrome C) in widely different organisms. The striking fact is that such comparisons entirely and independently confirm . . . the evolutionary relationships previously deduced on morphological and palaeontological grounds."

4. See, for example, Michael Denton, *Evolution: A Theory in Crisis* (Bethesda, Md.: Adler & Adler, 1985), and Michael J. Behe, *Darwin's Black Box* (New York: Simon & Schuster, 1996). For a brief summary of the issues, see Ian G. Barbour, *Religion and Science: Historical and Contemporary Issues* (San

Francisco: HarperCollins, 1997), 221–25. See also Kenneth D. Miller, *Finding Darwin's God: A Scientist's Search for Common Ground between God and Evolution* (New York: HarperCollins, 1999).

5. For a summary account, see Richard Fortey, *Life: A Natural History of the First Four Billion Years of Life on Earth* (New York: Alfred Knopf, 1998), 289–315.

6. Christopher F. Mooney, S.J., *Theology and Scientific Knowledge* (Notre Dame, Ind.: University of Notre Dame Press, 1996), 138.

7. See Peter Medawar, *The Threat and the Glory* (New York: Harper Collins, 1990), 144–77. More recently, in *NonZero: The Logic of Human Destiny* (New York: Random House, 2000), Robert Wright has argued for the continuity between biological and cultural evolution, pointing to the marked tendency in both toward increasing complexity.

8. Colin E. Gunton, *The One, the Three and the Many: God, Creation and the Culture of Modernity* (Cambridge: Cambridge University Press, 1993), 155–79.

9. Quoted in the *Catechism of the Catholic Church*, par. 292.

10. J. N. D. Kelly, *Early Christian Creeds*, 3rd ed. (New York: David McKay, 1972), 232.

11. Jaroslav Pelikan, *The Emergence of the Catholic Tradition (100–600)* (Chicago: University of Chicago Press, 1971), 203.

12. Message to the Pontifical Academy of Sciences, par. 4, 5, and 6.

13. For a discussion of these ways of relating science and religion, see Barbour, *Religion and Science*, 77–105. See also Avery Dulles, S.J., "Science and Theology," in *John Paul II on Science and Religion*, ed. Robert John Russell, William R. Stoeger, S.J., and George V. Coyne, S.J. (Vatican City: Vatican Observatory, 1990), 9–18.

14. See the survey by Ernan McMullin, "Evolution and Creation," in *Evolution and Creation*, ed. Ernan McMullin (Notre Dame: University of Notre Dame Press, 1985), 1–56. On the classical exegesis of the hexaemeron, see E. Mangenot, "Hexaméron," in *Dictionnaire de Théologie Catholique* 1:2335–9; William A. Wallace, O.P., Appendices 7–10, in Thomas Aquinas, *Summa Theologiae*, Blackfriars Edition (New York: McGraw-Hill, 1967), 10:202–29. The need for exegesis to keep informed of scientific developments was emphasized by Pope John Paul II in his address to the plenary assembly of the Pontifical Academy of the Sciences in 1992 *(Acta Apostolice Sedis* 85, 764–72). For a general orientation to these issues, see the Pontifical Biblical Commission, *The Interpretation of the Bible in the Church* (Vatican City: Libreria Editrice Vaticana, 1993).

15. Impelled partly by a certain biblical literalism and partly by acknowledged discrepancies in evolutionary theory, "creationism" or "creation-science" tries to show that it can furnish a more adequate explanation of the scientific evidence than can "evolution-science." In her essay, "Let There Be Light: Scientific Creationism in the Twentieth Century," in *Darwinism and Divinity*, ed. John Durant (New York: Blackwell, 1985), 181–204, Eileen Barker draws the following definition of creation-science from an Arkansas statute enjoining its balanced treatment: " 'Creation-science' means the scientific evidences for creation and inferences from those scientific evidences . . . that indicate: (1) Sudden creation of the universe, energy and life from nothing; (2) the insufficiency of mutation and natural selection in bringing about the development of all living things from a single organism; (3) changes only within fixed limits or originally created kinds of plants and animals; (4) separate ancestry for man and apes; (5) explanation of the earth's geology by catastrophism, including the occurrence of a worldwide flood; and (6) a relatively recent inception of the earth and living kinds" (191). For more complete and recent studies of creation-science, see Ronald Numbers, *The Creationists: The Evolution of Scientific Creationism* (New York: Knopf, 1998), and Robert T. Pennock, *Tower of Babel: The Evidence against the New Creationism* (Cambridge: MIT Press, 2000). For a Catholic critique, see Stanley L. Jaki, *The Savior of Science* (Grand Rapids: Eerdmans, 2000), 224–41.

16. On this topic in general, see the important essay by Ernan McMullin, "How Should Cosmology Relate to Theology?" in *The Sciences and Theology in the Twentieth Century*, ed. A. R. Peacocke (Notre Dame, Ind.: University of Notre Dame Press, 1981), 17–57; on the tentative character of scientific reasoning in relation to theology, see especially 49–52.

17. Pope John Paul II, "Message to the Pontifical Academy of Sciences on Evolution," par. 5, *Origins* 26 (1996), 415.

18. Although it was reaffirmed by Pope Pius XII in *Humani Generis* (1950) in response to materialist evolutionary theories (DS 3896), the doctrine of the immediate creation of the human soul has been continuously held by the Church and was not originally formulated with a view to issues raised by evolutionary theories (see DS 190, 201, 285, 360, 455, 685).

19. In addition to the works of Catholic and other Christian authors already cited, the following works are worthy of note for their synthetic scope: Benedict Ashley, O.P., *Theologies of the Body* (Braintree, Mass.: Pope John Center, 1985) and Jacques Arnould, O.P., *La théologie après Darwin: Elements*

pour une théologie de la creation dans une perspective évolutionniste (Paris: Editions du Cerf, 1998).

20. McMullin, "How Should Theology Relate to Cosmology?" 38.

21. Ibid.

22. The writings of St. Thomas Aquinas have been influential in the development and articulation of this account of divine causality. Among the many texts that could be cited, see especially, *Summa Theologiae* 1a: 14, 19, 45; and 105; *Summa Contra Gentiles* III: 66, 67, 70; *De Potentia* II: 7.

23. On this account, as Brian Hebblethwaite has put it in his essay "Providence and Divine Action," *Religious Studies* 14 (1978): 226, "the whole web of creaturely events is to be construed as pliable or flexible to the providential hand of God."

24. See discussions of the relevance of this understanding of divine causality for issues of science and religion in Ernan McMullin's "Evolution and Creation," and his essay, "Natural Science and Belief in a Creator: Historical Notes," in *Physics, Philosophy and Theology*, ed. Robert John Russell, William R. Stoeger, S.J., and George V. Coyne, S.J. (Vatican City: Vatican Observatory, 1988), 49–79

25. Thomas F. Tracy, "Particular Providence and the God of the Gaps," in *Chaos and Complexity: Scientific Perspectives on Divine Action*, 2d ed., ed. Robert John Russell, Nancey Murphy, and A. R. Peacocke (Notre Dame, Ind.: University of Notre Dame Press, 1997), 311. Tracy's entire essay (289–324) is indispensable for the consideration of the issues under discussion here.

26. See J. D. Barrow and F. J. Tipler, *The Anthropic Cosmological Principle* (Oxford: Oxford University Press, 1986). At the beginning of his book, *Nature's Destiny: How the Laws of Biology Reveal Purpose in the Universe* (New York: Free Press, 1998), the biologist Michael Denton expresses a strong version of this principle when he states that his aim is "first, to present the scientific evidence for believing that the cosmos is uniquely fit for life as it exists on earth and for organisms of design and biology very similar to our own species . . . and, second, to argue that this 'unique fitness' of the laws of nature for life is entirely consistent with the older teleological religious concept of the cosmos as a specially designed whole, with life and mankind as its primary goal and purpose" (xi). See also William A. Dembski, *Intelligent Design: The Bridge Between Science and Theology* (Downers Grove, Ill.: InterVarsity Press, 1999), and, for a preliminary theological analysis, Jean-Michel Maldamé, O.P., *Le Christ pour l'univers* (Paris: Desclée, 1998), 91–126.

27. See Peter D. Ward and Donald Brownlee, *Rare Earth: Why Complex Life is Uncommon in the Universe* (New York: Copernicus/Springer-Verlag, 2000). A complementary perspective can be found in Martin Rees, *Just Six Numbers: The Deep Forces that Shape the Universe* (New York: Basic Books, 2000).

28. See McMullin, "Evolution and Creation," especially 27–32; and Tracy, "Particular Providence and the God of the Gaps."

29. For a theological defense of this position, see Karl Rahner, *Hominisation* (New York: Herder & Herder, 1965); and Ashley, *Theologies of the Body*, 307–44. For a recent philosophical discussion of the origin of the soul, see Richard Swinburne, *The Evolution of the Soul* (Oxford: Clarendon, 1986), 174–99. For the classical discussion of this issue, see St. Thomas Aquinas, *Summa Theologiae* 1a: 90–92.

30. Message to the Pontifical Academy of Sciences, par. 6.

Chapter 6: Crucified Also for Us under Pontius Pilate

1. *Lutheran Book of Worship: Minister's Desk Edition* (Minneapolis: Augsburg, 1978), 142–43.

2. Faith and Order Commission, *Confessing the One Faith: An Ecumenical Explication of the Apostolic Faith as It Is Confessed in the Nicene-Constantinopolitan Creed*, Faith and Order Paper 153 (Geneva: WCC Publications, 1991), 55.

3. I use "mainline" to denote those church traditions in the modern West that have close and friendly relations with cultural and social modernity. The term is no longer sociologically accurate—*oldline* or *sideline* would capture the real situation more precisely—but it is still useful as a description of the self-understanding of these communities.

4. The good reasons are briefly that the penal doctrine posits a conflict between love and justice in God that is impossible to justify, and that it ascribes to *punishment* a role in the soteriological problem that is not proportionate to the witness of Holy Scripture.

5. The chief function of the anecdote with which many sermons begin is often to facilitate this sidestepping.

6. This diagnosis of contemporary preaching rests largely on personal observation and anecdotal evidence, though it is supported (I would suggest) by Charles Campbell's critical review of contemporary homiletic theories in *Preaching Jesus: New Directions for Homiletics in Hans Frei's Postliberal Theology* (Grand Rapids: Eerdmans, 1997), as well as by Marsha Witten's study of Protestant preaching in *All Is Forgiven: The Secular Message in American Protestantism* (Princeton: Princeton University Press, 1993).

7. P. T. Forsyth, *The Cruciality of the Cross* (London: Hodder and Stoughton, 1909), 60–61.

8. Cyril, *Third Letter to Nestorius*, in *The Nicene and Post-Nicene Fathers*, 2d series, vol. 14: *The Seven Ecumenical Councils*, 201–5.

9. Ibid., 203.

10. For the reading of St. Maximus summarized here, see my article "Jesus of Nazareth and Cosmic Redemption: The Relevance of St. Maximos the Confessor," *Modern Theology* (April 1996). See also the exposition and translated texts in Andrew Louth, *Maximus the Confessor* (New York: Routledge, 1996).

11. Maximus, *Ambiguum 5*, MPG 91:1056AB; the whole text is translated in Louth, 171–79.

12. See Maximus, *Opusculum 7*, in Louth, 180–91.

13. For a broader response to this critique, see Leanne Van Dyk, "Do Theories of Atonement Foster Abuse?" *dialog* (Winter 1996): 21–25.

14. See Isaiah 2:3; Isaiah 60:1–7; Ezekiel 36:20–23; Zechariah 8:20–23.

15. It is here that the language of priesthood, as foregrounded especially by the Epistle to the Hebrews, comes into its own. Precisely in fulfilling the priestly vocation of Israel, Jesus is the great high priest who has offered himself to God for all. The idiom of priesthood is useful especially to disclose the interconnections between the purpose of God for humankind as a whole, the priestly vocation of Israel, the death of Jesus, and the call of the church to live in the world as a community of worship and doxological witness.

16. See my essay, "The Bread of Life: Patristic Christology and Evangelical Soteriology in Martin Luther's Sermons on John 6," *St. Vladimir's Theological Quarterly,* Summer 1995.

17. Translations of Luther are my own from *D. Martin Luther's Werke. Kritische Gesamtausgabe* (Weimar, 1883ff.), cited as *WA.* I will provide reference where possible to the English translation in *Luther's Works* (Concordia & Fortress, 1955-), cited as *LW.* Here the reference is to *WA* 33:176; *LW* 23:114–115. Emphasis added.

18. *WA* 33:165; *LW* 23:107.

19. *WA* 36:188.

20. More precisely, insofar as the death on the cross was something done *to* Jesus by those who wanted to exclude him from the human world, the resurrection overcomes the cross; insofar as dying on the cross was something done *by* Jesus, who offered himself to the Father for the good of God's creatures, the resurrection is the affirmation of the cross.

21. *Lutheran Book of Worship,* 142–43.

Chapter 7: The Reality of the Resurrection

1. A. J. M. Wedderburn, *Beyond Resurrection* (Peabody, Mass.: Hendrickson, 1999), 154.

2. Robert W. Funk, *Honest to Jesus* (New York: HarperCollins, 1996), 258.

3. Carl E. Braaten, "Can We Still Be Christians," *Pro Ecclesia* 4 (Fall 1995): 395–97.

4. W. Stephen Gunter, *Resurrection Knowledge, Recovering the Gospel for a Postmodern Church* (Nashville: Abingdon, 1999), 51.

5. A. J. M. Wedderburn, *Resurrection*, 249 n. 2.

6. Albert Schweitzer, *The Quest of the Historical Jesus* (New York: Macmillan, 1961), 3–4.

7. Schubert Ogden, *Christ without Myth* (New York: Harper & Brothers, 1961), 136.

8. David Griffin, *A Process Christology* (Philadelphia: Westminster, 1973), 12.

9. Walter Kunneth, *The Theology of the Resurrection* (St. Louis: Concordia, 1965).

10. Karl Barth, *The Epistle to the Romans*, trans. Edwyn C. Hoskyns (Oxford: Oxford University Press, 1933), 203.

11. Rudolf Bultmann, "The New Testament and Mythology," *Kerygma and Myth*, ed. H. W. Bartsch, trans. Reginald Fuller (London: SPCK, 1954), 1:41.

12. Karl Barth, *Church Dogmatics* IV/1, 341, 351.

13. Ernst Troeltsch, "Historical and Dogmatic Method in Theology," in *Religion in History*, Fortress Texts in Modern Theology (Minneapolis: Fortress, 1991), 11–32.

14. Wolfhart Pannenberg, "History and the Reality of the Resurrection," *Resurrection Reconsidered* (Oxford: Oneworld Publications, 1996), 64.

15. Willi Marxsen, *Anfangsprobleme der Christologie* (Kassel: Gutersloher Verlagshaus Gerd Mohn, 1960), 51.

16. Bultmann, *Kerygma and Myth,* 39.

17. Quoted by Gerald O'Collins in *The Resurrection of Jesus Christ* (Valley Forge: Judson, 1973), 97.

Chapter 8: Confession and Confessions

1. O. Weber, *Foundations of Dogmatics* (Grand Rapids: Erdmans, 1981), 1:29.

2. Karl Barth, *Credo* (London: Hodder and Stoughton, 1936), 7.

3. Edmund Schlink, *Theology of the Lutheran Confessions* (Philadelphia: Fortress, 1961), 16.

4. Weber, *Foundations of Dogmatics,* 1:29.

5. Karl Barth, *Church Dogmatics* I/2 (Edinburgh: T & T Clark, 1956), 639.

6. Ibid., 39.

7. Karl Barth, *Die Theologie der reformierten Bekenntnisschriften* (Zürich: Theologischer Verlag, 1998), 33.

8. Schlink, *Theology of the Lutheran Confessions,* 12.

9. Immanuel Kant, *Religion within the Boundaries of Mere Reason* in *Religion and Rational Theology*, ed. A. W. Wood, G. di Giovanni (Cambridge: Cambridge University Press, 1996), 202–6.

10. Dietrich Bonhoeffer, *Christology* (London: Collins, 1978), 75.

11. Kant, *Religion within the Boundaries*, 205ff.

Chapter 9: Confessing Christ Coming

1. See Col. 3:1–3, 1 John 3:2. It may be noted with B. Marthaler (*The Creed* [Mystic, Conn.: Twenty-Third Publications, 1987], 204) that the above refrain was restored to the liturgy by Pope Paul VI.

2. The Gnostic tendency is toward a complete reversal of the subjective and objective values traditionally assigned to the eschatological articles. The objective pole is no longer the actual resurrection and ascension of Jesus; rather, it is the transformed subjectivity of those who hear the Gnostic "gospel" (see Tertullian, *Res.* 19). Hegel saw this especially clearly and deployed it to good effect: it is our faith in the dead Christ as the ground of God's self-reconciliation that is the real basis of what we may call his resurrection and ascension into heaven (*Philosophy of History* [New York: Dover, 1956], 325; cf. *Lectures on the Philosophy of Religion* [Berkeley: University of California 1988], 468).

3. Albert Schweitzer, *The Quest of the Historical Jesus* (London: Macmillan, 1966), 370ff.

4. I follow here the older fashion of enumerating individual segments of the creed; cf. e.g., John Pearson's *Exposition of the Creed*, rev. J. Nichols (London: William Tegg, 1857).

5. καὶ ἀνελόντα εἰς τοὺς οὐρανούς,
καὶ καεζόμενον ἐκ δεξιῶν τοῦ πατρός,
καὶ πάλιν ἐρχόμενον μετὰ δόξης κρῖναι ζῶντας καὶ νεκρούς
οὗ τῆς βασιλείας οὐκ ἔσται τέλος.

6. See also, e.g., Luke 1:33 (cf. Dan. 7:14) and Acts 10:42.

7. Cf. J. N. D. Kelly, *Early Christian Doctrines*, 5th ed. (London: A & C Black, 1985), 240ff.; T. H. Bindley, *The Oecumenical Documents of the Faith*, 4th ed., rev. F. W. Green (London: Methuen, 1950), 40ff., 64ff.

8. Rudolf Bultmann, for one, belittles the ancients with his comment that "no one who is old enough to think for himself supposes that God lives in a local heaven" (*Kerygma and Myth* 1, ed. H. W. Bartsch [London: SPCK, 1953, 4ff.]). The scientific outlook, he says, no longer permits us, as the ancients did, to "accept the story of Christ's descent into hell or his Ascension into heaven as literally true." He adds: "We can no longer look for the return

of the Son of Man on the clouds of heaven or hope that the faithful will meet him in the air."

9. "To this day stands Mount Olivet, still to the eyes of the faithful all but displaying him who ascended on a cloud, and the heavenly gate of his ascension. For from heaven he descended to Bethlehem, but to heaven he ascended from the Mount of Olives; at the former place beginning his conflicts among men, but in the latter, crowned after them" (Cyril of Jerusalem, *Cat.* 14.23, *Nicene and Post-Nicene Fathers*, 2nd series, 7: 100, capitalization altered.)

10. That appears to be the conclusion, e.g., of *Confessing One Faith* (Faith and Order #140, Genena 1987, §158), which consequently has nothing much to say about the ascension.

11. "Growing in Faith: A Sunday School Course: He Ascended into Heaven," *Church Times*, 12 May 1995, 14 (under the rubric "Sunday School/Cookery"!).

12. Origen, *Prayer* 23.2; cf. my *Ascension and Ecclesia* (Edinburgh: T & T Clark; Grand Rapids: Eerdmans, 1999), 96ff.

13. Gregory Nazianzen, *Ep. ad Cled*. (*Nicene and Post-Nicene Fathers*, 2nd series, 7: 440, capitalization altered.)

14. This is the logic still followed, e.g., by the deeply learned John Pearson, sometime master of Jesus College and of Trinity College, who invites us to make the following confession: "I am fully persuaded, that the only-begotten and eternal Son of God, after he rose from the dead, did, with the same soul and body with which he rose, by a true and local translation convey himself from the earth on which he lived, through all the regions of the air, through all the celestial orbs, until he came unto the heaven of heavens, the most glorious presence of the majesty of God. And thus I believe in Jesus Christ who 'ascended into heaven'" (*Exposition*, 396). But of course Pearson (unawares) was writing more or less at the close of Christendom, just prior to the publication of Newton's *Principia* and to the Enlightenment, which followed. His affirmation of "a true and local translation" above the celestial orbs, however contrary both to the conventional Ptolemaic and the new Copernican cosmology, only serves to highlight the need for a good deal of fresh thought. Must we not concede to Bultmann that the situation has changed more dramatically between Newton and the present than between Gregory, patriarch-for-a-day in fourth century Constantinople, and (as Pearson became in 1673) the Lord Bishop of Chester? And will we not then be forced to admit, after all, that the section of the creed we are now examining can no longer be maintained in anything quite like its traditional form? A bodily departure and a bodily return—are these ideas not hopelessly mired in

some hybrid mythology which must fail to speak even to the Christian man or woman of today? Or can the traditional form be redeemed without resorting to something like Bultmann's program of demythologization? Obviously I believe that it can, though in the present context my reasoning must remain largely implicit rather than explicit. Let it be said, however, that deciding this matter is one vitally important challenge for the ecumenical movement, for it is perfectly plain that a church divided in its understanding of the ascension-*parousia* framework must be divided also in its self-understanding. Divided, too, in its understanding of the present age, it can hardly hope to be united in its message or mission to this age.

15. See Acts 2:29–36. Of course, we may rightly speak of an enthronement already on the cross, for this is how Christ exercises his kingship among us. Yet on the cross he is still the king in exile. God has another and better throne for his Son than the one we devised! (Cyril asks that we "not curiously pry into what is properly meant by [this latter] throne, for it is incomprehensible" [*Cat.* 14.27ff.].)

16. Oliver O'Donavan, *Desire of the Nations* (Cambridge: Cambridge University Press, 1996). Cf. Thomas Hobbes, *Leviathan* 3: 39; Jean-Jaques Rousseau, *The Social Contract* 4: 8.

17. There is nothing partial or incomplete about his authority—"all power in heaven and on earth has been given to me"—but the David typology is instructive here.

18. I have treated these things at greater length in *Ascension and Ecclesia*.

19. *STh* III:57 (art. 6)

20. See my "Ascension and Atonement," in *The Theology of Reconciliation*, ed. C. Gunton (Edinburgh: T & T Clark, forthcoming).

21. See William Milligan, *The Ascension of Our Lord* (London: Macmillan 1892), and John Zizioulas, "Preserving God's Creation: Three Lectures on Theology and Ecology," *King's Theological Review* 12 no. 1 (1989), 12 no. 2 , 13 no. 1 (1990).

22. Cf. *AH* 4.8.3, 4.17.5, 4.18, 5.28.4, 5.34.3.

23. Cf. the words of Prisca, quoted by Tertullian (*Res.* 11): "They are carnal, and yet they hate the flesh."

24. Mr. Chrétien was elected to his third term of office in November 2000.

25. Here was a pretty sight—a "Catholicism" called to heel by Rousseau, whose language and logic were emulated to good effect!

26. This is Rousseau's victory over "priestly religion" (*Social Contract* 4: 8), which perversely refuses to divide neatly and without conflict into inner and outer, spiritual and civil, religion. W. Cavanaugh offers a thought-provoking counterattack on Hobbes and Rousseau in his article, "The City: Beyond Sec-

ular Parodies" in *Radical Orthodoxy*, ed. J. Milbank et al. (London: Routledge, 1999), 182ff.

27. *Cat.* 4.1; cf. Justin, *Trypho* 32.

28. For a thumbnail sketch consult Zechariah, from which is drawn much of the language and imagery employed in the New Testament to speak of the *parousia* and related events.

29. This is not the place to quibble with Protestant orthodoxy's triple advent *in carne, in gratia, in gloria,* or with Karl Barth's doctrine of a threefold *parousia* (but cf. *Ascension and Ecclesia,* 248 n. 386).

30. See Sir. 50:4ff.; cf. N. T. Wright, *The New Testament and the People of God* (London: SPCK, 1992), 409ff.

31. "God the Father," avers Augustine, "in his personal presence will judge no man, but has given all judgment unto his Son, who shall shew himself as man, to judge the world even as he shewed himself as man to be judged by the world" (*Civitas Dei* 20.30, trans. J. H.; [London, Griffith, Farran, Okeden, and Welsh, 1610], capitalization altered).

32. A point nicely captured (as Tom Smail reminds me) by Charles Wesley's familiar lines: "Those dear tokens of his passion / still his dazzling body bears. . . ."

33. Likewise, on that great and terrible day Jesus will show himself to be the Spirit of life's only sure foothold in a fallen and doomed race. That there is such a foothold is the best of news, yet in a culture that compensates for its materialism by priding itself, Gnosticlike, on its spirituality, this claim only heightens the awkwardness of the gospel. Is it true that "no one can say 'Jesus is Lord,' except by the Holy Spirit" (1 Cor. 12:3 NIV)? Then it is also true that until he has been confessed as Lord in this way, no one may go on to say, "I believe in the Holy Spirit, the Lord and giver of life."

34. *Cat.* 15.18

35. See *Cat.* 15.7.

36. *Cat.* 15.7. In those days, says Ammianus (*Hist.* 21.16, quoted ed. n. 3, p. 106), "The highways were covered with troops of bishops, galloping from every side to the assemblies, which they called synods; and while they laboured to reduce the whole sect to their own particular opinions, the public establishment of the posts was almost ruined by their hasty and repeated journeys." Today the posts may not be under threat, but the church still is. St. Hilary takes us to the heart of the matter: "It is a thing equally deplorable and dangerous that there are as many creeds as opinions among men, as many doctrines as inclinations, and as many sources of blasphemy as there are faults among us; because we make creeds arbitrarily, and explain them as arbitrarily" (quoted ibid.; see *ad Const.* 2.4ff.).

37. "Hatred of the brethren," warns Cyril, "makes room . . . for Antichrist; for the devil pre-

pares beforehand divisions among the people, that he who is to come may be acceptable to them" (*Cat.* 15.9).

38. Jesus' coming is not merely instrumental to the coming of God. He returns not as Elijah returns, or the Hidden Imam, but as the one he is—Emmanuel. In his offering up of all things together with himself to the Father, however, it will become entirely manifest that this indeed is the coming of God (cf. 1 Cor. 15:20–28, Rev. 21–22; and with both, Ezek. 36–37).

39. The problem is the opposite of Mary's (Luke 1:29–37), for what is no longer virginal (namely, the present creation) must first be made virginal again. Or *was* this also Mary's problem—the problem whose controversial answer is attempted in the notion of the immaculate conception?

40. Provoked by Schleiermacher (*The Christian Faith* 157–63) especially, I have tried to make a small contribution in a paper delivered at McMaster University in Hamilton, entitled "Life and Immortality: Continuity and Discontinuity in the Christian Tradition" (forthcoming).

41. "The last judgment," says Augustine (Civitas Dei 20.30; op cit. 290ff.), "is that which he shall settle on earth; coming to effect it out of heaven. . . . And this judgment shall consist of these circumstances, partly precedent and partly adjacent: Elijah shall come, the Jews shall believe, Antichrist shall persecute, Christ shall judge, the dead shall arise, the good and bad shall sever, the world shall burn and be renewed. All this we must believe shall be, but in what order, our full experience then shall exceed our imperfect intelligence as yet."

42. Oliver O'Donovan, *On the Thirty-Nine Articles* (Exeter: Paternoster 1986), 37ff. I am convinced, for my part, that we can and should see the post-passion history of Jesus as an extension and fulfillment, in several distinct temporal modes, of the priestly and kingly work that began with his baptism and reached its (preliminary) goal on the cross. But this I will have to sketch out further elsewhere.

43. As O'Donovan remarks, he is not then "killing time," to use the colloquial expression, until his coming again (ibid.), nor is he in some secret place nearer or farther from our own. Rather he is with God, "in the Father's house," as the mediator of all times, past, present, and future. That is to say, he is in a place and a time that bears an indescribable—a strictly eschatological, yet eucharistically and pneumatologically accessible—relation to our own.

44. Hence the famous vision of Daniel (7:13–14) is rightly appealed to with respect to both.

45. I have Moltmann in view, for whom the *apokatastasis* is universalistic because it is panentheistic. See *The Coming of God* (Minneapolis: Fortress,

1996), 235ff. On *anakephalaiosis* or recapitulation, cf. *Ascension and Ecclesia*, 52ff.

46. *AH* 5.27 (cf. 1.10.1, 4.4.3). For "the Word comes preparing a fit habitation for both" according to their option for life in communion or for death through self-alienation (5.28.1; cf. 3.25.1f., 4.28.3, 4.41.2). Epitomizing the latter is the Antichrist, who is called "'the other,' because he is alienated from the Lord" (5.25.4; cf. again 2 Thessalonians 2).

47. "For those who are bearers of the Spirit of God are led to the Word, that is, to the Son; but the Son takes them and presents them to the Father; and the Father confers incorruptibility" (Irenaeus, *Demo.* 7; cf. *AH* 5.36).

48. Note that if the credal "whose kingdom shall have no end" underlines against Sabellians and Arians the triune nature of God, it also guards against any attempt to marginalize the incarnate Son. That is, it refuses to allow us to remythologize everything at the last, or to transform the eschaton into a timeless affair—as if the judgment and the offering to be rendered by Jesus at his return amount to a folding up of the creaturely world with its spatiotemporal structures into the eternal recesses of the divine mind. Rather, it insists that the humanity assumed by God is something he has not, and will not, let go; hence it is only the form now known to us, not the substance of our creaturely reality as such, that will pass away at the last judgment (see Cyril, *Cat.* 15.27ff.).

49. Martyrdom is understood here not only as the deed, i.e., as a possible final act of witness, but (with the Apocalypse) as the life that prepares for the deed. See my *Ascension and Ecclesia*, 188ff., 270ff., and "Eucharist, Eschatology and Ethics," in *The Future as God's Gift*, ed. D. Fergusson and M. Sarot (Edinburgh: T & T Clark, 2000), 199ff.

Chapter 10: The Holy Spirit in the Holy Trinity

1. Gregory of Nyssa, "On the Holy Spirit" in *A Select Library of Nicene and Post-Nicene Fathers*, vol. 5, ed. P. Schaff and H. Wade (Grand Rapids: Eerdmans, 1979), 317.

2. Augustine of Hippo, *On the Trinity*, Book 15, Para. 47.

3. Alasdair Heron, "The *Filioque* in Recent Reformed Theology" in *Spirit of God, Spirit of Christ*, ed. Lucas Vischer (Geneva: World Council of Churches, 1981), 187.

Chapter 11: He Spoke Through the Prophets: The Prophetic Word Made More Sure

1. Athanasius, *Con. Gent.* 5, 30; 30; *De Synodis*, 46; *Contra Ar.* 1.37, 52ff., 3.28, 35; *Ad Ser de morte Arii*, 5.

2. T. F. Torrance, *Divine Meaning: Studies in Patristic Hermeneutics* (Edinburgh: T & T Clark 1995), 235 n. 24.

3. Ibid., 235.

4. Athanasius, *Con Ar.* 3.29; Torrance, 195, 239.

5. Frances M. Young, *Biblical Exegesis and the Formation of Christian Culture* (Cambridge: Cambridge University Press, 1997), 29ff.

6. See, for example, Athanasius, *De decretis* 18ff., 19.4.

7. Athanasius, *De decr. Nic Syn.* 11, 21; Torrance, *Divine Meaning*, 236.

8. Young, *Biblical Exegesis*, 40.

9. Justin Martyr, *Apology*, see 1.6.2, 1.13, and 1.31.7, but especially 1.61.10, where the context is baptism.

10. Iranaeus, *Epideixis* 6; see also *Adv. Haer.* 1.10.1.

11. Polycarp, *Phil.*, 6, 3.

12. William Contryman, "Tertullian and the *Regula Fidei*," *Second Century* 2 (1982): 233.

13. Ellen Flesseman-van Leer, *Tradition and Scripture in the Early Church* (Assen: VanGorcum 1953), 178.

14. James Kugel and Roman Greer, *Early Biblical Interpretation* (Philadelphia: Westminster 1986), 198–199.

15. Karl Barth, *Church Dogmatics* III/2, ed. G. W. Bromiley and T. F. Torrance (Edinburgh: T & T Clark, 1960).

16. Stephen Sykes, "The Role of Story in Christian Religion: An Hypothesis," *Journal of Literature and Theology* 1 (1987): 21; Paul Blowers, "The *Regula Fidei* and the Narrative Character of Early-Christian Faith," *Pro Ecclesia* 6 (2): 220.

17. Kathryn Greene-McCreight, "The Logic of the Interpretation of Scripture and the Church's Debate over Sexual Ethics," in *Homosexuality, Science, and the Plain Sense of Scripture*, ed. David Balch (Grand Rapids: Eerdmans, 2000).

Chapter 12: I Believe in One Holy, Catholic, and Apostolic Church

1. Alfred Loisy, *The Gospel and the Church* (Philadelphia: Fortress, 1976), 166.

2. See especially Aleksei Stephanovich Khomiakov, "On the Western Confessions of Faith," in *Ultimate Questions: An Anthology of Modern Russian Religious Thought*, ed. Alexander Schmemann (New York: Holt, Rinehart and Winston, 1965), 29–69.

3. The issue initially is one of collegiality within the church. However, I remain unconvinced by contemporary efforts to argue for the eternal procession of the Son from the Spirit from texts that focus on the temporal sending of the Spirit at Pentecost. Fresh suggestions on how to enrich the material on

the Holy Spirit should be kept strictly as theological midrash.

4. I have argued this case at length in my *Canon and Criterion in Christian Theology: From the Fathers to Feminism* (Oxford: Clarendon, 1998).

5. One option worthy of consideration is the possibility of permitting claims about papal infallibility without the whole church endorsing them. This was the position of Newman prior to Vatican I; he believed in papal infallibility but did not think that the church as a whole should formally accept it. I doubt if Rome would welcome this olive branch, but if she did, then the possibilities for the reunion of East and West would be greatly enhanced.

6. This theme is pursued with rare sensitivity by Ephraim Radner in *The End of the Church: A Pneumatology of Christian Division in the West* (Grand Rapids: Eerdmans, 1998).

Chapter 13: I Acknowledge One Baptism for the Forgiveness of Sins

1. This point is made by Henri de Lubac in *La foi chrétienne: essai sur la structure du Symbole des Apôtres* (Paris: Aubier-Montaigne, 1970), 217–34.

2. Even where the Rite of Christian Initiation for Adults (RCIA) is not formally adopted, this same *ordo* is acknowledged ecumenically. See Gordon Lathrop, "Baptismal *Ordo* and Rite of Passage in the Church," in *Baptism, Rites of Passage, and Culture*, ed. S. Anita Stauffer (Geneva: The Lutheran World Federation Department for Theology and Studies, 1998), 27–46; Thomas F. Best and Dagmar Heller, eds., *Becoming a Christian: The Ecumenical Implications of Our Common Baptism*, Faith and Order Paper No. 184 (Geneva: WCC Publications, 1999), 30.

3. Ibid.

4. de Lubac, *La foi chrétienne*, 217–34.

5. Catechism, 1253.

6. Ibid., 1124.

7. Ibid., 1123.

8. Avery Dulles, *The Assurance of Things Hoped For: A Theology of Christian Faith* (New York: Oxford University Press, 1994), 44.

9. Bernard Marthaler, *The Creed: The Apostolic Faith in Contemporary Theology* (Mystic, Conn.: Twenty-Third Publications, 1993), 323.

10. *Baptism, Eucharist and Ministry*, Faith and Order Paper No. 111 (Geneva: World Council of Churches, 1982), 13.

11. Nn. 473–501 of the English *editio typica* of the RCIA. It is an appendix to the Latin text.

12. RCIA n. 480.

13. RCIA n. 400.

14. *Unitatis redintegratio*, 22.

15. The text, however, speaks of a "fullness of unity which flows from baptism" in the next para-

graph even though this is apparently contradicted in the preceding paragraph that associates completeness of unity only with eucharistic communion.

16. *Unitatis redintegratio*, 2.

17. The Roman Catholic Church differs from many other communions in that it allows for the administration of baptism in case of necessity by a person of another tradition or even by an unbaptized person as long as that person intends to do what the church intends in baptism. This, however, does not affect normal pastoral practice.

18. Avery Dulles, "The Church as Communion," in *New Perspectives on Historical Theology: Essays in Memory of John Meyendorff*, ed. Bradley Nassif (Grand Rapids: Eerdmans, 1996), 134.

19. *Lumen gentium*, 8.

20. Jean-Marie R. Tillard, *L'Eglise locale: Ecclésiologie de communion et catholicité* (Paris: Cerf, 1995), 373.

21. See, for example, Joseph Komonchak, "The Church Universal as the Communion of Local Churches," in *Where Does the Church Stand?* Concilium 146 (Edinburgh: T & T Clark, 1981), 30–35.

22. *The Code of Canon Law*, 1983, can. 857, stipulates that "adults are to be baptized in their own parish church and infants in the parish church proper to their parents, unless a just cause suggests otherwise." Can. 862 states that "outside the case of necessity, it is not lawful for anyone without the required permission, to confer baptism in the territory of another, not even upon his own subjects."

23. Congregation for the Doctrine of the Faith, *Dominus Jesus*: "On the Unicity and Salvific Universality of Jesus Christ and the Church," available in *Origins* 30 no. 14 (September 14, 2000): 209, 211–22.

24. John Zizioulas, *Being as Communion* (Crestwood, New York: St. Vladimir's Seminary Press, 1985).

25. J. N. D. Kelly, *Early Christian Creeds* (London: Longman, 1972), 344.

26. Jaroslav Pelikan, *The Christian Tradition: A History of the Development of Doctrine*, vol. 1: *The Emergence of the Catholic Tradition (100–600)* (Chicago: The University of Chicago Press, 1971), 316–17.

27. Synod of Carthage (418) Can. (Mansi 3:811).

28. See also Acts 11:18; 16:31; 26:18.

29. RCIA, 1.

Chapter 15: To Desire Rightly: The Force of the Creed in Its Canonical Context

1. Athanasius, *De Synodis* 1:5. All subsequent references to patristic material, including translated citations, can be found in the appropriate volumes of the *Nicene and Post-Nicene Fathers*, Series One and Two (Peabody, Mass.: Hendrickson, 1995).

2. All this is confirmed by other historians; Socrates, *History*, 1:8.

3. Eusebius, *The Life of Constantine*, 3:18ff.

4. E.g., Socrates, in his *History*, 2:27; Basil, *Epistle*, 204:6.

5. See "Letter to the Eusebians," quoted in Athanasius's *Defence against the Arians*, c. 2.

6. Ibid.

7. *Encyclical Epistle to Bishops throughout the World*, 1.

8. Cf. the phrase in the Synodal Letter of the 341 (?) Synod of Antioch.

9. Andre de Halleux, "Toward a Common Expression of the Faith According to the Spirit of the Fathers" in *Faith to Creed: Ecumenical Perspectives on the Affirmation of the Apostolic Faith in the Fourth Century*, ed. S. Mark Heim (Grand Rapids: Eerdmans, 1991), 43.

10. "The Importance of the Conciliar Process in the Ancient Church," sec. 5; this and the Faith and Order Commission documents cited below can be found in *Documentary History of Faith and Order*, ed. Gunther Gassmann (Geneva: World Council of Churches, 1993).

11. E.g., Robert Wuthnow, *The Restructuring of American Religion* (Princeton: Princeton University Press, 1988), and *The Struggle for America's Soul* (Grand Rapids: Eerdmans, 1989).

12. Faith and Order Commission, "Towards a Common Expression of the Apostolic Faith Today," sec 1:10–15.

13. Cf. the Faith and Order document "The Ecumenical Movement and Church Law."

14. *Encyclical Epistle*, 1 and 6.

15. Cf. especially Athanasius's *Defence against the Arians*, passim.

16. But cf. Basil's *On the Spirit*, c. 15, where "imitation" of the "pattern" of Christ's life in the "flesh" fulfills the purpose of the incarnation, which is to make us "like" him, a process Basil links to the initiating grace of baptism.

17. See Athanasius, *On the Incarnation*, 29, 48.

18. See the "Letter" of the Council of Sardica to the Church of Alexandria, in Athanasius, *Defence against the Arians*, c. 3:38.

19. Gregory of Nazianzen, *Oration*, 2.

20. Ibid., 87, 95.

21. Ibid., 69, 102.

22. Ibid., 87.

23. See the wonderful chapter on this topic in H. Reginald Buckler's small classic *The Perfection of Man by Charity* (London: Blackfriars, 1954).

Contributors

William J. Abraham, Southern Methodist University, is the author of *Canon and Criterion: From the Fathers to Feminism.*

Carl E. Braaten, cofounder of the Center for Catholic and Evangelical Theology, is the author of *Mother Church: Ecclesiology and Ecumenism.*

J. Augustine Di Noia, Dominican House of Studies (Washington, D.C.) is a coauthor of *The Love That Never Ends: A Key to the Catechism of the Catholic Church.*

Douglas Farrow, McGill University, is the author of *Ascension and Ecclesia: On the Significance of the Doctrine of the Ascension.*

Kathryn Greene-McCreight, Smith College, is the author of *Feminist Reconstruction of Christian Doctrine: A Narrative Analysis and Appraisal.*

Colin Gunton, King's College, London, is the author of several books, including *The Triune Creator: A Historical and Systematic Study.*

Vigen Guroian, Loyola College in Maryland, is the author of *Incarnate Love: Essays in Orthodox Ethics.*

Robert W. Jenson, the Center for Theological Inquiry, has authored several books, most recently his two-volume *Systematic Theology.*

Ephraim Radner, rector of the Church of the Ascension (Episcopal), in Pueblo, Colorado, has written *The End of the Church: A Pneumatology of Christian Division in the West.*

Christopher R. Seitz, the University of St. Andrews, is the author of *Figured Out: Typology and Providence in Christian Scripture.*

Thomas Smail, formerly of Fuller Thelogical Seminary, is the author of *The Forgotten Father.*

Alan Torrance, the University of St. Andrews, has written *Persons in Communion: An Essay on Trinitarian Description and Human Participation.*

Philip Turner, formerly of Berkeley Divinity School, Yale University, is the editor of *Men and Women: Sexual Ethics in Turbulent Times.*

John Webster, Oxford University, is the author of *Word and Church.*

Susan K. Wood, St. John's University, is the author of *Sacramental Orders.*

David S. Yeago, Lutheran Theological Seminary, Columbia, S.C., is a frequent contributor to *Pro Ecclesia* and other theological journals.